WINDOWS 2000

quick *fixes*™

WINDOWS 2000

JIM BOYCE

O'REILLY®

Beijing · Cambridge · Farnham · Köln · Paris · Sebastopol · Taipei · Tokyo

JUN 2 9 2004

Windows 2000 Quick Fixes
by Jim Boyce

Published by O'Reilly & Associates, Inc., 101 Morris Street, Sebastopol, CA 95472.

Editor: Troy Mott

Production Editor: Leanne Clarke Soylemez

Cover Designer: Hanna Dyer

Printing History:

January 2001:   First Edition.

ISBN: 0-596-00017-0   [6/01]

[M]

Table of Contents

Preface

Use an operating system day in and day out, and you're sure to become intimately familiar with it, reaching one of three states: love, hate, or mere tolerance. When you have to switch to a new operating system or new version, or even just try to use features you've never used before, that state can certainly change. Sometimes the problem and its solution are simple; sometimes they are not.

Windows 2000 Quick Fixes targets a selection of common problems, first-time tasks, and infrequently used features and provides quick and (usually) simple solutions to those issues. New users and users who are experienced but not familiar with the Windows 2000 interface will find tips on customizing a wide range of operating system parameters that control everything from the way the desktop looks and functions to how the operating system does its job behind the scenes. Users of all levels will find quick and concise instructions that address problems and features in many areas of Windows 2000, including hardware and software configuration, security, networking, remote access, and a range of other features and functions.

Like most computer books, *Windows 2000 Quick Fixes* isn't meant to be read from front cover to back (surely no one is that much of a masochist). Instead, the book provides chapters covering specific topic areas, each with simply stated problems and concise instructions on how to work through the issue. You can find a topic quickly when the need occurs and turn to that section, working out a solution in a matter of minutes. *Windows 2000 Quick Fixes* assumes you have a solid computer background, are comfortable using a computer, and have a relatively high level of confidence in your computer skills. This book won't teach you how to use every feature in Windows 2000. Rather, it focuses on specific problems and features that you may be aware of but aren't sure exactly how to deal with. As you browse the book you're sure to run across solutions you already know, but read anyway—you might find a simpler solution or one that better fits your need.

Organization of this book

This book contains thirteen chapters.

Chapter 1, *Installing Windows 2000*, covers problems you might run across when installing Windows 2000, as well as problems that have the potential to bite you shortly after installation. Among other things, you'll learn about dual-boot solutions and alternatives, how to address specific installation issues, and a forgotten Administrator password.

Chapter 2, *Configuring Hardware*, will help you deal with hardware configuration problems, set up and use hardware profiles, optimize your system's hard disk(s), and take advantage of Windows 2000's new dynamic disk features.

Chapter 3, *Configuring System Software/Components*, focuses on configuring the Windows 2000 operating system's core components and adding components. You'll learn how to work with services, remove several "hidden" components, customize Microsoft Management Consoles (MMC), configure and use offline folders, and other similar topics.

Chapter 4, *Configuring the Windows 2000 Interface*, addresses those myriad questions about tweaking and fine-tuning the Windows 2000 GUI and its behavior. You'll learn how to configure multiple monitors, customize the Start menu and taskbar, add to and sort the Start menu items, and find new and easier ways to accomplish tasks. Chapter 4 also covers potential GUI annoyances like the sometimes irritating special effects, as well as how to start applications with switches and other interface topics.

Chapter 5, *Printing*, assumes you're up to speed on installing and using printers in Windows and focuses on new features like the Internet Printing Protocol (IPP), which enables a client to print to a printer across an intranet or even the Internet. You'll find several tips in Chapter 5 to make printing easier, such as how to quickly switch printer settings by maintaining multiple instances of the same printer driver.

Chapter 6, *Console (Command) Prompt*, goes where many users dread going: to the Windows 2000 command console. If you're a diehard DOS user, you'll be right at home in the command console, but this chapter will give you several tips to make your character mode tasks easier. Those of you who cut your teeth on the GUI will find tips to help you get the most out of the console prompt as well, and make it a little less intimidating (and more useful!).

Chapter 7, *Network Configuration*, will help you configure your computer's network interfaces and settings for both performance and security. You'll learn how to bind and unbind protocols to a client or service, restrict traffic with IP filters and IPSec, and address problems such as errors caused by duplicate protocols on multiple adapters. Chapter 7 also addresses several security-related questions, among them enforcing strong passwords, forcing users to change their passwords, and other logon and security topics.

Chapter 8, *Sharing and Accessing Network Resources*, offers tips on sharing folders and files, controlling access to resources, moving between workgroups and domains, and networking home computers. The chapter also covers scripts, access permissions and rights, and *roaming profiles*, which enable you to have the same working environment regardless of which computer you use to log on to the LAN.

Chapter 9, *Using and Troubleshooting TCP/IP*, will help you configure TCP/IP for your system, including using DHCP and APIPA to assign IP addresses and related settings to client computers automatically. Troubleshooting is a big part of this chapter, and you'll learn about several tools you can use in Windows 2000 to identify and fix specific connectivity problems.

Chapter 10, *Using and Sharing Dial-Up Networking Connections*, is the place to turn for answers about remote access, Internet connections, virtual private networks (VPNs), and related topics like credit card dialing. You'll learn how to share a single dial-up Internet connection with other users on the LAN and use multilink to combine multiple connections to provide a single, higher-speed connection.

Chapter 11, *Web Services and Security*, will help you make the most of Windows 2000's web services. You'll learn how to host multiple web sites on one computer with a single IP address, build a web site directory structure from multiple computers, pull a few neat tricks with FTP, and jazz up those boring web site error pages. Chapter 11 also looks at remote web site management, configuring sites to use Secure Sockets Layer (SSL), and related topics.

Chapter 12, *Users, Policies, Certificates, and Security*, provides quick solutions to a variety of security-related issues. You'll learn how to issue your own certificates, copy certificates between computers or users, work with secure email, and encrypt your files. This chapter also covers topics that will help you protect your computer from potential problems, including limiting the tasks that others can perform on your computer. You'll also learn about group policies and how to use them to configure specific security features and apply certain restrictions to the system.

Chapter 13, *Backup/Recovery and Repair*, is targeted at users who need to know what steps to take to prevent disaster and how to plan for the worst in case it does happen. You'll learn how to back up your system's configuration, create an emergency repair disk, and perform backups to network drives and writable CDs. Chapter 13 also covers some potentially catastrophic problems such as a forgotten Administrator password, a system that refuses to boot, and others. You'll also learn about the new Windows 2000 Recovery Console, which will help you boot an otherwise unbootable system and resurrect it from the dead.

Conventions used in this book

The following typographical conventions are used in this book:

Constant width

Indicates command-line computer output and code examples.

Constant width italic

Indicates variables in examples and in registry keys. It also indicates variables or user-defined elements within italic text (such as pathnames or filenames). For instance, in the path *Windows\username*, replace *username* with your name.

Constant width bold

Indicates user input in examples.

Constant width bold italic

Indicates replaceable user input in examples.

Italic

Introduces new terms and indicates URLs, variables in text, user-defined files and directories, commands, file extensions, filenames, directory or folder names, and UNC pathnames.

This is an example of a note, which signifies valuable and timesaving information.

This is an example of a warning, which alerts a potential pitfall. Warnings can also refer to a procedure that might be dangerous if not carried out in a specific way.

Path notation

We use a shorthand path notation to show you how to reach a given Word or Windows user interface element or option. The path notation is relative to a well-known location. For example, the following path:

Start → Programs → Accessories

means "Open the Start menu, then choose Programs, then choose Accessories."

Keyboard shortcuts

When keyboard shortcuts are shown, a hyphen (such as Ctrl-Alt-Del) means that the keys must be held down simultaneously, while a plus (such as Alt+F+O) means that the keys should be pressed sequentially.

How to contact us

We have tested and verified the information in this book to the best of our ability, but you may find that features have changed (or even that we have made mistakes!). Please let us know about any errors you find, as well as your suggestions for future editions, by writing to:

> O'Reilly & Associates, Inc.
> 101 Morris Street
> Sebastopol, CA 95472
> (800) 998-9938 (in the United States or Canada)
> (707) 829-0515 (international/local)
> (707) 829-0104 (fax)

To comment or ask technical questions about this book, send email to:

> *bookquestions@oreilly.com*

We have a web page for this book, where we list errata, examples, and any additional information. You can access this page at:

> *http://www.oreilly.com/catalog/qfwin2000/*

For more information about our books, conferences, software, Resource Centers, and the O'Reilly Network, see our web site at:

> *http://www.oreilly.com*

Acknowledgments

Although I've authored and co-authored some 48 or so books on computers, this is my first with O'Reilly, and I can say it has truly been a pleasure, in the development stage, through writing, and final polishing. There are certainly many people behind the scenes at O'Reilly that made this experience so pleasant, but I can only name those with whom I worked directly. To the rest I offer heartfelt but regrettably anonymous thanks.

First and foremost, special thanks go to Simon Hayes and Troy Mott, who helped bring the project from concept to reality. Both fellows did a super job of shepherding the project along. I'd also like to thank Tim O'Reilly for his support of the concept and the book, and my agent, David Fugate, for taking on with such relish those aspects that used to keep me away from writing (now, it's the golf that keeps me away from writing). I'd also like to thank Walter Glenn and David Karp for their on-point review and excellent comments on the material.

Finally, many authors acknowledge their spouse or children for the time the project development took away from family time. My wife, Julie, has always been a great support and help, and the kids did miss a few evenings with Dad. But hey, I have six kids . . . I needed the quiet time!

—Jim Boyce
September 2000

CHAPTER 1

Installing and Booting
Windows 2000

Windows NT offered a relatively easy installation process, and Windows 2000 makes that process even easier. In most cases you can simply pop in the CD and start Setup, and Windows 2000 installs successfully with very little input from you.

In some situations, however, you might run across problems with installation. For example, Setup could have problems locating the hard disk for installation if you have a host adapter not supported directly by Windows 2000. In RAID installations you might need to specify SCSI device IDs manually rather than letting the RAID hardware assign them for you. And a handful of other potential problems can prevent Setup from finding the installation hard drive. This chapter addresses those situations with relatively painless solutions.

Windows 2000 includes a new feature called the Recovery Console; you'll find it helpful in diagnosing Setup difficulties and problems that crop up after a successful installation. You can install the Recovery Console to the hard disk or run it from the Windows 2000 installation disks. The Recovery Console provides a console environment with several commands for manipulating the filesystem and performing other tasks.

This chapter also addresses a selection of problems you might run across after installation: a lost Administrator password, incorrect drive letter assignments, inability to boot Windows 2000, and problems logging on after hardware configuration changes. You'll also find a discussion of NTFS versus FAT and how to convert FAT volumes to NTFS, as well as tips on setting up a dual-boot system and avoiding the need to reinstall all your applications for a clean install.

1.1   Create Setup diskettes to install Windows 2000 or the Recovery Console

The Windows 2000 Setup diskette set enables you to install Windows 2000 on systems that can't access the CD-ROM drive without a driver, such as systems that don't support boot from CD and don't have an existing operating system installed. You also can use the Setup diskette set to install and run the Recovery Console if you have a problem booting Windows 2000. The Recovery Console is a command-line environment much like the command console you can run within Windows 2000, but with a limited command set. The Recovery Console is indispensable for repairing problems that prevent a normal boot. See Section 1.9, "The Recovery Console," for a more detailed description of the Recovery Console.

Unlike Windows NT, Windows 2000 does not come with a set of Setup diskettes, but the Windows 2000 CD does include the files necessary to create them. If you're making a disk set because you're having trouble booting Windows 2000, you'll need to boot another operating system or use a bootable DOS/Windows diskette with the necessary drivers to access the CD-ROM drive. (You could also make the disk set on a functioning computer.)

 If you have only one system and can't boot it to install the Recovery Console, you can run Setup, install a minimal copy of Windows 2000 in a new folder, and then use it to install the Recovery Console.

Creating boot diskettes

Follow these steps to create the Windows 2000 Setup floppy disk set:

1. Have four high-density diskettes on hand.

2. Boot the system and open a command console.

3. Change to the \Bootdisk folder on the Windows 2000 CD.

4. Execute the program *makeboot.exe* if you're running DOS, Windows 3.x, or Windows 9x. Run *makebt32.exe* if you're running Windows NT or Windows 2000.

5. Follow the prompts to complete the creation of the disk set. The program will format the disks if necessary and overwrite any data currently on them.

1.2   Setup doesn't find my hard disk

When you're attempting to install Windows 2000, Setup might encounter problems locating your computer's hard disk. Setup's inability to find a drive that you know is available is not only an annoyance, but it also makes it impossible to install Windows 2000. One potential cause of this problem is that Setup doesn't have the appropriate driver loaded for your SCSI or RAID adapter. Problems with disk geometry configuration in the system's BIOS or the size of the drive itself can also be potential problems. Also, the location that Setup places the temporary installation files can cause problems. Depending on the cause, overcoming the problem can be as simple as installing an additional driver during setup, changing a few BIOS settings, or directing Setup to use a different location for temporary files. When you run Setup again it should find the drive without any problems.

Adding a driver during Setup

If your SCSI or RAID controller isn't recognized and supported directly by Windows 2000 Setup, but instead requires a third-party device driver, Setup will generally fail to recognize your hard disk during Windows 2000 installation. Loading the driver during Setup enables Windows 2000 to recognize and use the drive or array. If you have multiple adapters, Setup might detect one but not the other(s), so you might still need to add a driver manually during Setup.

Follow these steps to load a mass storage driver during Setup:

1. Start Setup normally. You should see the message "Setup is inspecting your computer's hardware configuration" on a black screen.

2. When the initial Setup blue screen appears, press F6 (as indicated by the prompt at the bottom of the display) to specify a third-party driver. If Setup continues with installation without prompting you for a device driver disk, Setup is not detecting the adapter at all. Contact your system or adapter manufacturer for support as you may have a bad controller or other problem with the system.

3. If Setup does detect the host adapter, insert the disk containing the third-party driver when prompted by Setup and continue with the installation.

Changing SCSI ID assignment manually

In some systems all SCSI drives are configured for ID 0 and are assigned a SCSI ID by the SCSI host adapter. In such a system, Setup may have difficulty locating the drives or might incorrectly detect the desired boot drive.

You need to configure the drives manually for specific SCSI IDs rather than allowing the adapter to configure them. This requires installation of jumpers on each drive to configure it for a specific SCSI ID.

1. Check the drive documentation to determine which jumpers to use to configure the SCSI ID. Some drives come with an installation booklet that specifies the settings, while others have the information printed on the drive itself. As a last resort you may be able to find the information you need on the drive manufacturer's web site.

2. Shut down the system and remove each drive in turn, configuring the drives as explained in the following steps.

    Make sure you touch a metal part of the case before handling any equipment to ensure you discharge any static electricity that has built up in your body.

3. The boot drive should be configured for SCSI ID 0, and on most drives, you omit a jumper to assign ID 0 to the drive (no ID jumpers installed). Configure the boot drive as ID 0 according to the requirements of the drive as indicated by the drive documentation.

4. Install jumpers to configure the other hard drive(s) using unique IDs that do not conflict with other devices (CD-ROM drive, tape drive, removable drive, etc.) in the system. Each device must have a unique ID or the devices won't function properly.

5. Verify that the last device on the SCSI chain is terminated. Usually this is accomplished by installing a manufacturer-supplied resistor pack or, more commonly, installing a jumper on the device. Check the device for a label that indicates which pin sets termination.

6. Reinstall each drive and restart the system to install Windows 2000.

Changing the location of the temporary files

By default Setup places temporary files for Windows 2000 installation on the first available drive with adequate free space. If you run *winnt.exe* or *winnt32.exe* from within another operating system, such as Windows 98, it's possible for *winnt.exe* or *winnt32.exe* to see and place the temporary files on drives not supported by Setup. This can include compressed volumes, unsupported SCSI drives, or drives on secondary IDE or ESDI controllers. The solution is simple: just direct Setup to use a different location for the temporary files.

Start Setup using the command **winnt.exe /t:*drive*** or the command **winnt32.exe /tempdrive:*drive***, where *drive* is the letter of the drive on

Installing
and Booting

which Setup should copy the temporary installation files. Select a drive that Setup can recognize. If no such drives exist, you'll have to repartition or replace drives to enable Setup to install Windows 2000.

 The /t or /tempdrive option also specifies the installation partition for Windows 2000. This means the drive you specify must be the same partition in which you intend to install Windows 2000.

Checking and changing IDE/EIDE drive type settings

It's possible for Setup to have problems locating the hard drive(s) in the system if their configuration data in the BIOS is incorrect. For example, you might have the system configured to auto-detect the drives but the BIOS is not detecting them properly. In this situation you need to enter the BIOS Setup program and configure the drive settings according to the drive specifications:

1. Determine the correct settings for your IDE/EIDE hard drives, including number of cylinders, number of heads, etc., using the documentation for the drives.

2. Boot the computer and watch for a message that explains how to enter the BIOS Setup program. Typically, you press Delete, F2, or Esc during the initial boot screen to enter BIOS Setup. Check your system documentation if you're not sure how to get into the BIOS Setup program.

3. Once you're in BIOS Setup, note the current drive configuration settings on a piece of paper for reference in case you need to restore the original settings.

4. In BIOS Setup, check the configuration for the hard drives against the actual drive configuration and correct if necessary. You might need to configure the drives using the user-defined type, manually specifying the appropriate parameters, rather than auto-detection.

5. Save the changes to the BIOS and reboot the computer, then restart Setup.

1.3   Using winnt and winnt32 switches

The *winnt.exe* and *winnt32.exe* commands support several switches in addition to the temporary drive option explained in the previous topic. These switches enable you to specify the source location for the Windows 2000 files, specify an answer file for unattended installation, specify commands to

---

Eliminating an MBR virus

Another reason Setup may not find your hard drive is the presence of a Master Boot Record (MBR) virus. Just deleting a partition doesn't necessarily kill an MBR virus, since the drive can still have an MBR without a partition being present. Run a virus detection and repair program on the drive and direct it to scan the MBR for viruses. Make sure the virus definition file you use with the detection program is up to date. You might also be able to repair an MBR virus infection using *fdisk*. Boot the system to a command console (DOS Mode, for example) and execute the fdisk /mbr command, which rewrites the MBR.

---

execute at completion of Setup, and more. The following is the syntax for *winnt.exe*, and Table 1-1 lists the command switches for *winnt.exe*:

```
winnt [/s[:sourcepath]] [/t[:tempdrive]] [/u[:answer_file]]
[ic:ccc][/udf:id[,UDF_file]] [/r:folder] [/rx:folder] [/e:command] [/a]
```

Table 1-1. winnt.exe command switches

Option	Function
/s[:sourcepath]	Location of Windows 2000 source files; must be full local or UNC pathname.
/t[:tempdrive]	Location for temporary Setup files and installation partition.
/u:[answer_file]	Perform unattended Setup using specified answer file; requires /s option.
/udf:id[,UDF_file]	Specify unique ID and use Unique Database File (UDF) to modify answer file for unattended Setup. ID determines which answers in UDF file are used.
/r[:folder]	Create optional folder that remains after installation; specify folder name as folder.
/rx[:folder]	Copy folder during Setup but delete after installation.
/e	Specify command to be executed after GUI-mode Setup completes.
/a	Enable accessibility options.

The following is the syntax for *winnt32.exe*, and Table 1-2 lists the command switches for *winnt32.exe*:

```
winnt32 [/s:sourcepath] [/tempdrive:drive_letter]
[ic:ccc][/unattend[num]:[answer_file]] [/copydir:folder_name]
[ic:ccc][/copysource:folder_name] [/cmd:command_line]
[ic:ccc][/debug[level]:[filename]] [/udf:id[,UDF_file]]
[ic:ccc][/syspart:drive_letter] [/checkupgradeonly] [/cmdcons]
[ic:ccc][/m:folder_name] [/makelocalsource] [/noreboot]
```

Table 1-2. winnt32.exe command switches

Option	Function
/s:*sourcepath*	Location of Windows 2000 source files; you can specify multiple sources with multiple /s switches.
/tempdrive:*drive_letter*	Location for temporary Setup files and Windows 2000 installation partition.
/unattend	Upgrade previous version of Windows 2000 in unattended Setup mode; implies acceptance of the End User License Agreement.
/unattend[*num*]:[*answer_file*]	Fresh install in unattended mode; *num* is the number of seconds between file copy and system restart and *answer_file* is the answer file for Setup options.
/copydir:*folder_name*	Copy optional folder specified by folder to the system root folder during Setup; use multiple switches to copy multiple folders. Folder(s) remain after Setup completes.
/copysource:*folder_name*	Copy optional folder specified by folder to the system root folder during Setup; use multiple switches to copy multiple folders. Folder(s) deleted after Setup completes.
/cmd:*command_line*	Execute specified command after Setup but before final system restart.
/debug[*level*]:[*filename*]	Log information to specified file; levels are 1 (errors), 2 (warnings), 3 (information), and 4 (detailed).
/udf:id[,*UDF_file*]	Specify unique ID and use Unique Database File (UDF) to modify answer file for unattended Setup. ID determines which answers in UDF file are used.
/syspart:*drive_letter*	Copy Setup startup files to drive, mark drive active for install in another computer, which continues Setup on boot. Requires /tempdrive switch. Not available for Windows 9x.
/checkupgradeonly	Analyze system for upgrade compatibility but don't install; creates *Upgrade.txt* (Windows 9x) or *Winnt32. log* (Windows NT) log file in current OS system root folder.
/cmdcons	Install Recovery Console during Setup.
/m:*folder_name*	Copy files from specified folder (if it exists) rather than default source location.
/makelocalsource	Copy all installation source files to local hard disk; for cases where CD is not available after Setup starts.
/noreboot	Don't restart system after final Setup phase.

1.4   Only one CPU shows up in a multiprocessor system

While this problem doesn't happen often, it can occur if Setup incorrectly detects your PC type and installs the wrong system driver. There are a handful of ways for you to determine whether Windows 2000 is using only one CPU in a multi-CPU system:

- Open the Computer Management console, and then open the System Information\System Summary branch. Look for multiple Processor entries. If there is only one, Windows 2000 is not using all processors.

     Right-click My Computer and choose Manage to open the Computer Management console, or choose Start → Settings → Control Panel → Administrative Tools → Computer Management.

- In the Computer Management console, open the Device Manager and expand the Computer branch in the right pane. If Device Manager doesn't list a multiprocessor PC, Windows 2000 is using only one processor. Figure 1-1 shows Device Manager on a multiprocessor system.

- Open the Performance console by choosing Start → Settings → Control Panel → Administrative Tools → Performance. Right-click in the right pane and choose Add Counters. Select Processor from the Performance Object drop-down list. Verify that there is more than one processor instance listed in the Select Instances from List control.

Once you've determined for sure that Windows 2000 is using only one processor, there are a couple of ways to correct the problem.

Reinstall Windows 2000 with a different system driver

The best solution is to reinstall Windows 2000 with the correct computer driver. Follow these steps to select a different system driver set during Setup:

1. Back up any data you need to retain in the event the installation fails.

2. Start the Windows 2000 Setup program.

3. When you see the message "Setup is inspecting your computer's hardware configuration," press F5.

4. Setup will prompt you to select the appropriate driver for your system, or choose Other to supply a disk provided with your computer.

5. After specifying the appropriate driver, complete Setup normally.

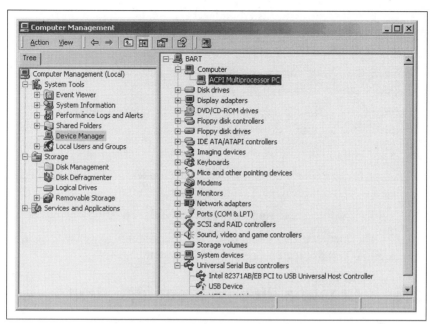

Figure 1-1. Device Manager lists the type of system driver in use under the Computer node

6. Boot Windows 2000 after installation and use the methods described earlier in this section to verify that Windows 2000 is using all processors in the system.

Change system driver

The best solution is to reinstall Windows 2000, particularly if some of your applications are multiprocessor-aware, and install a different version on a single-processor system. But if you've already installed applications and configured your system and don't want to reinstall Windows 2000, you could try to replace the system driver with a different one.

 Replacing the system driver with the wrong one will probably lead to a system that won't boot, requiring a reinstall. Back up your critical data before replacing the system driver.

Follow these steps to replace the driver:

1. Open the Computer Management console and select the Device Manager node.

2. In the right pane, expand the Computer branch.

3. Double-click the driver listed under the Computer branch, or right-click the driver and choose Properties. Either action opens the property sheet for the driver.

4. Click the Driver tab, then click Update Driver to start the Upgrade Device Driver Wizard.

5. Click Next, select "Display a list of the known drivers for this device so I can choose a specific driver," then click Next.

6. Select Show all hardware of this device class.

7. Select the appropriate manufacturer and model, or click Have Disk to use a disk supplied by your computer manufacturer.

8. Follow the prompts to replace the driver, and then reboot the computer.

9. Use the methods described earlier in this section to verify that Windows 2000 is using all processors in the system.

1.5   Create a dual-boot configuration

If necessary, you can retain your existing Windows 9x or Windows NT operating system and boot Windows 2000 as well (called a *dual-boot system*). A dual-boot system is particularly useful if you need to run applications that won't run under Windows 2000 or want to retain your existing configuration and run Windows 2000 primarily for testing and learning purposes.

Microsoft recommends that you place Windows 2000 in its own partition, but you can install Windows 2000 in the same partition as Windows 9x or Windows NT. However, Windows 2000 uses some of the same folders that these other operating systems do to store applications (such as the Program Files folder). This means that you could run into problems with certain common applications such as Internet Explorer or Outlook Express if you're not using the same version under your existing OS that you'll be using under Windows 2000. If at all possible, create another partition to contain Windows 2000.

There's one other potential snag as well. Setup won't install Windows 2000 as a dual-boot option if Windows NT is present. You'll need to clone your existing copy of Windows NT and then upgrade the installation, leaving the cloned copy as your NT installation. The following procedure explains how to set up a dual-boot system with Windows 9x. See Section 1.6, "Clone your original OS for a dual-boot system," to configure a system for dual-boot with Windows NT and Windows 2000.

VMWare is an alternative to a dual-boot system

An alternative for Windows NT users that can help you avoid potential problems and enable you to install Windows 2000 in the same partition as NT is VMWare for Windows NT. VMWare lets you create virtual machines and run other operating systems in a window under your Windows NT base OS. Each guest OS can reside in its own virtual file, safely protecting it from the others. VMWare provides virtual networking support, so the VMs act like physical computers on the network. Another advantage is that you can run DOS, Windows 3.x, Windows 9x, Linux, NT Server, or 2000 Server in a window if needed. You'll find more information about VMWare at *http://www.vmware.com.* Figure 1-2 shows a Windows 2000 system running Windows 98 in one window with Windows ME in a second window.

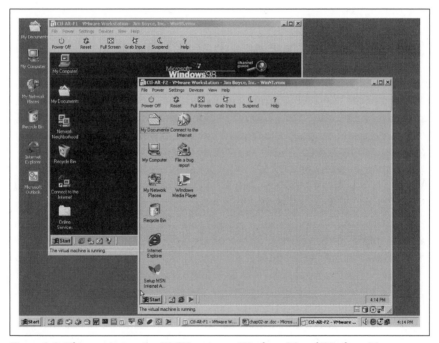

Figure 1-2. This system is using VMWare to run Windows 98 and Windows Me concurrently on a Windows 2000 Professional platform

Setting up a dual-boot system—Windows 9x

Setting up a dual-boot system is easy, but you should take some time to back up your important data beforehand to make sure nothing gets lost. Follow these steps to create a dual-boot system:

1. If they're not already installed, install and configure Windows 9x and your applications.

2. Back up any critical data such as mail folders, application data, etc.

3. Make a bootable Windows 9x system disk. To do so, open the Control Panel, then open the Add/Remove Programs object. Click the Startup Disk tab then click Create Disk. Insert the Windows 9x CD when prompted and follow the remaining instructions to create the boot diskette. You can use this diskette to boot the system if you have problems with the Windows 2000 installation.

4. Run Windows 2000 Setup from the Windows 2000 CD or Setup disks and install Windows 2000 to a new folder on the same partition as or a different partition from your existing OS.

5. Boot the system and note that the boot menu's default option is to boot Windows 2000. Select that option to boot Windows 2000 or the other option to boot your previous OS.

1.6   Clone your original OS for a dual-boot system

A nice option that lets you retain your existing OS and applications while still upgrading to Windows 2000 is to clone your existing OS to a new folder or partition and upgrade the copy. Your original installation remains as-is, and you end up with a Windows 2000 installation that incorporates all your application and customized OS settings. You can upgrade Windows 9x or Windows NT Workstation to Windows 2000 Professional, or upgrade Windows NT Server to Windows 2000 Server.

Both of the next two procedures require that you replace several instances of a given string in the registry. For example, you need to change all instances of *C:\Windows* in the Windows 9x registry to *C:\Win9x*, and in the Windows NT registry, from *C:\Winnt* to *C:\Win2k*. Although you can make the changes manually, it's impractical to do so because there are so many. Instead, you should use a third-party utility that enables global search-and-replace in the registry. There are a handful of utilities that provide that capability, and a search on the Internet or popular download sites should turn up at least one or two. The one used in this example is Registry Toolkit from Funduc Software, Inc. (*http://www.funduc.com*), which is licensed as shareware with a nominal fee.

 You can also clone your operating system from one drive to another using a third-party utility such as PowerQuest's Drive-Copy (*http://www.powerquest.com*).

Cloning Windows 9x

Cloning Windows 9x to a new folder is relatively easy—you can do it from within Windows using the *xcopy32* command. Getting everything to work properly afterwards, however, takes a little planning and attention to detail. Don't skip any of the steps in the following procedure:

> Note that the following steps for cloning Windows 9x will not work if you boot your computer to a DOS environment. You must be working within Windows for *xcopy32* to be able to clone your installation.

1. Create a bootable Windows 9x diskette if you don't already have one. Don't skip this step—if you have a problem booting the system after making the changes in this procedure, you'll need the bootable diskette to fix the problem.

2. Back up your system in case you experience problems with this process. At a minimum, back up your data.

3. Create a directory called *Win9x* to contain your cloned copy of Windows 9x (or a different folder name of your choosing—*Win9x* is used in this example).

4. Boot the system to Windows and open a DOS prompt (Start → Programs → MS-DOS Prompt). At the DOS prompt type the following command:

   xcopy32 C:\Windows C:\Win9x /h /i /c /k /e /r /y

   If Windows is installed in a folder other than *C:\Windows*, change the command accordingly to specify the correct source location for the *xcopy32* command.

> For a description of the switches referenced in the previous *xcopy32* command example, type xcopy32 /? at the console prompt.

5. After the files are copied, open My Computer and configure folder options to show all files. Look in the root folder for the following files: *io.sys*, *msdos.sys*, *autoexec.bat*, and *config.sys*. Create the folder *Win9x\Bootfiles* and copy these four files to that directory.

6. Right-click the copy of *msdos.sys* in the root folder and remove the read-only attribute to make the file editable.

7. Open *msdos.sys* in Notepad and change the values of WinDir and WinBootDir to both point to *C:\Win9x*, then save the file.

8. Restart the system to boot your cloned copy of Windows in the *Win9x* folder.

9. Perform a global search and replace in the registry, replacing all instances of *C:\Windows* with *C:\Win9x*. This "refocuses" the registry to the current Windows folder, which is *\Win9x*.

10. Modify the copy of *msdos.sys* in the root folder again to restore the values of WinDir and WinBootDir to *C:\Windows*.

11. Restart the system to boot the copy of Windows in *\Windows*.

12. Insert the Windows 2000 CD and perform an upgrade. This will upgrade the copy of Windows 9x in the *\Windows* folder to Windows 2000. *Do not upgrade the disk to NTFS!*

13. Make backup copies of *autoexec.bat* and *config.sys* in *\Windows\ Bootfiles*, and then restore your original *autoexec.bat* and *config.sys* files from the *\Win9x\Bootfiles* folder to the root folder.

14. Modify *autoexec.bat* and *config.sys* in the root folder to change references, if any, of *C:\Windows* to *C:\Win9x*. This includes changing the PATH statement (if any) to remove references to *C:\Windows*.

15. Modify *autoexec.bat* to include the *win* command as the last line of the file. If you omit this step, a DOS command prompt boots when you select the Windows 9x boot option, and you can enter **win** at the command prompt to start Windows.

16. Change the properties of *boot.ini* in the root folder to remove the read-only attribute to make it editable.

17. In the [operating systems] section, add the following line:

    ```
    C:\="Windows 9x"
    ```

    Save the file and replace the read-only attribute.

18. Configure the folder options again and select the Hide Protected Operating System Files option.

19. Restart the computer and test to verify that you can start Windows 9x. Review shortcuts in the Start menu and on the desktop for references to *C:\Windows*, replacing them with references to *C:\Win9x*. (The MS-DOS Prompt object in the Start menu is a good example, as are the shortcuts in the Accessories menu.)

20. Restart again to test Windows 2000.

Cloning Windows NT

You can clone Windows NT just as you can Windows 9x, although the process is a little different:

1. Boot your current installation of NT and execute **rdisk /s** to update the repair data and update the Emergency Repair Disk (ERD). This is a precautionary measure only but one you should do any time you begin modifying your NT environment.

2. Perform a full backup of your system just in case problems arise during this process. At a minimum, back up your data.

3. Create a directory called *Win2k* to contain Windows 2000 (or a different folder name of your choosing—*Win2k* is used in this example).

4. Boot the system and open a console prompt. At the command prompt type the following command:

   ```
   xcopy C:\Winnt C:\Win2k /h /i /c /k /e /r
   ```

   If Windows NT is installed in a folder other than *C:\Winnt*, change the command accordingly to specify the correct source location for the *xcopy* command.

5. Open My Computer and locate the file *boot.ini* in the root folder of the boot drive. Change the file's properties to remove the read-only attribute. (You might need to configure folder options to show all files if *boot.ini* doesn't appear in the folder.)

6. Open *boot.ini* in Notepad and in the [operating systems] section, select and copy the line that defines your Windows NT installation, such as,

   ```
   multi(0)disk(0)rdisk(0)partition(1)\Winnt="Microsoft Windows NT Workstation
   Version 4.0"
   ```

7. Insert a new line in the [operating systems] section and paste the copied line into the file at that point.

8. Modify the inserted line to reference the *\Win2k* folder rather than the *\Winnt* folder, and name it "Windows 2000." This will give you a menu option to boot the copy of NT in the *\Win2k* folder.

9. Save the file and restore the read-only attribute.

10. Holding down the Shift key to prevent an autorun, insert the Windows 2000 CD. Open a console prompt and change to the *\i386* folder on the CD.

11. Execute the following command to install the Windows 2000 Recovery Console:

    ```
    winnt32 /cmdcons
    ```

12. After the Recovery Console is installed, restart the system and boot the option "Microsoft Windows 2000 Recovery Console."

13. When prompted to select the installation for logon, select the backup copy stored in *\Win2k*. Since *xcopy* did not copy the Security Account

Manager (SAM), you won't be prompted to provide an administrator password.

14. Change to the *\Winnt\System32\config* folder, then use the *copy* command to copy all of the files in the folder to *\Win2K\System32\config*. Since *copy* doesn't support wildcards in the Recovery Console you'll have to copy the files one at a time. (This step copies the registry from your *\Winnt* installation to the *\Win2k* installation.)

15. Restart the system and select the option "Windows 2000." This will boot the cloned copy of Windows NT in the *\Win2k* folder.

16. Log on as administrator, then perform a global search and replace in the registry, changing all instances of *C:\Winnt* to *C:\Win2k*.

17. Review all shortcuts on the Start menu and desktop, changing references to *C:\Winnt* to *C:\Win2k*.

18. Restart the system and select the option "Windows 2000" to boot the cloned copy of Windows NT. Insert the Windows 2000 CD and perform an upgrade.

19. Upon successful completion of the upgrade, test both operating systems to verify that you can boot both and that both work properly.

1.7   Avoid reinstalling applications for a dual-boot system

If you create a dual-boot system with Windows 2000 and your previous OS (Windows 9x or Windows NT), you'll probably want to run at least some of the same applications under both operating systems. Many applications that don't use the registry to store their settings (not too common these days) can run without reinstalling—you simply create shortcuts in Windows 2000 to their existing locations. If an application does use the registry or requires some of its files (such as DLLs) to be located in the *systemroot\System* or *systemroot\System32* folder, you'll probably have to reinstall the application to be able to use it under Windows 2000 as well as your other OS. However, you probably won't have to duplicate the files by installing the application to a new folder. In most cases you can simply reinstall the application to its current location. Finally, some applications will recreate their registry keys to "heal" themselves automatically if the registry keys are missing. You can try running the application after installing Windows 2000 to see if it behaves this way.

Make sure to back up customized files such as templates prior to reinstalling the application. In most cases, reinstalling an application to the same folder overwrites any customized settings from the previous installation. Make sure you know which files you'll need to restore afterwards. Also, be aware that some customization settings are probably stored in the registry, so these might be lost when you reinstall.

Before you begin worrying about reinstalling applications you should test them to see if they work in Windows 2000 without reinstalling. Open My Computer and browse to the location of the application's executable file. Double-click the file to start the application. If you're not sure which file to execute, boot your other operating system and check the location as explained in the following procedure.

You can also clone the existing OS and then upgrade the cloned copy to avoid reinstalling applications. See Section 1.6, "Clone your original OS for a dual-boot system," for more information.

Locating and testing your applications

Before you reinstall applications you should test them to see if they'll run without reinstalling. Because they aren't technically installed under Windows 2000, however, you won't find any shortcuts to them in the Start menu or on the desktop. Instead, you'll have to locate and run their executable files manually to see which ones, if any, need to be reinstalled or imported into Windows 2000.

Checking a shortcut

If you start the application from a shortcut on the desktop or in a folder, or if you start it from the Windows 98 Start menu, you can view the shortcut's properties to determine what file it executes:

1. Right-click the shortcut and choose Properties. You'll see a property sheet for the shortcut.

2. Click the Shortcut tab and look in the Target text box. This is the command line that executes when you double-click the shortcut. Make a note of the path and filename.

3. After you reboot to Windows 2000, browse to and double-click the file referenced in the shortcut to see if the application runs properly. If it does, you should be able to simply copy the shortcut to your Windows 2000 Start menu or desktop and execute it from there. See "Creating shortcuts to existing applications," later in this chapter, for more information.

Windows 95 and Windows NT Start menu

Although most of the objects on the Windows 95 and Windows NT Start menu are shortcuts, you can't right-click them to display a context menu and get to the shortcut's properties like you can in Windows 98. Instead, you need to view the properties of the shortcut through Explorer:

1. Right-click the taskbar and choose Properties.

2. Click the Start Menu Programs tab, then click Advanced. This opens Explorer with a focus on the Programs folder where the Start menu's Programs items are located.

3. Browse through the Programs folder to locate the shortcuts you want to check.

4. Right-click a shortcut and choose Properties, then click the Shortcut tab after the object's property sheet opens.

5. Make a note of the path and filename in the Target box.

6. After you reboot to Windows 2000, browse to and double-click the file identified in step 5 to determine if the application can run in Windows 2000 without reinstalling.

Creating shortcuts to existing applications

If you determine that the applications can run without reinstalling them, you can simply copy shortcuts to the desired locations in your Windows 2000 interface to make them readily accessible, such as to the desktop or the Start menu. To do so, start Windows 2000, then open Explorer and locate the object you want to copy (either the shortcut or the application itself). Right-drag the object to the desired location and choose Create Shortcut(s) Here. You can drag objects to the Start menu to create shortcuts there as well.

 See Section 4.5, "Change or rearrange the contents of the Start menu,," for additional information on modifying the Start menu.

Copying registry keys and DLLs

In some cases you can "import" an application into Windows 2000 from your other OS by copying its registry key from the other OS to the Windows 2000 registry. If the application uses custom DLLs in the *systemroot\System* or *Systemroot\System32* folders, you will also have to copy those DLL files to the corresponding Windows 2000 folder. There is no guarantee that the application will run, but it could be easier than reinstalling the application and is worth a try, particularly if your installation media is lost, damaged, or otherwise not readily available.

1. Boot the system to your other OS and run *regedit* (click Start → Run, and enter **regedit** in the Run dialog box).

2. In Regedit, open HKEY_LOCAL_MACHINE\Software.

3. Browse for the application's registry key (indicated by the application name as the key name). Figure 1-3 shows an example.

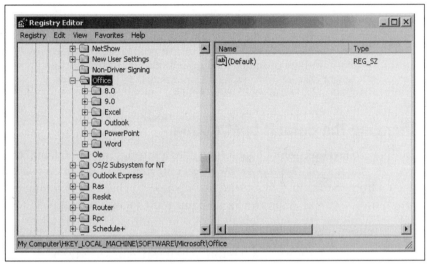

Figure 1-3. Registry Editor showing the registry key for an application prior to exporting it to a file

4. Select the key and choose Registry → Export Registry File.

5. In the Export Registry File dialog, browse to the location where you want to save the registry file. Specify a name for the file and click Save.

6. Reboot the system to Windows 2000.

7. In Explorer, browse for the registry file you created in step 5, then double-click the registry file to import it into the registry. The file will have a *.reg* file extension.

8. Try running the application. If you receive an error that a specific DLL is missing, locate that DLL in the *systemroot\System* or *systemroot\ System32* folder of your other OS and copy it to the corresponding folder in your Windows 2000 installation.

9. Repeat step 8 until all required DLLs are copied and the program runs properly.

1.8 Change the boot menu options

Windows 2000 displays a boot menu that lets you choose which operating system to boot on a multi-boot system or to boot the repair console if installed. Depending on your preferences, you might want to change which option boots by default and how long the menu is displayed before the default option is booted. You can change these options from the Windows 2000 GUI or modify the source of the options, *boot.ini*, within Windows 2000 or from a console prompt.

 If you choose to modify the boot menu by editing *boot.ini*, make a backup of the file first in case you have problems editing the file. Also, keep in mind that you can modify the labels for each boot option by modifying *boot.ini*. For example, you might change "Windows 2000 Professional" to just "Windows 2000." Or you might change "MS-DOS" to "Windows 98."

Changing the default boot option

The [boot loader] section of *boot.ini* includes a setting named "default" that specifies the option that boots by default if you don't select any other options from the menu. Usually the main reason to change this setting is if your system contains Windows 9x and you want to switch from Windows 2000 to Windows 9x as the default boot option (or vice versa). Making the switch is as easy as modifying the value of the default setting. The easiest way to do that in Windows 2000 is through the System property sheet:

1. Right-click My Computer and choose Properties, or select My Computer and press Alt+Enter.

2. Click the Advanced tab, then click Startup and Recovery (see Figure 1-4).

3. From the Default Operating System drop-down list, select the OS that you want to boot by default. Click OK to save the changes and close the dialog.

You also can change the value of the default setting manually, which is useful for changing the value from Windows 9x:

1. Open My Computer and locate *boot.ini* in the root folder of the boot drive. If you're running Windows 2000, choose Tools → Folder Options, then click View and deselect the option Hide Protected Operating System Files so that you can view *boot.ini*.

2. Change the properties of *boot.ini* to remove the read-only attribute. In the GUI, right-click the file and choose Properties to access the

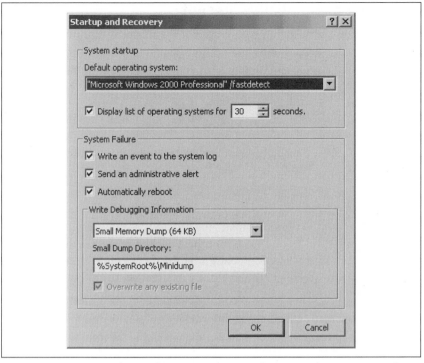

Figure 1-4. You can use the Windows 2000 GUI to configure some boot options, rather than directly modifying boot.ini

attribute. From a command line, use the following two commands to remove the read-only attribute (removes read-only and restores hidden and system attributes):

```
attrib -s -h -r boot.ini
attrib +s +h boot.ini
```

3. Open the *boot.ini* file with Edit, Notepad, or another text editor. Change the value of the default setting in the [boot loader] section to the OS you want to boot by default. Look in the [operating systems] section and note the value to the left of the = sign for the desired boot option. This is the value to use for "default." To configure Windows 98 as the default, for example, you would use the value default=c:\. Use copy and paste to make sure you get the entry right.

4. Save the file, and if desired, restore the read-only attribute (not required, but a good idea).

Changing menu display timeout

The boot menu remains on the screen for 30 seconds if you don't select a menu option. Windows 2000 boots the default operating system after the timeout period expires. Changing the timeout period is a simple matter of changing the timeout value in *boot.ini*. Follow these steps to change the value through the Windows 2000 GUI:

1. Right-click My Computer, choose Properties, click the Advanced tab, then click Startup and Recovery.

2. Change the value using the option "Display list of operating systems for *n* seconds."

3. Click OK to save the change.

You also can modify the value manually, which is useful when the system is booted to Windows 9x or a DOS prompt. See the previous section, "Changing the default boot option," to learn how to edit *boot.ini*. Change the value of the "timeout" setting in the [boot loader] section to the number of seconds the menu should be displayed.

Press an arrow key on the keyboard to stop the countdown and allow the boot menu to remain until you select an option.

Hiding the boot menu

If you always boot the same option and don't need to see the boot menu, you can hide it by setting the timeout value to 0. See the previous section for an explanation of how to change the "timeout" setting.

1.9   The Recovery Console

Windows 2000 provides a new feature called the Recovery Console that essentially gives you a bootable command console environment for restoring files, modifying the registry, troubleshooting, and other testing and repair operations. The Recovery Console enables you to read NTFS volumes, a major advantage and important reason for installing the console. A bootable DOS or Windows 9x diskette wouldn't give you that capability.

A common use for the Recovery Console is to make system changes that are preventing you from booting the system. For example, you might have installed an application that installed a buggy or incompatible driver, and the driver is preventing the system from booting. You can boot the Recovery

Console, disable the driver, then reboot normally to fix the problem. You can also treat the Recovery Console as a sort of quick command console that lets you access your Windows 2000 system without booting the full GUI. On a dual-boot system, for example, you might use the Recovery Console to quickly copy a file from an NTFS volume to a FAT volume for access by Windows 9x. Whatever the need, the Recovery Console gives you a quick way to boot the system without the GUI and perform a variety of tasks, including system troubleshooting and repair.

Installing and using the Recovery Console

When you install the Recovery Console it is added to the boot menu and the corresponding files are copied to the hard disk. This enables you to access the Recovery Console directly from the system without the Windows 2000 Setup disks (assuming the hard disk hasn't failed or become inaccessible). Follow these steps to install the Recovery Console:

1. Insert the Windows 2000 CD in the system and select No if prompted to upgrade to Windows 2000 (or hold down the Shift key when inserting the CD to bypass autorun).

2. Open a command console and change to the \i386 folder on the CD.

3. Execute the following command to install the Recovery Console:

   winnt32.exe /cmdcons

4. Follow the prompts to complete the installation.

Running the Recovery Console
from the Setup disks

You can run the Recovery Console from the Setup disks if you can't access the CD-ROM drive or boot the system from the hard disk. Follow these steps to run the Recovery Console from the Setup disks:

1. Insert the Windows 2000 Setup boot disk in the floppy drive and restart the system.

2. Provide the other Setup disks when prompted by Setup.

3. When prompted to install or repair Windows 2000, select the repair option.

4. Windows 2000 Setup gives you two repair options: use the Recovery Console or use the emergency repair process. Press C to use the Recovery Console.

Using the Recovery Console

When you start the Recovery Console it prompts you to select which Windows 2000 installation you want to access. Only one will be listed if you have only one installation of Windows 2000 on the system. Enter the number of the installation to use. The Recovery Console then prompts you for the Administrator password. Once you're logged in you'll see a familiar console prompt. Enter **help** to view a list of commands you can use in the console, or enter **help** *command*, where *command* is the name of the command for which you need syntax and description. For example, **help fixboot** displays information about the *fixboot* command, which you can use to repair the boot sector.

1.10 Drive letter assignments need to be changed

In some cases, particularly if you add a new CD drive or hard drive, you might need to change the drive IDs assigned to one or more drives. If you installed Windows 2000 on a Windows 9x system that contains a compressed volume, Windows 2000 won't see the compressed volume, and all volumes after that will have different drive IDs from those in your Windows 9x environment.

Changing a drive letter

You can't change the ID of a system or boot volume in Windows 2000, but you might be able to change drive order in the BIOS. However, you'll need to edit *boot.ini* to boot from the appropriate partition, as changing drive IDs in the BIOS will change the logical partition order.

In some cases Windows 2000 might assign a drive letter to the CD-ROM drive lower than one or more of the hard drives, and you might want to group all of the hard drives together in terms of ID. Or, you might simply prefer a different drive ID for your CD-ROM drive. You also might want to rearrange hard drive IDs on a system with multiple physical drives or logical volumes. Whatever the case, changing the drive letter is easy:

1. Right-click My Computer and choose Manage to open the Computer Management console.

2. Click the Disk Management branch, then right-click the drive in the right pane and choose Change Drive Letter and Path. If you're changing a CD-ROM drive and it doesn't appear in the right pane, switch to Disk List or Graphical View.

3. In the Drive Letter and Paths dialog, click Edit.

4. Select a drive ID, click OK, and confirm the change.

1.11   I forgot the Administrator password

Forgetting the Administrator password can range from a nuisance to a complete disaster. If you've just performed a clean install of Windows 2000, forgetting the Administrator password you assigned during Setup is a nuisance—you can simply perform the installation again, losing an hour or so but no data or accounts. If you upgraded your previous installation or if you've been using the system for a while, forgetting the Administrator account can be a real problem. In this situation, recovering from the problem relies a lot on preparation before the fact. Even without any preparation, however, you can recover the system through the use of some third-party utilities.

Before you agonize over the lost password, take a few seconds to check for a simple mistake. If you're relatively certain of the password but it won't work, check the caps lock key. The password is case sensitive. If the caps lock key is off, try entering the password with it on. You might have inadvertently had the caps lock key on when you entered the password for the Administrator account during installation. If so, log on and change the password to be lowercase using the Users and Groups branch of the Computer Management console.

Use a different account

Hopefully, you have at least one other account that is a member of the administrators group. If so, you can simply log in using that account and change the password for the Administrator account using the Local Users and Groups branch in the Computer Management console.

Delete the SAM hive

If you can boot the system and get read/write access to the system folder (the one containing Windows 2000), you can delete from the registry the Security Account Manager (SAM) hive, which contains the accounts. You'll lose all accounts other than the Administrator account (which will then have a blank password), but at least you'll be able to boot the system and access your applications and data without having to reinstall Windows 2000. You should not consider using this procedure on a server with numerous accounts that would be difficult to recreate. In that situation, see "Recovering the system," later in this section.

You can't use the Recovery Console to delete the SAM, since the Recovery Console requires the Administrator password to log on to the selected Windows 2000 installation.

Follow these steps to delete the SAM hive:

1. Boot the system using a bootable DOS/Windows 9x diskette (FAT volumes only) or a bootable disk with a driver capable of reading NTFS volumes (such as Winternals' ERD Commander—see *http://www. winternals.com*).

2. At the command prompt, change to the *systemroot\System32\Config* folder.

3. Enter `ren sam sam.old` to rename the SAM, or simply delete the file.

4. Restart the system.

5. At the Windows 2000 logon prompt, enter the Administrator account with no password.

6. After logon, open the Local Users and Groups branch of the Computer Management console, change the Administrator password, and recreate any lost accounts.

Back up and reinstall

If you can boot the system with an account that has the ability to back up the system, you can reinstall Windows 2000 to assign a new Administrator account and password, then restore the backup set to recover your application settings. Since Windows 2000 Backup doesn't require a tape drive like Windows NT's version, you can back up to a local file or network server, provided you have enough space to contain the system.

 This option is useful on systems with NTFS boot volumes when you don't have a means of booting to a floppy with NTFS support.

Before you go this route, consider the catch: you're going to lose all accounts in the original installation. If you're dealing with a workstation with only a few accounts, it's not critical. You can easily recreate the accounts after reinstalling Windows 2000. On a server with numerous accounts, however, you should strongly consider the solution in the next section, "Recovering the system," which will enable you to retain all of your current accounts and does not require reinstallation of the OS.

Here's how to reinstall Windows 2000 while retaining your program and customization settings:

1. Boot the system using the account that has the necessary permissions and rights to back up the system. Back up the Windows 2000 folder as well as the Documents and Settings folder.

2. Run Setup and install Windows 2000 either to a new folder or to the original location. Don't forget the Administrator password you assign during Setup!

3. After installation boot the system and run Backup. Start the Restore wizard and click Next. In the Restore Wizard dialog, click Import File. Locate the backup set you created in step 1 and restore it. If you installed Windows 2000 to a new folder, remember to redirect the files to the new folder rather than the original one.

4. After the restoration is complete, restart the system and log on with the new Administrator password, then check your system to make sure your applications run properly.

Recovering the system

If reinstalling is not an appealing solution or you don't have an account that can back up the system, there is one other method you can use to recover the system. This option is most useful if you've been working with the system for some time and don't want to lose or have to recreate the current configuration. It'll cost you a little money, but that could be a small price to pay if you simply can't go through a reinstall.

While there are multiple tools on the market for Windows 2000 repair and recovery, two products from Winternals (*http://www.winternals.com*) are targeted specifically at system recovery. Both *ERD Commander Professional* and *NTRecover* with the *NT Locksmith* add-on provide a means of changing any password, including the Administrator account. In addition, both tools provide the ability to boot a completely dead system and recover data from the system. Check out Winternals' Web site for more information about their products.

1.12   Windows 2000 runs chkdsk at startup

Windows 2000 provides recoverability of the filesystem, which means it can recover filesystem errors, particularly for NTFS volumes. To that end, Windows 2000 writes data to the disk at shutdown to indicate that the volume has been shut down properly, meaning that there are no open files and no uncompleted disk I/O. When Windows 2000 starts, it checks the filesystem to determine if it was shut down properly, and if not, it automatically runs *chkdsk* at startup to analyze and repair the filesystem.

Shut down properly

The best way to keep *chkdsk* from running automatically at startup is to make sure you shut down the system properly. Choose Start → Shutdown, then Shut down or Restart, as needed. Don't just turn off the machine, as you could not only lose some data but also potentially corrupt your Windows 2000 installation. While I've never had it happen in the several times it has been necessary to shut off the system rather than shut it down, you shouldn't run the risk if you don't have to.

Disable automatic chkdsk execution

It's possible to configure a system to run *chkdsk* at startup even when there is no problem with the drive. If your system is running *chkdsk* at startup even after you shut down the system properly, this could be the case. You can check a setting in the registry to determine if Windows 2000 is forcing a check at startup. Here's how:

1. Click Start → Run, and enter **regedit** in the Run dialog box.

2. In the Registry Editor, open the branch HKEY_LOCAL_MACHINE\
   SYSTEM\CurrentControlSet\Control\Session Manager.

3. Make note of the current setting for BootExecute in case you decide to restore it.

4. Change the value of BootExecute to read **autocheck autochk *** and then close the Registry Editor.

 The value for BootExecute referenced in step 4 is the default value and restores the default behavior to *chkdsk*.

1.13   Can't log on after adding a hard drive or breaking a mirror

Your system boots, you specify a valid username and password, and you receive messages indicating a logon in process. But then Windows 2000 displays the logon dialog again rather than displaying the desktop. This behavior can occur if the Windows 2000 boot partition drive letter does not match the drive letter assigned during Windows 2000 Setup. This situation can arise in the following circumstances:

- You install a new drive, which implicitly changes drive order.

- You change drive order in the BIOS.

- You break a system/boot mirror and try to boot from the old former shadow drive with the old primary drive missing or unavailable.

Windows 2000 records drive letters in the registry and reassigns drive letters on the basis of a Globally Unique Identifier (GUID) that it records for each volume. If the GUID changes, it's possible the original drive letter might not be reassigned to the boot volume. The solution to the problem depends on the cause.

Restoring the original drive configuration

If you added a new drive to the system or changed the order of drives through the BIOS, the immediate solution is to restore the original configuration by undoing what you did. For example, remove the new drive or change its configuration (as in restoring the original SCSI IDs), or restore the original BIOS order. Try these tasks as appropriate to fix the problem:

- If you've added any cloned hard disks to the system, remove them and restart, then try to log on.

- Restore the BIOS order of drives if you've modified the BIOS configuration.

- Remove any newly added hard drives.

- For SCSI drives, restore the SCSI ID of the boot/system disk to what it was when you installed Windows 2000.

If you can't restore the original configuration, you need to modify the registry, as explained next.

Restoring drive ID assignments remotely through the registry

In situations where you can't make changes in the BIOS or change physical drive configuration to restore the original GUIDs, you must modify the registry to restore the original settings. Since you can't log on locally through the Windows 2000 GUI, you'll have to either connect to the system's registry from another computer on the network or use the Recovery Console locally to accomplish the change.

This option relies on the problem computer being networked and you having the ability to modify the problem computer's registry from another computer on the network. This example assumes you need to swap drive IDs C and D:

1. Log on to a Windows 2000 or Windows NT system on the network.

2. If the problem computer is not part of a domain, map a connection to the computer's IPC$ share using that computer's local administrator account, using the following command (include the asterisk at the end):

   NET USE *problem_computer_name*\IPC$ /user:administrator *

3. Open Regedt32. Choose Registry → Select Computer, then enter the name of or browse to the problem computer to open its registry.

4. Open the registry key HKEY_LOCAL_MACHINE\SYSTEM\Mounted-Devices.

5. In Regedt32, select the MountedDevices key and choose Security → Permissions. Verify that the Administrators group has full control.

6. Close Regedt32 and open Regedit, then locate and open the HKEY_LOCAL_MACHINE\SYSTEM\MountedDevices key.

7. Locate the drive currently assigned as the boot drive ID (in this example assume \DosDevices\C:). Right-click \DosDevices\C: and choose Rename. Rename the entry to \DosDevices\Z: to make C: available for the correct boot drive.

8. Rename the correct boot drive to \DosDevices\C: substituting the appropriate drive ID if your installation originally booted from a drive other than C.

9. Rename \DosDevices\Z: to whatever drive letter is appropriate for your installation, such as \DosDevices\D:.

10. Quit Regedit and start Regedt32, then set the permissions on the MountedDevices key back to its original settings for Administrators.

11. Close Regedt32 and restart the problem computer to verify that you can now log on.

Restoring drive ID assignments locally through the registry

If you prefer to do the majority of the registry editing locally rather than across the network, you can make one change from across the network, then make the remaining changes locally:

1. Log on to a Windows 2000 or Windows NT system on the network.

2. If the problem computer is not part of a domain, map a connection to the computer's IPC$ share using that computer's local administrator account. Use the following command (include the asterisk at the end):

   NET USE *problem_computer_name*\IPC$ /user:administrator *

3. Open Regedt32. Choose Registry → Select Computer, then enter the name of or browse to the problem computer to open its registry.

4. Open the key HKEY_LOCAL_MACHINE\Software\Microsoft\Windows NT\Current Version\Winlogon.

5. Change the value of Userinit:Reg_SZ:C:\WINNT\System32\userinit.exe to Userinit:Reg_SZ:userinit.exe, changing the absolute path to a relative path.

6. You should now be able to log on locally to the computer. Follow steps 5 through 11 in the previous section to modify the drive IDs in the registry.

Restoring drive ID assignments with a duplicate System32 folder using the Recovery Console

You can still recover the system to enable you to log on and change drive IDs even if the problem computer isn't on a network or doesn't allow remote registry modification:

1. Boot the system using the Recovery Console, either through the installed console or through the Setup boot disks.

2. At the console prompt, issue the following commands:

   set allowwildcards = true
   set allowallpaths = true

3. If you receive an error in step 2 indicating that the *set* command is disabled, you need to enable the command. Use one of the following tools to modify the policies in Local Policies\Security Options to include the two policies Allow Automatic Administrative Logon and Allow Floppy Copy And Access To All Drives And All Folders:

   — Security Configuration and Analysis MMC console

   — Domain Controller Security Policy

   — Domain Security Policy

   — Local Security Policy

4. In the Recovery Console, create a *Winnt**System32* folder on the drive that is being incorrectly assigned as the boot drive.

5. Expand and copy the file *userinit.exe* from the Windows 2000 CD to this folder using the *expand* command.

6. Restart the system and log on as administrator.

7. Follow steps 5 through 11 in the procedure "Restoring drive ID assignments remotely through the registry," earlier in this section, to change the drive assignments.

1.14   Boot problems in systems with multiple drives

The inability to boot from a drive you think is good can be caused by changes to the active partition or by the value of the setting in *boot.ini* for the given boot option. For example, you might have cloned a drive to replace your old drive but not made the partition on the new drive active, preventing Windows 2000 from booting from the drive. Or you might have marked a partition active in Windows 2000 that doesn't contain a bootable OS, then tried to reboot.

Only one partition can be active at a time, and the one that is active is used to boot the operating system at startup. How you reactivate the appropriate partition depends on whether or not you can boot Windows 2000.

Making a partition active

You use the Disk Management console in Windows 2000 to activate a partition. The Fdisk program lets you perform the same function from a command prompt. Fdisk isn't included with Windows 2000, however, so you'll need a bootable Windows 9x or DOS diskette to activate the partition and boot Windows 2000. Here's how to mark a partition active if you're able to boot Windows 2000, which is useful when you want to boot an OS in a different partition:

 If you can boot to a Linux or Unix partition, you can use the *fdisk* command to activate the Windows 2000 partition.

1. Right-click My Computer and choose Manage, or open the Computer Management object in the Control Panel, to open the Computer Management console.

2. Click the Disk Management branch in the Computer Management console.

3. In the right pane, right-click the partition you want to make active and choose Mark Partition Active.

4. Close the console and reboot.

If you can't boot Windows 2000 because it resides on an inactive partition, you'll need to use Fdisk to activate the partition. Unfortunately, you can't just boot a Windows 2000 system to a command prompt and use Fdisk to activate the partition, since Windows 2000 doesn't include Fdisk. So, you'll need a bootable DOS diskette with the Fdisk program on it. Follow these steps to activate a partition with Fdisk:

1. Insert a bootable DOS or Windows 9x disk containing *fdisk.exe* in drive A and boot the system.

2. At the command prompt, type **fdisk** and press Enter.

3. When Fdisk opens, press Y if it asks if you want to enable large disk support.

4. Select item 2, "Set active partition."

5. Select the partition you want to make active.

6. Exit Fdisk and reboot the computer.

 Be careful with Fdisk. It's possible (and quite easy) to delete a partition and all the data it contains if you don't pay attention to what you're doing.

Modifying boot.ini (FAT/FAT32 partitions only)

In rare circumstances you might have problems booting Windows 2000 because of the entry in *boot.ini* that defines the Windows 2000 boot option. The default entry looks like this:

```
multi(0)disk(0)rdisk(0)partition(1)\Winnt
```

The numbers could vary depending on which drive and partition contains Windows 2000. For example, if Windows 2000 is on the second partition in a folder called *Win2k*, the entry would look like this:

```
multi(0)disk(0)rdisk(0)partition(2)\Win2k
```

If you have problems booting Windows 2000, use a bootable DOS or Windows 9x diskette to boot the system. Then, edit *boot.ini* to modify the line according to your disk configuration. (You won't be able to edit *boot.ini* if it is stored on an NTFS partition unless you use a third-party utility that enables you to boot from a floppy with an NTFS driver.) If everything looks correct and Windows 2000 is installed on a SCSI drive, try replacing multi with scsi, as in:

```
scsi(0)disk(0)rdisk(0)partition(1)\Winnt
```

1.15 Convert a FAT partition to NTFS

Windows 2000 supports three filesystems: FAT, FAT32, and NTFS. FAT stands for File Allocation Table, the original filesystem used in DOS (although modified somewhat over the years). FAT is supported by all Microsoft operating systems, making it the most compatible filesystem and a necessity on dual-boot systems if you want all volumes to be available from each OS.

FAT32 is a 32-bit version of the FAT filesystem, introduced in Windows 95, that offers better performance and efficiency. Windows NT does not support FAT32, but Windows 2000 does.

The third filesystem, NTFS (which stands for New Technology File System), offers much better security than FAT and much better fault tolerance to recover from filesystem errors. NTFS is supported by Windows NT and Windows 2000, but it requires a third-party driver for access by Windows 9x.

 You'll find a discussion of an NTFS driver for Windows 9x in the next section.

When you install Windows 2000 you have the option of formatting (new filesystem) or converting (existing filesystem) to NTFS. You can convert to NTFS at any time, however, with very little effort.

 If you need to reconfigure partitions, including resizing them without having to backup and restore the data, consider using one of the third-party partition applications. Two possibilities are Partition Magic (*http://www.powerquest.com*) and PartitionIt (*http://www.quarterdeck.com*).

Using the Convert command

Follow these steps to convert a volume from FAT or FAT32 to NTFS:

1. Boot the system and open a command console.

2. At the command prompt enter the following command:

   `convert c: /fs:ntfs`

   Replace **c:** with the appropriate drive letter if you are converting a drive other than C.

3. Windows 2000 will perform the conversion immediately unless you are converting the system volume. In that situation, Windows 2000 schedules the conversion for the next time you restart the system. Restart to complete the conversion.

1.16   Windows 9x can't see NTFS volumes on a dual-boot system

Although Windows 2000 now supports FAT32, something Windows NT did not do, Windows 9x systems don't natively support NTFS. This means that on systems that dual-boot Windows 9x and Windows 2000, the Windows 9x OS can't see any NTFS volumes. In many dual-boot situations it is very useful for both operating systems to see all available volumes. There are two ways to approach the problem: revert from NTFS to FAT32 or install a third-party NTFS driver for Windows 9x.

Converting to FAT32

Although Windows 2000 provides a utility to convert from FAT/FAT32 (hereafter referred to simply as FAT) volumes to NTFS, there is no corresponding utility to migrate from NTFS back to FAT. It is possible, although the conversion is somewhat cumbersome and time-consuming. If you don't need the security or other benefits offered by NTFS (such as mounted volumes, encryption, recoverability, etc.), spending a little time to convert to FAT could be a solution for you. You might even see a minor improvement in performance, since NTFS imposes more overhead than FAT.

Converting from a FAT filesystem to NTFS requires that you completely back up the volume, format it as FAT, and restore the files. If the volume hosts only programs and data, it's not such a chore. If the volume happens to contain Windows 2000, however, you're in for a little more work. Before you perform the following, perform a test backup and restore of a few files to make sure that you can successfully restore the files—a backup set won't do you any good if you can't restore it.

Converting a data volume to FAT32

1. Back up the NTFS volume to tape, CD-R, CD-RW, or other mass storage media. If you use the Windows 2000 Backup utility you can back up the volume data to a file, although you'll need enough disk space on another volume to contain the data.

2. In Windows 2000, format the volume as FAT. To do so, right-click the drive in My Computer and choose Format. In the Format dialog, select FAT or FAT32 as desired for the filesystem.

3. Restore the files from the backup to the newly formatted volume.

4. Boot Windows 9x and verify that you can access the volume.

Converting a Windows 2000 volume to FAT32

1. Have a bootable DOS or Windows 9x disk on hand that contains a copy of Fdisk.

2. In Windows 2000 Backup, update the ERD from the Welcome tab, and select the option to copy the registry to the repair folder.

3. Back up the NTFS volume using Windows 2000 Backup. Select the entire Windows 2000 NTFS volume and system state data. Select the option to verify the files after backup to ensure a good backup. You can back up the files to a network server if available, but bear in mind that the backup could consume several hundred megabytes of space.

4. Run Windows 2000 Setup again. Select the option to install a clean copy of Windows 2000 rather than upgrade.

5. After the system restarts to begin installation, Setup will ask if you want to repair the existing installation. Press Esc to indicate that you want to install rather than repair.

6. Setup will prompt for the location to install Windows 2000. Delete the existing partition and specify the unpartitioned space as the location. Direct Setup to format the volume using FAT. If Setup doesn't allow you to delete the partition, boot the system using a DOS or Windows 9x boot disk that contains the Fdisk utility. Run *fdisk* and delete the NTFS partition (which will show up as a non-DOS partition). Create a primary DOS partition, then reboot. Run Setup again and install to the new partition, formatting it as FAT.

7. After installation, boot the new copy of Windows 2000. Open the Backup utility and restore the backup set created in step 2.

8. Reboot the system to incorporate application, security, and other settings from the restored installation.

Using an NTFS driver for Windows 9x

There's another approach to take if you don't want to go through the hassle of a backup/reinstall/restore, or if you want to retain the benefits of the NTFS filesystem for Windows 2000. You can add a driver to Windows 9x that will enable it to access the NTFS volume.

You'll find such a driver, called NTFS for Win98, at *http://www.winternals. com*. Winternals offers a demo version for download that provides read-only support of NTFS volumes in Windows 9x. The full version supports read/ write access to NTFS volumes. One limitation of NTFS for Win98 is that it doesn't support any of the security of NTFS, making all files accessible from

Windows 9x regardless of the security settings in Windows 2000. The other limitation is that NTFS for Win98 doesn't support Windows 2000's Encrypting File System (EFS). Any files stored on the NTFS volume using EFS will not be accessible under Windows 9x.

Even with these limitations, NTFS for Win98 is a great way to gain access to your NTFS volumes from Windows 9x on a dual-boot system.

CHAPTER 2

Configuring Hardware

Although Setup does a great job of configuring your system's hardware—in many cases with little or no input from you—occasionally you'll need to either modify the existing configuration or add new devices. In some cases the configuration change is required because of a conflict between two devices. In this chapter you'll learn about *hardware profiles*, how to create and use them, and how to avoid hardware conflicts by disabling devices under specific configurations. You'll also learn how to make a backup of your system's critical files so you can restore the system if a problem occurs.

Disk space is another issue that will eventually crop up. This chapter covers installation of a new hard disk and how to clone your system from one disk to another. You'll learn about other steps you can take to increase available disk capacity, such as converting from FAT to FAT32 or NTFS, removing unneeded Windows 2000 components, using mounted volumes, employing disk quotas, and using compression.

You might also want to take advantage of some of the benefits offered by Windows 2000's new dynamic disk structure, which overcomes the four-partition limitation of the basic disk structure used by previous Microsoft operating systems. You'll need to use dynamic disks if you intend to create volume or stripe sets on your system, because Windows 2000 only supports existing volume and stripe sets on basic disks (those created with Windows NT).

Finally, this chapter offers quick solutions for a handful of other configuration issues, such as how to readily view and manipulate IRQ and other resource settings, and how to obtain system configuration summaries.

2.1   View or change IRQ and other resource settings

Windows 2000's support for plug-and-play and its incorporation of a Windows 9x–like hardware interface mean that configuring hardware settings is much easier than it is in Windows NT. As with Windows 9x, you use the Device Manager to view and configure device resource settings such as IRQ, I/O base address, and RAM address. In most cases it isn't necessary to modify settings, but you might occasionally need to modify device resource settings to resolve a conflict between devices or to configure a device with a non-default setting.

Use the Device Manager to manage device resources

The Device Manager resides in the Computer Management console. With the Device Manager you can view devices installed in the system, configure their resource settings, update their drivers, perform troubleshooting, and accomplish other device management tasks. Follow these steps to configure a device's resource settings through the Device Manager:

1. Right-click My Computer and choose Manage to open the Computer Management console, then click the Device Manager branch.

2. Right-click Device Manager, choose View, then select the desired view option using the following list as a guide. When configuring a specific device's resources, viewing devices by type is the most useful method. Figure 2-1 shows the view by resource type.

   Devices by type
   > View the list of devices sorted by device type, such as Computer, Disk Drives, Display Adapters, DVD/CD-ROM Drives, etc.

   Devices by connection
   > View the list of devices sorted by how they interact with the system.

   Resources by type
   > View a list of resources used, sorted by resource type, including DMA, I/O base address, IRQ, and memory assignment.

   Resources by connection
   > View a list of resources used, sorted by how the device interacts with the system.

3. Locate the device whose resources you want to modify, then either double-click the device, or right-click the device and choose Properties.

4. Click the Resources tab to view the current resource settings for the device. Typically Windows 2000 automatically assigns a default set of resources to a device.

5. Deselect the option "Use automatic settings."

6. Select the resource you want to change, then click Change Setting. If you get an error message that you can't change the setting using the current

Configuring Hardware

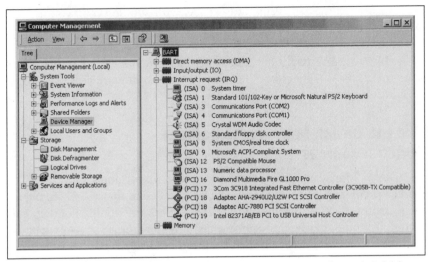

Figure 2-1. Viewing devices by type is the default, but other view modes are helpful for configuration and troubleshooting

configuration, select a different configuration set from the Settings based on drop-down list. Then click Change Setting again to display a dialog enabling you to select the desired resource setting.

7. When you've finished configuring the device, close the Device Manager. Depending on which device you configured, you might need to restart Windows 2000 for the change to take effect.

2.2 Create a system summary

In addition to using the Device Manager to view and manage device settings, you also can use it to create printed reports of your system's configuration. You can generate a system summary report, a report of a specific device or device class, or a combination report showing all devices and settings along with a summary.

Use the Device Manager to create system reports

Follow these steps to create a report with the Device Manager:

1. Open the Computer Management console and then the Device Manager branch.

2. Right-click Device Manager and choose View → Print.

3. If you want to print a report for a specific device or device class, select that device or class.

4. In the Print dialog box, select the report type you want to see (system summary, selected class or device, or all devices and system summary), select the target printer, and click Print.

2.3 Turn off or remove conflicting or unneeded devices

Windows 2000 makes configuring hardware much easier than it is in Windows NT. Its support for plug-and-play means that in many cases you can simply install a device, then boot Windows 2000 and let it detect and install support for the device. In the case of legacy devices or a system containing several devices, there is the possibility of a resource conflict. For example, a device might share the same interrupt or base I/O address as another device.

While you might be able to change the resource allocation for a device and clear up a conflict, in some cases you can't. For example, there might not be any available IRQs for reassignment, or the conflicting devices may not support the available IRQs. In such situations, you can turn off the conflicting device and enable it only when you need it, or remove the device altogether.

 An alternative to removing or disabling a device is to use hardware profiles.

Disable a device temporarily

Turning off a device resolves the conflict (because Windows 2000 no longer loads the driver or uses the device), and it has the advantage of leaving the device installed so you can use it later if needed. Turning off or disabling a device is easy:

1. Right-click My Computer and choose Manage to open the Computer Management console. Then click the Device Manager branch to open the Device Manager.

2. In the list of installed devices, locate the device with the conflict. Windows 2000 should recognize the conflict and show an exclamation icon beside the device.

3. Right-click the device and choose Properties, or simply double-click the device to open its property sheet.

4. In the General page, select "Do not use this device" from the Device usage drop-down list.

5. Click OK, then close the Computer Management console.

Remove a device

You can remove a device if you don't intend to use it anymore. This can clear up conflicts or problems caused by a buggy or incompatible driver. The benefit of removing a device rather than disabling it is that Windows 2000 removes the device driver files. While this isn't usually a major issue, it's a good housecleaning move and frees up a small amount of space on your drive.

1. Right-click My Computer and choose Manage to open the Computer Management console. Then click the Device Manager branch to open the Device Manager.

2. Locate and select the device, then choose Action → Uninstall. Or, simply right-click the device and choose Uninstall.

3. Windows 2000 prompts you to confirm that you want to uninstall the device. Click OK to confirm the deletion.

2.4 Use different hardware settings at different times

Although disabling a device to overcome a conflict isn't difficult, it does take a few steps to complete. A *hardware profile* can give you the same results and works automatically at startup. Each hardware profile stores a system configuration by name. You can select the hardware profile to use at startup, or, in many cases, Windows 2000 can detect the appropriate profile automatically.

For example, assume you use a PC Card network adapter in your notebook computer at some times, and a network adapter in a docking station at other times. Also assume the two adapters need to use the same resources, so they conflict if both are enabled. To resolve the conflict without requiring that you disable one of the adapters each time you boot, you can create two hardware profiles called *Docked* and *Undocked*, each of which has the appropriate driver enabled and the other disabled. When Windows 2000 boots, it automatically detects whether or not the system is docked and uses the appropriate hardware profile automatically. If Windows 2000 is unable to determine which hardware profile to use, it prompts you at startup to select the desired profile.

Set up hardware profiles

Setting up hardware profiles is a two-phase process: first you create a profile, then you selectively disable devices in the profile. By default, Windows 2000 enables a device for all hardware profiles, but you can boot with a specific profile, then configure the device in Device Manager to not be active in the selected profile.

First, create the profile:

1. Right-click My Computer and choose Properties to open the System Properties sheet. Then click the Hardware tab.

2. Click Hardware Profiles to open the Hardware Profiles dialog.

3. Current profiles are listed in the Available hardware profiles list. Select a profile to copy from, then click Copy.

4. Enter a name for the new profile that describes its purpose.

5. Select one of the following options:

   Wait until I select a hardware profile
   Select this option if you want Windows 2000 to wait indefinitely at startup until you select the desired profile.

   Select the first profile listed if I don't select a profile in
   Select this option to have Windows 2000 automatically select the first profile in the list if you haven't selected a profile within the specified time. Set the time with the associated spin control.

6. Use the up and down arrow buttons to move the profiles into the desired order and then click OK.

After you create the profile, you need to restart the system and boot with the profile in which you want to disable a given device. Then disable the device with the Device Manager:

1. Restart the system and select the hardware profile in which you want to modify devices.

2. Open the Computer Management console and select the Device Manager branch.

3. Locate and select the device you want to disable, then choose Action → Properties or simply double-click the device.

4. From the Device Usage drop-down list, choose "Do not use this device" in the current hardware profile (see Figure 2-2).

5. Repeat steps 3 and 4 for any other devices you want to disable in the current profile.

6. Restart the system and select another hardware profile, then disable any devices as needed per steps 3 and 4.

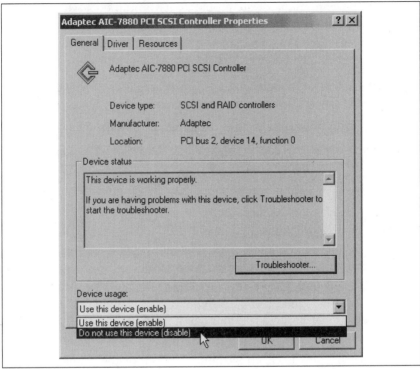

Figure 2-2. Disable devices in the current profile through the property sheet for the device

2.5   Take a snapshot of the current settings for safekeeping

Installing Windows 2000 and your applications and then configuring everything just the way you want it takes a lot of time. One hardware problem or
failed software installation could force you to redo much of that work. It's
therefore a good idea to make a backup of your system's configuration information after you have the system set up and configured, and prior to making any system changes, such as adding or removing hardware or software.

Windows 2000 stores its configuration data in the registry, a group of several files stored in the *systemroot\System32\Config* folder. The registry stores
settings that define the way Windows 2000 looks and functions and also
stores application settings. If you experience a problem with the registry, having a backup copy of it can make it relatively simple to recover the system.

Backing up the registry is just one task you should perform on a regular
basis. Consider the following tasks as a good guideline to follow to ensure
that you can recover your system quickly in the event of a hardware failure

or other problem that causes your system configuration to become corrupted or lost.

 Backing up the registry and system state data is no substitute for a complete backup of the filesystem. Having the registry and system state data backed up can help you recover the system, but it doesn't address problems such as new drivers being replaced by older ones, lost data files, or hardware failures. Make sure you also implement a regular backup strategy for your entire filesystem.

Back up system state data

The system state data comprises the registry, the COM+ class registration database, the system boot files, and protected files in the *dllcache* folder. On a Windows 2000 domain controller, the system state data also includes the registry and other system components such as the *Sysvol* folder.

It's extremely important that you have a backup of the system state data in order to restore the system should the need arise. The system state data can include 200 megabytes or more of data, so plan your backup accordingly.

You back up the system state data through the Windows 2000 Backup utility:

1. Choose Start → Programs → Accessories → System Tools → Backup to open the Backup application.

2. Click the Backup tab, then select the System State box in the path tree.

3. Select any other files you want to back up, then specify location and filename (if applicable) for the backup.

4. Click Start Backup and follow the prompts to complete the backup operation.

If you need to restore the system state data, run Backup again, select the backup set containing the system state data backup, then restore the set to the system. Restart the system to incorporate the restored files and settings.

Any time you perform a full backup of the system you should include the system state data in the backup to make it easier to restore the system should the need arise.

Back up the registry with the Backup utility

The registry stores the majority of a Windows 2000 system's configuration and is a critical part of the system. As mentioned earlier, the registry comprises several files in the *systemroot\System32\Config* folder. Windows 2000 loads the files at startup and builds the working registry from them.

Backing up the registry is an important step in ensuring that you can recover your system in the event of a problem. You should always back up the registry before making any changes to the system. One of the easiest ways to back up the registry is to use the Windows 2000 Backup utility:

1. Choose Start → Programs → Accessories → System Tools → Backup to open the Backup utility.

2. Click the Welcome tab, then click Emergency Repair Disk.

3. Select the option "Also backup the registry to the repair directory" (see Figure 2-3).

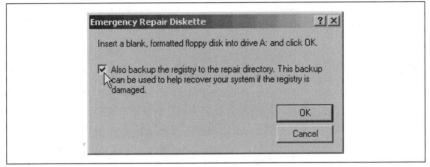

Figure 2-3. Back up the registry to the Repair folder through the ERD wizard in Backup

4. Click OK. Backup copies the registry files to *systemroot\Repair\RegBack*.

5. If there is a floppy disk in the drive, Backup also updates the repair data on the diskette. (See "Create a repair disk" later in this section for detailed information on the ERD.)

Back up the registry manually with the Recovery Console

The Backup utility offers the quickest and easiest way to back up the registry to the repair folder. If you can't log on to the system for some reason, or if you want to copy the registry files to a removable disk or other storage media, you can use the Recovery Console to do so. You also can use the Recovery Console to restore the registry files manually. However, you'll need to be able to configure the Recovery Console to allow all paths if you want to copy files to or from a removable media (such as a Zip disk).

1. Configure the local security policy or domain policy to enable the use of the *set* command in the Recovery Console. To do so using the Local

Security Policy snap-in, choose Start → Programs → Administrative Tools → Local Security Policy. Or select Local Security Policy from the Administrative Tools folder in the Control Panel. Expand Local Policies\Security Options, then enable the option "Recovery Console: Allow floppy copy and access to all drives and all folders."

2. Run the Backup utility and back up the repair data as explained in the previous section.

3. Restart the system and select the Recovery Console option from the boot menu, or start the Recovery Console from the Windows 2000 Setup disks if you don't have the Recovery Console installed on the system.

4. Log in to the desired Windows 2000 installation through the Recovery Console, and at the command prompt issue the following command:

   `set AllowAllPaths = true`

5. Change to the *systemroot\Repair\RegBack* folder, then copy each file in the folder to the desired destination.

If it becomes necessary to restore the registry files using the Recovery Console, simply copy the files from their backup location to the *systemroot\System32\Config* folder and restart the system.

Create a repair disk

In Windows NT the Emergency Repair Disk (ERD) contained system boot files *config.nt* and *autoexec.nt* along with registry files. In Windows 2000, however, the ERD contains only *config.nt*, *autoexec.nt*, and *setup.log*. The registry is no longer copied to the ERD, which makes it doubly important that you back up the registry using one of the methods described previously.

Even without the registry, the ERD is an important part of your system recovery strategy, so you should make sure to update the ERD any time you make changes to the system. Follow these steps to create the ERD:

1. Insert a blank, formatted disk in the floppy drive.

2. Choose Start → Programs → Accessories → System Tools → Backup to open the Backup utility.

3. Click the Welcome tab and click Emergency Repair Disk.

4. Select the option "Also backup the registry to the repair directory."

5. Click OK. Backup copies the registry files to *systemroot\Repair\RegBack* and updates the ERD.

2.6   Running low on disk space

With hard disk prices much lower than they were just a few years ago, adding another drive or replacing an existing drive is a good way to gain more storage space. If that isn't practical, however, there are some other steps you can take to gain more storage space.

Clean out files

Perhaps the most obvious way to gain more space is to get rid of files and applications you don't need:

- Use the Add/Remove Programs object in the Control Panel to remove applications you no longer need.

- Empty the Recycle Bin on a regular basis.

- Right-click the Internet Explorer icon and choose Properties, then click Delete Files to clear the cache.

- Archive those documents you no longer need to tape, diskette, network server, or removable storage.

Convert from FAT to FAT32 or NTFS

If you're using FAT, 30% or more of the drive could be wasted through *cluster slack*. The OS allocates space on the drive using *clusters*. A cluster is the smallest allocation unit and comprises a fixed number of disk sectors, the number of which depends on disk geometry and other factors. As cluster size increases, the chance that a cluster won't be completely filled with data increases. That unfilled space in the cluster is cluster slack and is essentially wasted space.

Because of the difference in structure between FAT and FAT32 or NTFS volumes, you can improve storage efficiency considerably by converting from FAT to either FAT32 or NTFS. Windows 2000 does not include a conversion utility to convert FAT volumes to FAT32. If the system dual-boots to Windows 9x, you can use the Windows 9x FAT32 Converter (Start → Programs → Accessories → System Tools → Drive Converter) to convert to FAT32. Simply boot the system to Windows 9x and use the utility to convert the volume.

You also can convert FAT volumes to NTFS, keeping in mind that NTFS volumes are not accessible to Windows 9x without a third-party driver. Converting to NTFS will give you much the same benefit in terms of storage efficiency as FAT32, and it offers the additional benefits of greater security, mountable volumes, encryption, compression, and several other features not supported by FAT. See Section 1.15, "Convert a FAT partition to NTFS," to learn how to convert a FAT volume to NTFS.

Remove unneeded Windows components

Windows 2000 Setup installs a lot of services, some of which you might not need. You can use the Add/Remove Programs object in the Control Panel to remove Windows 2000 components, but before you rush off to the Control Panel, here's a tip: it doesn't list all of the installed components. For example, Accessories, Fax, Imaging, and a handful of other items don't appear in the list of components you can remove. With a simple modification of a text file, however, you can make these show up in the Add/Remove Programs object so you can remove them:

1. Open the folder *systemroot\Inf*. The folder is hidden, so you'll need to turn on display of hidden files if you haven't already done so.

2. Find the file *sysoc.inf* and copy it to *sysoc.inf.old*.

3. Open the original *sysoc.inf* file in Notepad. Search for occurrences of the word HIDE and delete them. Here's an example of a before and after line from *sysoc.inf*:

   Before: Games=ocgen.dll,OcEntry,games.inf,HIDE,7

   After: Games=ocgen.dll,OcEntry,games.inf,,7

   Don't delete the commas on either side of HIDE, and don't leave a space between the commas.

4. Save the file and exit Notepad.

5. Open the Add/Remove Programs object in the Control Panel and click Add/Remove Windows Components.

6. Deselect the objects you want to remove and click Next. Then follow the prompts to remove the component.

Add a mounted volume

NTFS in Windows 2000 supports *mounted volumes*, which enable you to mount a basic or dynamic volume to an empty NTFS folder. The contents of the volume appear as the contents of the folder, even though they're actually located on a different volume (another physical drive or a logical volume on the same drive).

For example, assume you have one 4GB drive in your system and you've run out of space for more applications. So you add a new 8GB drive, keeping the existing drive as is. You then move the contents of *C:\Program Files* to the new drive, leaving the original *Program Files* folder empty. You then mount the new 8GB volume to *C:\Program Files* and voila! you have a total apparent capacity on drive C of 12GB, with *C:\Program Files* now having several gigabytes of free space for more programs.

Adding a mounted volume is easy. It requires only that you have an empty folder on an NTFS volume in which to mount the volume. Any volume can be mounted, whether FAT/FAT32 or NTFS:

1. Create the volume if it doesn't already exist.

2. Create an empty folder on an NTFS volume. The name you assign the volume is the path through which the mounted volume is accessed.

3. Right-click My Computer and choose Manage to open the Computer Management console, then open the Disk Management branch.

4. Right-click the volume to be mounted and choose Change Drive Letter and Path.

5. Select the currently assigned drive ID and click "Mount in this NTFS folder," then click Browse or type the path to the folder (see Figure 2-4).

6. Click OK to apply the change.

Using Dfs for a distributed filesystem on Windows 2000 Server

Mounted volumes enable you to create a homogenous filesystem structure from multiple physical volumes on a single computer. You can create a homogenous filesystem structure from multiple computers under Windows 2000 Server through its Distributed File System, or Dfs. Unlike mounted volumes that are limited to the same computer, Dfs enables you to build a file structure that incorporates volumes on the local server as well as folders and volumes shared by other computers on the network. These remote shares can be hosted by computers running Windows 2000 Server or Professional, Windows NT, and Windows 9x.

The primary advantage to Dfs is that the distributed filesystem appears under a single logical structure to users across the network, although the contents might actually reside on several different servers. Dfs therefore enables you to simplify resource access by consolidating multiple resources under one logical share. Rather than search several servers for the resources they need, users can get access to all resources from a single share point.

Use compression

You can use compression on NTFS volumes to increase the amount of available space, gaining as much as 40–50% in some situations. (Windows 2000 doesn't support compression on FAT/FAT32 volumes.) NTFS compression

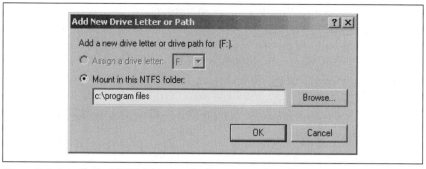

Figure 2-4. Specify the NTFS folder in which to mount the volume

is transparent to the user, handling compression and decompression on the fly. You can configure compression on an entire volume, individual folders, or even individual files.

 Compression and encryption are mutually exclusive features. Selecting compression deselects encryption and vice versa. See Chapter 12, *Users, Policies, Certificates, and Security,* for a discussion of several security issues, including encryption.

1. Open Explorer and locate the volume, folder, or file you want to compress.

2. Right-click the item and choose Properties.

3. On the General tab, click Advanced.

4. Select the option "Compress contents to save disk space" and click OK, then click OK again to close the property sheet.

5. (Optional) Choose Tools → Folder Options → View and select the option "Display compressed files and folders with alternate color," then click OK. Compressed items will now appear with a blue label.

Use quotas

You can reduce disk usage by multiple users through the use of disk quotas, which are supported only on NTFS volumes. Quotas let you limit individual users or groups to a specific amount of storage space on a volume. When the limit is reached, Windows 2000 will either deny further storage or only warn the user that he has reached his quota limit, depending on how you have quotas configured.

Quotas are applied on a volume basis, not a folder-by-folder basis. Quotas are determined based on file ownership and are independent of file location on the volume. Moving files from one location to another, for example, does not affect a user's total quota.

Follow these steps to configure quotas on a volume:

1. Log on as Administrator and open My Computer or Explorer.

2. Right-click a volume and choose Properties, then click the Quota tab.

3. Configure options using the following list as a guide:

   Enable quota management
   > Select to turn on quotas. Deselect to prevent Windows 2000 from applying quotas.

   Deny disk space to users exceeding quota limit
   > Select to prevent users from using more space when they exceed their quota limits.

   Do not limit disk usage
   > Select to warn users when the quota limit is reached but not deny additional space.

   Limit disk space to
   > Specify the default quota limit for the volume. You can change the value on an individual basis when you assign new quotas or modify existing ones.

   Set warning level to
   > Specify the default warning level for the volume. When the user reaches his quota limit Windows 2000 displays a warning message to the user. You can change the value on an individual basis when you assign new quotas or modify existing ones. This value should be lower than the default quota value.

   Log event when a user exceeds their quota limit
   > Log an event to the event log when a user exceeds his quota limit.

   Log event when a user exceeds their warning limit
   > Log an event to the event log when a user exceeds his warning limit.

4. Click Quota Entries to open the Quota Entries window.

5. Choose Quota → New Quota Entry or click the New button in the tool-bar to define a new quota.

6. Select the user or group to which the quota will apply and click Add → OK.

7. In the Add New Quota Entry dialog specify the quota limit and warning limit for the specified user or group, then click OK.

8. In the Quota Entries window double-click any users or groups for which you want to change quota levels, make the changes, and click OK.

9. Close the Quota Entries window.

2.7   Use more than four partitions

Basic disks in Windows 2000 are limited to no more than four partitions, just as in DOS, Windows 9x, or Windows NT. *Dynamic disks*, a new feature in Windows 2000, let you create more than four partitions on a disk. Aside from this distinction, dynamic disks are essentially the same as basic disks. However, dynamic disks are not supported by or visible to other operating systems, including Windows NT. If Windows 2000 is your only operating system on the computer, or if you don't need to see the dynamic disk and its contents from your other OS, this isn't a problem.

See Section 2.9, "Install a new hard disk or add a volume from unpartitioned space," to learn how to create a dynamic disk.

2.8   Replace the existing boot disk

When a data drive runs low on space, it's relatively easy to add additional space—just install a new drive. If desired, you can copy the data from the old drive to the new one and remove the old drive. With a system drive, however, it's not so easy. You have to perform a few extra steps to make the new drive bootable and change the drive sequence.

There are a couple of ways to approach the problem, but one of the easiest is simply to copy the files to the new drive, then remove the old one. If you have a tape backup system, you could also back up the system to tape, install the new drive, install Windows 2000 on it, and then restore the system. Both methods require several steps.

 The following two methods do not use disk cloning software but rely instead on the *xcopy32* and Backup utilities included with Windows 2000. There are a handful of third-party disk cloning tools such as PowerQuest's Drive Copy (*http://www. powerquest.com*) and Symantec's Ghost (*http://www.symantec. com*). These tools are particularly useful when you need to clone multiple drives or perform the task frequently.

Cloning the drive

You can clone the existing drive to the new one, then remove the existing drive or reconfigure it as a data drive. The following steps assume you'll be keeping the old drive as a data drive. Read through the procedure to make sure you understand the process before starting:

1. Configure the new drive as a slave (IDE) or with a SCSI ID other than 0 (which is used by the boot drive).

2. Shut down the system and install the new drive.

3. If installing an IDE drive, open the BIOS Setup utility and configure the BIOS so it detects the new drive.

4. Restart the system and log on as Administrator.

5. Open Disk Management in the Computer Management console and create the same partition structure as on the original disk. Naturally, you'll want to create a larger partition on the new disk than your existing system partition on the old disk. If the old disk contains more than one partition, create the same number of partitions on the new drive.

6. Format the newly created partition(s) using the desired filesystem. Use the same filesystem for the system volume as on the old disk. You can always convert from FAT to NTFS later if you wish.

7. Open the Windows 2000 Backup utility and update the emergency repair disk (Start → Programs → Accessories → System Tools → Backup → Welcome → Emergency Repair Disk). Select the option "Also back up the registry to the repair folder." This is a precautionary measure only but one you should do any time you begin modifying your NT environment.

8. If possible, perform a full backup of your system just in case problems arise during this process. At a minimum, back up your data.

9. Open a console prompt. At the command prompt type the following command:

```
xcopy C:\ D:\ /h /i /c /k /e /r
```

This example assumes you have only one volume in the system and the new volume is recognized as drive D.

10. If you have multiple partitions on each disk, also copy those volumes to the new disk in the appropriate sequence. For example, if the original drive is partitioned into C and D, the new drive will probably show up as F and G, assuming a CD-ROM drive at E. So, you would use the following commands to clone both volumes:

```
xcopy C:\ F:\ /h /i /c /k /e /r
xcopy D:\ G:\ /h /i /c /k /e /r
```

Replace drive letters as necessary if your system's volumes are assigned different letters.

11. Holding down the Shift key to prevent an autorun, insert the Windows 2000 CD. Open a console prompt and change to the \i386 folder on the CD.

12. Execute the following command to install the Windows 2000 Recovery Console:

```
winnt32 /cmdcons
```

13. After the Recovery Console is installed, choose Start → Programs → Administrative Tools → Local Security Policy to open the Local Security Settings console.

 If the Administrative Tools menu doesn't appear on the Start menu, open the folder from the Control Panel.

14. In the Local Security Settings console, open the Local Policies\Security Options branch and double-click "Recovery Console: Allow floppy copy and access to all drives and all folders." Select Enabled and click OK, then close the console.

15. Restart the system and boot the option, "Microsoft Windows 2000 Recovery Console."

16. In the Recovery Console, enter the following command to enable you to access the new volume:

    set AllowAllPaths = TRUE

17. Change to the *C:\Winnt\System32\Config* folder, then use the *copy* command to copy all of the files in the folder to *D:\Winnt\System32\Config*. Because *copy* doesn't support wildcards, you'll have to copy the files one at a time. (This step copies the registry from the current installation to the new one.) Make sure you copy them all.

18. Shut down the system. For IDE systems, reconfigure the new drive as the master and the old drive as the slave (or simply remove the old drive). Make changes in the BIOS Setup accordingly so the BIOS recognizes the drives properly at their new locations. For SCSI systems, reconfigure the drives so the new drive is SCSI ID 0 and the old drive has a different SCSI ID that doesn't conflict with other SCSI devices in the system. Use ID 1 if available.

19. Restart the system, which should boot from the new drive.

20. Log on as Administrator, open My Computer or Explorer, and verify that the new drive has all the files from the old drive. If all is well, delete all files from the old drive or reformat it to use as a data drive.

Backup/reinstall/restore method

If you have a tape backup system or other backup media sufficient to back up the entire system, you can do a reinstallation and restore of Windows

2000 to move your system to a new volume. Read the entire following procedure to make sure you understand the process before beginning:

1. Log on as Administrator, open the Backup utility, and back up the entire system. *Make sure to select the System State Data option to back up the registry.* Back up other volumes if they are located on the same physical disk as the system volume and you will be removing the old drive after the upgrade. If you'll be leaving the old drive in, you don't need to back up the other volumes (although it's a good idea as a precaution, if possible).

2. Shut down the system and install the new drive, either removing the old drive (if you backed up all volumes) or configuring the drives so the new one is first. For IDE drives, configure the new drive as the master and the old drive as a slave. For SCSI drives, configure the new drive as SCSI ID 0 and the old drive with a different ID that doesn't conflict with other SCSI devices in the system. In either case, make sure the new drive is configured as the boot device.

3. Restart the system and perform a clean install of Windows 2000 on the new drive, creating a new partition for the system volume that is larger than the old system volume. If the old drive contained multiple volumes and you are going to remove the old drive, leave enough unpartitioned space on the new drive to accommodate the other volumes. If you are going to retain the old drive in the system, you can use the entire new drive for the boot volume. Format the volume using the same filesystem as the original system volume. You can convert from FAT to NTFS later, if you wish.

4. Boot Windows 2000, open the Backup utility, and restore the backup set created in step 1. Remember to restore the system state data. You'll have to use the Restore Wizard and click Import File to import the backup set, since it was created with a different installation of Windows 2000.

5. Restart the system to incorporate the registry changes.

6. Log on as Administrator, then open My Computer or Explorer to verify that the new volume duplicates the old one. Also open the Local Users and Groups branch of the Computer Management console to verify that all your accounts transferred.

7. Open the Disk Management branch of the Computer Management console. If you are removing the old drive and left space on the new one for

the other volumes (if any), create the partitions on the new drive to hold the other volumes. Copy the files from the old volumes to the new ones through Explorer or *xcopy* or by restoring from the backup set, redirecting to the new location.

If you are not removing the old drive, format the volume containing the old system installation, then reassign drive letters as needed to restore the original drive letters of your data volume(s).

8. If you are removing the old drive, shut down the system and remove the drive, then restart and test the system.

2.9   Install a new hard disk or add a volume from unpartitioned space

Disk space seems always to be at a premium, so you may at some point need to add a hard drive or create a volume from unpartitioned space on an existing drive. Adding a drive is relatively easy, but you do have some options to consider.

 Refer to Section 2.8, "Replace the existing boot disk," for details on replacing your primary drive to gain more disk space. That section explains how to clone your existing drive to the new one as well as related tasks.

Windows 2000 supports two types of disks: *basic* and *dynamic*. A basic disk is just like the type of disk you're probably used to in Windows 9x or Windows NT. Basic disks can contain up to four partitions and are supported by DOS, Windows 9x, and Windows NT. However, the filesystem used on a given volume on a basic disk determines whether or not you can read the drive in the given OS. NTFS is supported only on Windows NT and Windows 2000, and FAT32 is not supported under Windows NT.

Dynamic disks overcome the four-partition limit of basic disks. Windows 2000 supports dynamic disks for standard volumes as well as spanned, striped, and RAID volumes. If you want to create these latter types of volumes with Windows 2000, you'll have to do it on a dynamic disk, but you can use and modify in Windows 2000 these types of volumes created with Windows NT on basic disks. The only disadvantage of dynamic disks is that DOS, Windows 9x, and Windows NT do not support them and therefore won't even see the drives, much less let you access them. If Windows 2000 is your only system, however, this might not be a problem for you.

A *volume* is not the same as a *partition*. A primary partition can contain a single volume. An extended partition, however, can contain multiple volumes. For example, your system might include two partitions: a primary partition and an extended partition. The primary partition contains one volume, drive C. The extended partition contains multiple logical drives, such as D, E, F, and G. In this configuration the system has five volumes, but still only two partitions. So it's possible to have more than four volumes on a drive, but not more than four partitions.

Deciding which type of disk structure to use when you add a new drive depends on a few factors:

Compatibility
Use a basic disk if you boot any operating systems other than Windows 2000 on the same computer and need to access the disk from those operating systems.

Number of partitions
Use a dynamic disk if you want to create more than four partitions on the disk.

Recoverability
Since DOS and Windows 9x can't even see the partition structure on a dynamic disk, you won't be able to boot the system from a DOS or bootable Windows 9x disk to access the drive. If you're adding a data drive, this probably isn't a concern. Since you can read the dynamic disk from the Recovery Console, it isn't as big an issue with Windows 2000, but it's nevertheless something to consider when deciding on a disk type.

If you're adding a basic disk, you also need to decide what type(s) of partition to create on the disk. You can create up to four partitions on the disk. All four can be primary partitions, or one of the four can be an extended partition. Each primary partition will contain only a single volume (typically represented by a drive letter), but the extended partition can contain multiple logical volumes. So you can use an extended partition to create more than four volumes on the disk, if needed.

Add a basic disk

Adding a basic disk is fairly straightforward. As with other disk-related tasks in Windows 2000, you use the Disk Management branch of the Computer Management console to add the disk:

1. Shut down the system and install the new drive.

2. Boot the system and log on as Administrator, then right-click My Computer and choose Manage to open the Computer Management console.

Disk management changes happen immediately

In Windows NT, most changes you make to a disk with the Disk Administrator don't happen immediately. Instead, you must commit the changes to have them take effect. For example, you could delete a partition in NT, then close the Disk Administrator without actually deleting the partition. This ability was a nice security feature that helped avoid serious mistakes such as deleting the wrong partition.

In Windows 2000, however, changes you make with the Disk Management console snap-in happen immediately. If you delete a partition, it is gone with no means of recovering it (short of doing a restore operation from tape or other offline storage after recreating the partition). As you're working with the Disk Management console, keep in mind that changes will happen immediately.

---

3. Click the Disk Management branch.

4. The new drive will show up as a basic disk with unallocated space in the Disk Management window when using either Disk List or Graphical View display modes (use the View menu to change modes).

5. Right-click the unallocated space and choose Create Partition to open the Create Partition wizard, then click Next.

6. Select Primary Partition or Extended Partition, depending on the type of partition you want, and then click Next.

7. Specify the amount of space (in megabytes) to use for the partition. Windows 2000 displays the minimum and maximum allowable values. Then click Next.

8. Choose between the following options, then click Next:

   Assign a drive letter
   > Select the drive ID you want assigned to the new volume.

   Mount this volume at an empty folder that supports drive paths
   > Use this option to mount the volume to an empty NTFS folder, creating a mounted volume.

   Do not assign a drive letter or drive path
   > Select this option if you want to wait until later to assign a drive ID or mount the volume to a folder. You won't be able to use the volume until you do one of the two, however.

9. Select a filesystem (FAT, FAT32, or NTFS), cluster size, and volume label, and (optionally) enable file and folder compression for NTFS. Click Next and then Finish to complete and exit the wizard.

Add a dynamic disk

As explained earlier, a dynamic disk overcomes the four-partition limit of basic disks and is the only disk type Windows 2000 supports for creating new spanned, striped, or mirrored volumes. When you add a new disk, Windows 2000 adds it as a basic disk. You then can convert the disk to a dynamic disk, either before or after you create partitions on it. You can upgrade a basic disk to a dynamic disk without affecting any existing partitions or data, although the disk must have at least 1MB of free space prior to the upgrade. Reverting from a dynamic disk to a basic disk requires that you first delete any partitions and their corresponding data, so reverting to a basic disk requires a full backup of the disk and a restore operation afterward.

Most of the process for creating a dynamic disk is the same as for a basic disk. Other than the fact that you can create more than four partitions on the disk, the primary difference is that you must convert the disk from basic to dynamic. Here's how:

1. Open the Computer Management console, then open the Disk Management branch.

2. In Disk List or Graphical View, right-click the disk identifier (disk 1, disk 2, etc.) and choose Upgrade to Dynamic Disk.

3. Windows 2000 prompts you to verify which drives you want to convert, which also gives you the opportunity to select other drives for conversion. Select the disks to be upgraded and click OK.

4. After the conversion, right-click in the unpartitioned space on the disk and choose Create Volume to start the Create Volume Wizard, then click Next.

5. Choose Simple volume, Spanned volume, or Striped volume depending on the type you want to create, then click Next.

6. The process for creating volumes from this point on is very similar to creating a partition on a basic disk. You specify the capacity, filesystem, cluster size, and other options just as you do for a partition.

2.10 Schedule defrag for off hours

The Disk Defragmenter in Windows 2000 rearranges the data on the system's hard disk so that files are in contiguous clusters, improving performance and making available larger blocks of free space on the disk.

Unfortunately, the version of Disk Defragmenter included with Windows 2000 doesn't support command-line switches that would otherwise enable you to use the *at* or *winat* commands from the Windows 2000 Resource Kit to schedule a defragmentation operation for off hours.

To automate the process, you can obtain a third-party defragmentation tool that supports scheduling or use a third-party scripting utility to create a script that executes the Windows 2000 Disk Defragmenter. If using the latter option, you can use the Scheduled Tasks folder in Windows 2000 (choose Start → Programs → Accessories → System Tools → Scheduled Tasks) or the *at* command to schedule the script.

2.11   Convert a basic disk to a dynamic disk

The primary reason for upgrading a basic disk to a dynamic disk is to make it possible to create more than four partitions on the disk or to create striped, spanned, or mirrored volumes. When you upgrade an existing basic disk to a dynamic disk, any existing volumes on the disk are converted to basic volumes.

Before you upgrade a disk, however, understand that if you later decide to revert it to a basic disk, you'll first have to remove all volumes and data from the disk. This means you'll have to back up the data, revert the disk, and then restore the data.

It's easy to upgrade a basic disk to a dynamic disk. The only requirement is that the disk contain at least 1MB of free space. To upgrade a basic disk to a dynamic disk, follow these steps:

1. Open the Disk Management branch of the Computer Management console.

2. Right-click a disk in Disk List or Graphical View and choose Upgrade to Dynamic Disk.

3. Windows 2000 prompts you to verify the disks you want to upgrade. Place a check beside each disk to upgrade and click OK.

2.12   Revert a dynamic disk back to a basic disk

As indicated previously, you can revert a dynamic disk back to a basic disk. The primary reason for doing so is to enable other operating systems on the same computer to see the disk. Since Windows 2000 handles access from across the network, dynamic disks can be accessed by other operating systems across the LAN. The compatibility issue only applies to other operating systems on the same computer as the dynamic disk.

While it is a painless process to upgrade from basic to dynamic, there is a little pain involved in going the other way. All volumes and data on the disk must be removed prior to reverting the disk. If you intend to retain the data, this means you need to back it up to tape or other media, revert the disk, and then restore the data.

Follow these steps to revert a dynamic disk to a basic disk:

1. Back up all data on all volumes on the disk unless you don't want to retain the data.

2. Open the Disk Management branch of the Computer Management console.

3. Remove all volumes from the disk by right-clicking each volume and choosing Delete Volume.

4. After all volumes are removed from the disk, right-click the disk and choose Revert to Basic Disk.

5. Create partitions and volumes on the disk and restore the data to the volumes.

CHAPTER 3

Configuring System Software and Components

Windows 2000 configuration tasks fall into two distinct categories: hardware and system software. Chapter 2, *Configuring Hardware*, covered hardware configuration issues. This chapter covers Windows 2000 system software and components. For example, this chapter explains how to add and remove Windows 2000 components that don't normally show up in the Add/Remove Programs object. You'll also learn how to stop and start services, manage their startup behavior, and control what happens when a service fails.

System management is another important topic covered in this chapter, including how to customize the Microsoft Management Console (MMC) to incorporate the console snap-ins you need for various management scenarios. You'll also learn how to customize MMC consoles with taskpads that simplify performing various tasks.

Offline files—a new feature in Windows 2000—are also covered in this chapter. Offline files enable you to work with network files even when the computer hosting those files is offline or unavailable. You'll learn how to configure offline files, move the offline cache to a different drive, and manage folders you share from your computer. Synchronization of offline files is also covered, which will help ensure that you're always working with the most up-to-date copy of a file.

3.1   Enable or disable a service

Windows 2000 Setup by default installs a lot of system components, including some you might not really need or want. While you could remove these components altogether, you might prefer to simply disable them, particularly if you think you might use them in the future. Or, you might simply need to turn off a Windows 2000 component temporarily for performance reasons. The same could hold true for certain third-party applications that you install on the system—there could be an occasion when you want to temporarily turn off the application (such as turning off a virus monitor prior to installing software).

In many cases Windows 2000 components such as Fax, Index Server, Telnet, and ftp (to name just a few) operate as *services*. A service is essentially an application that Windows 2000 can start automatically and that can function outside the framework of the user interface. Unlike a word processor, for example, the service application can start up when the system boots and function even when no user is logged on. So most services run all the time, even when no one is logged on.

In some cases a Windows 2000 component actually comprises more than one service. Some third-party applications install as services, as well. In any case, you can stop a running service to stop the application if needed, as in the case of the virus monitor mentioned previously.

Windows 2000 provides a management console for configuring and managing services. In addition to letting you stop and start services, you can use the console to specify service properties such as how the service starts, if at all.

Start, stop, pause, and resume services

As mentioned previously, a service is really just an application, in most cases a special-purpose application designed specifically to run as a service. Like any application, a running service is resident in memory and working to perform its task. You can stop or pause a service, which causes it to stop doing its intended function. When you want it to operate again, you start or resume the service. If you stop a service with dependent services (other services that require the one you're stopping), Windows 2000 prompts you to determine whether you want to stop those dependent services as well.

Follow these steps to stop or pause a service from the Windows 2000 GUI:

1. Right-click My Computer and choose Manage to open the Computer Management console.

2. Open the Services and Applications\Services branch.

3. Locate the service you want to stop or pause. Right-click the service and choose Stop or Pause from the context menu, or double-click the service, and then click Stop or Pause on the service's property sheet.

4. When you need to start a stopped service or resume a paused service, select Start or Resume from the service's context menu or click Start or Resume from the service's property sheet.

Configure service startup

Each service has properties that control how the service starts and functions. One property is the startup type, which can be one of the following:

Manual
> The service does not start at system startup but can be started by a user or dependent service.

Automatic
> The service starts automatically when the system starts.

Disabled
> A user or dependent service can't start the service, nor does it start at system startup. You can switch a service to manual or automatic startup type if you need to start it.

If a given service is configured for Automatic startup but you don't want it to start until you start it manually, change its startup type to Manual. When you need to use the service you can open the Services console and start it as explained earlier in this chapter.

Follow these steps to configure a service's startup type:

1. Open the Services and Applications\Services branch of the Computer Management console.

2. Select the desired startup type from the Startup type drop-down list, then click OK.

3.2   Control services remotely

The Services console works great when you need to manage services locally (start, stop, pause, restart, etc.) In some cases you might also need to manage services for a computer remotely. For example, you might have a remote server that isn't readily accessible because it's located in a branch office several hundred miles away. If you have a Virtual Private Network (VPN) or leased line connection to the remote network, you can use the Computer Management console to manage the remote computer's services just as you would a local computer. You also can use a telnet session and manage services from a command console.

Connecting to a remote computer for management

You can use the Computer Management console to manage remote computers in the same way you manage a local computer. Some differences apply depending on the task you're performing, but in most cases management capabilities are the same. You need a connection to the remote network, but beyond that connecting through the console is easy:

1. If you don't currently have the ability to connect through a leased line or other WAN connection to the remote computer, create and establish a VPN connection to the remote network's VPN server.

 See Section 10.6, "Create a secure remote connection to your LAN," for details on setting up a VPN connection to a remote computer or network.

2. After you establish the connection, open the Computer Management console by right-clicking My Computer and choosing Manage.

3. In the Computer Management console, click the Computer Management branch, and choose Action → Connect to Another Computer.

4. Specify the computer name in the Name text box or click the computer name in the list of available computers, then click OK.

Control services from a command console

You can also start or stop a service from a command console. This ability is particularly useful when you need to remotely manage services on a server running the Telnet service. You can connect to the computer through Telnet, then stop and start services on the remote computer as needed. The advantage to this method over using the Computer Management console is that you don't need a VPN or WAN connection other than a standard Internet connection to the remote computer.

In order to control a service from a console you first need to know its *service name*. The service name appears on the service's property sheet at the top of the General page. For example, the Telnet service's name is TlntSvr and the Internet Connecting Sharing service is SharedAccess. Just double-click a service in the Services console to view its service name. Then at a command prompt, use the following commands to stop and start the service:

```
net stop servicename
net start servicename
```

For example, to stop the Index Service you would enter this command:

```
net stop cisvc
```

 You can use the *listsvc* command from the Recovery Console to view service names.

3.3   You changed the Administrator account and now a service fails to start

As a security measure, each service in Windows 2000 must log on with a valid account. Many services use a special System account built in to Windows 2000 for logon. In some cases, however, services (particularly those you install through an application) use a different account. Typically these applications prompt you to specify the service account when you install the application.

For example, assume you're installing a backup application that provides email notification of job status, and you'd like to use the same account for running the service as you use to generate the messages. You might create an account called BackupApp, give it the necessary rights required by the application and then use that account as the service account.

Pros and cons of account logon options

The main problem with assigning an account other than the System account for a service is the password. If you use the Administrator password for the service, you have to change the service's configuration every time you change the Administrator password. Since you hopefully change that often, you'd have to change the service configuration just as often. And perhaps that's why you're reading this section—you changed the Administrator password and suddenly one or more services are failing to start. The key is to choose an account whose password doesn't change. In most cases the best option is to use the System account. If that isn't feasible because of permission requirements or security concerns, create an account specifically for the service, then don't change the account unless something happens to suggest that the account could be compromised. Choose a cryptic username and password, or at least one with a mix of alpha, numeric, and punctuation characters, to lessen the possibility of cracking.

Changing or specifying service account logon and options

Here's how to specify a different account or change the password for the current account:

1. Open the Computer Management console.

2. If the account you want to use doesn't exist yet, open the Local Users and Groups branch and create the account. Grant it the necessary rights and privileges required by the service.

3. Open the Services and Applications\Services branch and double-click the service you want to modify.

4. Click the Log On tab to display the Log On property page.

5. Select the option This Account, type or browse for the account to use, and specify the password for the account.

6. Click OK to apply the change, then (if necessary) right-click the service and choose Start to restart it.

3.4   Specify what should happen if a service fails

A service failure isn't always a major problem, but in some cases it can certainly be a cause for concern. In other cases it *is* a major problem, particularly with critical services on a server. Windows 2000 enables you to specify what action the system should take if a service does fail. For example, you can direct Windows 2000 to try to restart the service. If the service fails again, you might have Windows 2000 execute a program that emails a notification to you or pages you. In some cases you might even want the system to restart if a service fails.

Windows 2000 lets you specify an action to take for the first, second, and subsequent failures of the service In the preceding example, you might have Windows 2000 try to restart the service on the first failure, send you an email on the second, and restart the system on the third.

Configuring service recovery properties

As explained previously, you can configure a service to take any of four different actions on failure: do nothing, restart the service, execute a file, or restart the system. You set each of these properties through the Recovery page of the service's property sheet. Here's how to configure those properties:

1. Open the Services and Applications branch of the Computer Management console, then open the Services branch.

2. Double-click the service whose properties you want to set and click the Recovery tab in the service's property sheet.

3. Select the desired action for first, second, and subsequent failures from the appropriate drop-down lists (see Figure 3-1).

4. If specifying a restart, use the "Reset fail count after *n* days" option to specify the number of days the service must run successfully before Windows 2000 resets the fail count to zero. (The fail count determines which of the specified actions Windows 2000 takes when the service

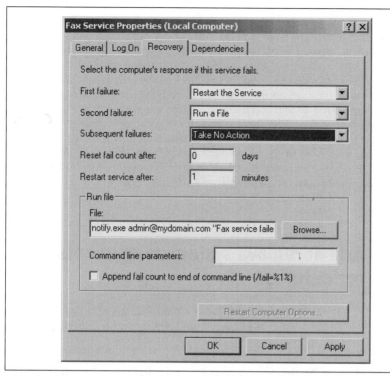

Figure 3-1. You can specify three different actions to take for service failures

fails.) Also use the option "Restart service after *n* minutes" to specify how soon after the failure Windows 2000 should attempt to restart the service. Depending on the service and system load, you might want to allow a few minutes for the system to "settle" before attempting to restart.

5. If specifying that Windows 2000 should run a file, use the File text box to specify the path to the file Windows 2000 will execute when the service fails. Add any command-line options for the file in the "Command line parameters" text box.

6. If the command specified in step 5 is designed to accept command-line arguments (which might be the case with a batch file) and you want to pass the fail count to the program, select the option "Append fail count to end of command line." Windows 2000 will append /fail=%1% as the last parameter of the command.

7. If configuring the system to reboot after a failure, click Restart Computer Options. Specify the number of minutes to wait after the service failure before rebooting and optionally specify a message to broadcast on the network prior to the reboot.

Getting notification when a service fails

The ability to execute a command on service failure is a great feature that enables remote notification. For example, you might execute the *blat.exe* utility available on the Internet (*http://www.interlog.com/~tcharron/blat.html*) to send an email message notifying you of the failure. Or perhaps you have another third-party application that you can use to page you when the problem occurs. In either case, having remote notification capability can be extremely important in situations where computer uptime is critical but you can't always be close to the computer for monitoring purposes. And even when you are in the same room as the computer you need to monitor, having an email or pager notification can get your attention when you're focused on another problem or project.

3.5   Add or remove system components or features

Windows 2000 installs a lot of components during setup, including perhaps some you don't want, like the Fax service or games. So you might at some point want to remove a component or two. You also might determine that Setup didn't install all the components you want to use, and you want to add a component or two. For example, you might want to remove the Accessibility Wizard, games, HyperTerminal, or other accessories if you never use them, particularly on a server. Removing a component removes not only its files, but also its services, if any.

Using the Windows Components Wizard to remove components

Like Windows 9x, Windows 2000 provides a wizard to help you automate the process of adding or removing system components. You'll find the Add/Remove Programs object in the Control Panel and the Windows Components Wizard as an option in Add/Remove Programs.

By default, the Windows Components Wizard doesn't display all installed components. Specifically, the wizard doesn't display the following components or component branches (some of these do appear under Windows 2000 Server):

Accessories and Utilities
    Contains Accessibility Wizard, Accessories, Communications, Games, and Multimedia.

COM+
> Provides support for developing and deploying distributed component-based applications.

Distributed Transaction Coordinator
> This component coordinates distributed transactions between multiple clients, servers, and resource managers.

Fax Service
> Enables sending and receiving of faxes through a fax modem.

Imaging
> Provides an image viewer/editor, ActiveX controls for imaging, and TWAIN support.

Microsoft made the conscious decision to install these components and hide them to provide a common set of applications and services and, in theory, simplify system configuration. In order to make all the components available in the wizard, you need to manually edit one of Windows 2000's *.inf* files:

1. Open the *systemroot\inf* folder. The folder is hidden, so you'll need to configure folder options to view all objects.

2. Locate the file *sysoc.inf* and make a backup copy called *sysoc.inf.hide*.

3. Open *sysoc.inf* in Notepad or Wordpad and remove all references of HIDE in the file. You'll find the references between two commas and followed by a number. Leave the commas and simply delete the word HIDE from between them.

4. Save the *sysoc.inf* file. If you later want to restore the original file, simply rename *sysoc.inf* to *sysoc.inf.all* and rename *sysoc.inf.hide* to *sysoc.inf*.

 Even removing the HIDE parameter doesn't enable you to remove COM+, DTC, or the Fax service through the wizard.

Removing components manually

In some cases you'll need to remove components manually. For example, even removing the HIDE parameter from the *sysoc.inf* file doesn't enable you to remove certain components, such as Fax. You can, however, remove components manually. You should exercise a little caution when doing so, however, to make sure you don't delete the wrong file or files or delete a shared file needed by another service.

Here's how to determine which files are included with a given Windows 2000 component and delete the files:

1. Open the file *systemroot\Inf\Sysoc.inf* in Notepad or Wordpad.

2. Locate in the file the component you want to remove, then determine the name of the component's setup information file from its entry. For the Fax service, for example, the file is *faxsetup.inf*.

3. Open the component's setup information file in Notepad or Wordpad. The files that Setup copies to the system when installing the component are listed in the *.inf* file, although they could be listed in more than one section in the *.inf* file. Make a note of the filenames.

4. If the component in question currently has services running, open the Services and Applications\Services branch of the Computer Management console and stop the service(s).

5. Locate the files listed in the component's *setup.inf* file and delete them manually.

6. If the component has an entry in the Start menu, manually remove the entry by right-clicking and choosing Delete.

3.6 Customize the Microsoft Management Console (MMC)

In Windows NT most administrative functions are handled with standalone utilities. The User Manager application, for example, provides the means for managing user accounts, groups, rights, and other properties. In Windows 2000, however, administrative functions are largely integrated under a common interface through the Microsoft Management Console (MMC) as console snap-ins (often referred to simply as *consoles*). User and group management, for example, has moved to the Local Users and Groups console.

The MMC functions as the framework for the individual consoles. The Computer Management console, for example, actually comprises several individual consoles. One of the nicest benefits of the new MMC/console architecture is that you can create your own custom console configurations that include sets of tools you use most often or that are related. If you're managing an Internet server, for example, you might integrate the DHCP, DNS, and IIS snap-ins into a single console so you'll have all of your management tools handy in one interface.

Taskpads are another handy feature of the MMC. A taskpad is a page on which you can add shortcuts to various functions inside and outside of a console. These shortcuts can execute commands, open folders, open web pages, and execute menu commands. A taskpad is essentially a page of organized tasks you can access quickly rather than using the existing menu provided by the snap-in. A console can contain multiple taskpads and must contain at least one snap-in. Figure 3-2 shows a taskpad for managing IIS.

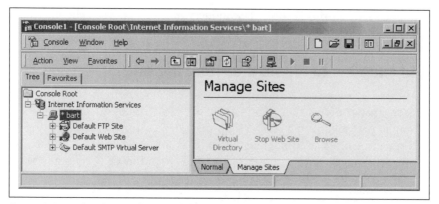

Figure 3-2. Taskpads provide a simplified interface and quick access to frequently used features or commands

You can work with consoles in one of two modes: author mode and user mode. In author mode you can make changes to the console. When you open the MMC application by itself, it automatically opens in author mode so you can add snap-ins. Use one of these methods to open the MMC in author mode:

- Double-click the application *mmc.exe* in the *systemroot\System32* folder.

- Choose Start → Run, and enter mmc in the Run dialog box.

- Choose Start → Run, and enter the name of the console you want to open followed by the /a switch, as in the following example that opens the Security Policy console:

```
c:\winnt\system32\secpol.msc /a
```

User mode applies restrictions to the console to prevent certain actions or capabilities, such as adding new snap-ins. There are three variations of user mode:

Full Access
    Allows access to all window management commands in the MMC but does not allow snap-ins to be added or removed or console properties to be changed.

Limited Access, Multiple Window
    Prevents changes to the view and shows the snap-ins in multiple windows.

Limited Access, Single Window
    Prevents changes to the view and shows snap-ins in a single window.

The default mode in Windows 2000 is user mode—limited access, single window. You can change the mode through the options for the console as explained later in this section. The mode you specify is used the next time the console is opened.

Add snap-ins to create a custom console

You can add snap-ins to an existing console or create from scratch a new console that contains the snap-ins you want. As discussed previously, for example, you might bring several snap-ins into a custom console to bring all of your most often used administrative tools into one interface. Figure 3-3 shows an example with a subset of the tools found in the Computer Management console.

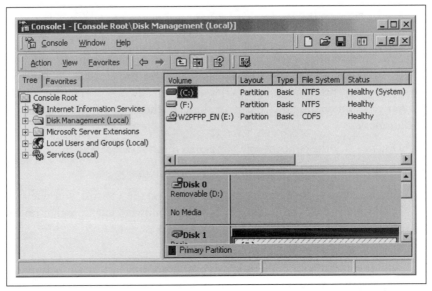

Figure 3-3. Custom consoles let you tailor the console to your needs and practices

Snap-ins come in two flavors: standalone and extensions. A standalone snap-in either functions by itself or with a collection of one or more extensions that provide specific features or capabilities within the snap-in. The Group Policy snap-in, for example, incorporates several extensions to provide the individual features available within the Group Policy snap-in. When you add snap-ins, you can add an entire snap-in or only those extensions you need.

Follow these steps to add a snap-in to a console:

1. If you are creating a custom console, open an empty console in author mode by choosing Start → Run, and entering `mmc.exe` in the Run dialog. If adding a snap-in to an existing console, enter `mmc.exe console /a` in

the Run dialog, where *console* is the name of the console you want to modify.

2. In the MMC, choose Console → Add/Remove Snap-In, or simply press Ctrl+M.

3. Click Add on the Standalone page, then select the snap-in you want and click Add. The MMC might prompt you for additional information such as the focus of the snap-in (the local computer, a remote computer, etc.) or provide a wizard that helps you specify the focus of function of the snap-in. Provide the information requested and click Finish.

4. Add other snap-ins as desired from the Add Standalone Snap-in dialog box and click Close.

5. Click the Extensions tab if you want to specify which extensions are added for a specific snap-in.

6. Select the snap-in from the "Snap-ins that can be extended" drop-down list, deselect Add All Extensions, and select or deselect extensions to specify which ones will be added. Click OK when you're finished.

7. Choose Console → Save or Save As to save the console by name.

8. Create a shortcut to the newly created console on the desktop or in My Documents to make it readily accessible.

Set console options such as default mode

Each console offers a handful of properties you can use to specify the mode in which the console starts (author or user) and other aspects of how the console functions. You also can change the icon associated with the console through these properties. Follow these steps to change console properties:

1. Open the console in author mode.

2. Choose Console → Options to display the Options dialog box.

3. Configure options using the following list of options as a guide, then click OK or Apply:

Change Icon
> Change the icon associated with the console. Several icons are provided in *systemroot\System32\Shell32.dll*.

Console mode
> Choose author mode, which allows full control over the console's function and appearance, or one of the three user modes that were explained previously.

Enable context menus on taskpads in this console
> Select this object to allow context menus to appear when you right-click a taskpad.

Do not save changes to this console
> Prevent the user from saving changes to the console, effectively write protecting it.

Allow the user to customize views
> Allow the user to add windows focused on specific items in the console.

Create a taskpad for frequent tasks

You can create taskpads for tasks you perform often in a console. A taskpad provides a more user-friendly interface to a specific console function. Because of that simplified interface, taskpads are particularly useful for users who aren't familiar with the MMC because of that simplified interface. For more advanced users, taskpads offer quicker, easier access to often-used functions or features in a given console, eliminating the need to drill down through a console to find the tool they need.

You create and modify taskpads with the console opened in author mode. Follow these steps to create a taskpad:

1. Open the console in author mode, right-click the object in the tree that you want as the focus of the taskpad, and choose New Taskpad View. The MMC starts a wizard to help you create the taskpad. Click Next to continue.

2. In the wizard, choose the display style for the taskpad using the options provided. When you select an option, Windows 2000 displays a sample of how the taskpad will look. Click Next to continue.

3. Specify whether the taskpad will apply to the selected tree item only or to all tree items that are the same type as the selected item, then click Next (see the following list as a guide):

Selected tree item
> Apply the taskpad only to the selected item in the tree. If you created a taskpad for Forward Lookup Zones in the DNS console, for example, this option would cause the taskpad to appear only when you clicked Forward Lookup Zones but not if you clicked Reverse Lookup Zones.

All tree items that are the same type as the selected tree item
> Apply the taskpad to all objects in the tree that are the same as the selected object. Using the same DNS console example, this option

would cause the taskpad to display when you clicked either For-ward Lookup Zones or Reverse Lookup Zones.

Change default display to this taskpad view for these tree items
Have MMC automatically switch to taskpad view when the user clicks the object in the tree associated with the taskpad. Deselect the option to have MMC default to the normal view instead.

4. Specify a name and description for the taskpad and click Next.

5. Select the option Start New Task wizard and click Finish.

6. Click Next when the New Task Wizard appears, then select the type of command you want to add to the taskpad using the following as a guide:

Menu command
Use this option to execute a menu command. You specify the source for the command and the command itself through the remaining wizard pages. Available commands fall within the con-text of the source you select. Select an object and then select the desired command.

Shell command
Use this option to start a program, open a web object, execute a script or shortcut, or perform any other command-line task. The wizard prompts you for the command, optional command-line parameters or switches, startup folder, and window state (mini-mized, normal, maximized).

Navigation
Use this option to add an icon for an existing item listed in Favorites.

7. Depending on the type of command you select the wizard prompts you for additional information. Specify the information (menu command, command line and switches, etc.). At the completion of the wizard, select the option "Run this wizard again" if you want to add other items, then click Finish.

Modify or remove a taskpad

After you create a taskpad, you can make modifications such as changing tasks, adding tasks, etc. To modify a taskpad, right-click the branch where the taskpad is configured and choose Edit Taskpad View. MMC displays a property sheet you can use to modify the taskpad's appearance or add or remove tasks.

To remove a taskpad, right-click the branch where the taskpad is defined and choose Delete Taskpad View.

Acquire add-on or third-party snap-ins

Many applications include MMC consoles as the primary means of managing the application or as an alternative. When you install the application the console typically gets installed as well. Because the MMC is modular in nature it lends itself well to third-party management consoles. You'll find additional information about customizing the MMC as well as additional Microsoft MMC console tools and links to third-party tools at *http://www.microsoft.com/management/mmc.*

3.7   Make files available when offline

Windows 95 introduced a feature called the Briefcase that provided the ability to synchronize a working copy of a file in the Briefcase with a copy on another computer such as a network server or the user's desktop system. Windows 2000 expands on and simplifies the concept with the introduction of *offline files.* You can use offline files to work with shared network resources when you're not connected to the network. For example, you might make a set of documents available offline while you're out of town on a business trip, allowing you to continue working on the documents while you're away. When you get back you synchronize the files with the server.

 The term *server* is used in this section generically to refer to any computer that shares its resources.

Set up offline files

Setting up your system to use files from a server when you're offline is easy, but you need to keep something in mind: caching the files actually copies them to your computer, so caching a folder containing a large number of files is going to use the equivalent amount of disk space on your computer. If you need only a few files from a folder on the server, and the folder contains a lot of other files, just make the selected files available offline, rather than the entire folder.

Follow these steps to make shared folders or files available to your computer offline:

1. Browse to the folder containing the folder or file you want to cache on your local hard disk.

2. Right-click the folder or file and choose Make Available Offline. Windows 2000 displays a status dialog box as the file or folder is copied to your system.

A deeper understanding of offline files

In essence, offline files work by copying the desired files from the network server to a hidden folder on your local system. Although Windows 2000 knows the files are not stored on the server, it continues to treat them that way as far as the user is concerned. You still browse for the files as you would when connected to the network (getting to them through My Network Places, for example). When the network server becomes available again, Windows 2000 synchronizes the files with the network copy, either automatically or manually through user direction depending on how you have offline folders configured).

Folders and files you share on your Windows 2000 computer also can be used offline by others on the network unless you specifically disable offline use through the sharing properties for the folder.

In order to use offline files you must have the permissions necessary to access them in their primary location on the file server. In other words, if you don't have the necessary permissions to access the files at the server, you can't cache them for use locally. Systems that support Server Message Block (SMB) file and printer sharing can share resources for offline use. This includes Windows 2000, Windows 9x, and Windows NT, but excludes Novell NetWare. Of these only Windows 2000 offers the ability to control offline access on the server side where the folder is shared, enabling you to prevent offline caching of the folder or its contents. There is no mechanism with the other SMB-capable platforms to prevent shared folders from being cached for offline use.

Moving the cache to a different location

By default Windows 2000 places the offline folders and files you cache in the hidden folder *systemroot\Csc* (CSC stands for *Client Side Cache*). Windows 2000 renames and tracks filenames for offline folders and files, so you won't recognize the contents of the CSC folder. You can use the *cachemov.exe* program included with the Windows 2000 Resource Kit to move the cache to a different location, if needed. For example, you might not have enough space on the system drive to contain a large set of files and therefore need to use a different volume. You can acquire the Resource Kit directly from Microsoft, from various retail outlets (including most bookstores), or on subscription content from Microsoft such as TechNet.

Set offline access properties for folders you share

As mentioned previously, you can make your shared folders and their contents available to others on the network as offline files. In fact, all you have to do is share the folder under Windows 2000 and the folder and its contents are available for offline use subject to any object permissions you apply to the folder and files.

You configure offline file properties through the sharing properties for the folder. You can share the folder and its contents but still prevent it from being made available offline, or you can specify how the folder and its contents can be cached to the client's computer. Follow these steps to configure offline file access on your system:

1. Open the folder containing the shared folder. In the case of an entire volume, open My Computer.

2. Right-click the shared folder and choose Properties, then click the Sharing tab.

3. Click Caching to display the Caching Settings dialog box.

4. To enable the files to be used offline by others, select the option "Allow caching of files in this shared folder." Deselect this option to prevent offline use.

5. From the Setting drop-down list choose one of the following options:

   Manual caching for documents
   This option is the default option. It enables caching for only those files specifically identified by the remote user. The user must right-click each file (or group of files) to be used offline and choose Make Available Offline to cache them to his computer.

   Automatic caching for documents
   This option enables caching of all files that are opened by the remote user. The file is cached automatically as soon as the user opens the file. Files he doesn't open are not cached to his computer.

   Automatic caching for programs
   With this option, offline files are always opened from the cached location, reducing network traffic. It is intended for folders containing shared applications. You should set the folder's permissions to read-only to prevent changes to the files.

3.8 Cached files on your computer are different from the server's copy

When you work with an offline file, its contents change from the original copy stored on the server, and the two files become unsynchronized. When you reconnect to the network (or the remote resource becomes available again), you need a means of synchronizing the copy on the server with the modified copy cached on your local system. Windows 2000 lets you easily synchronize offline files manually or automatically.

Synchronize offline files manually

You can synchronize a particular file or group of files separately from any other offline files, if desired, by performing a manual synchronization. Follow these steps to synchronize a locally cached file with the version on the server:

1. Browse to the location of the file, then right-click the file and choose Synchronize.

2. Windows 2000 synchronizes the file, displaying a status dialog box during the synchronization. The dialog box disappears when the synchronization is complete.

Synchronize offline files automatically

In addition to synchronizing files manually, you can configure your system to automatically synchronize items either selectively or on a global basis. Windows 2000 keeps track of your offline files and lets you specify synchronization properties for each one. You can choose to have the files synchronized when you log on or log off, when the system is idle, or at scheduled times.

You use the Synchronization Manager to specify how Windows 2000 handles offline file synchronization. Follow these steps to open the Synchronization Manager and configure options:

1. Choose Start → Programs → Accessories → Synchronize to open the Synchronization Manager.

2. Click Setup to display the Synchronization Settings dialog box.

3. Use the controls on the Logon/Logoff page to configure synchronization during logon and logoff. Use the following list as a guide:

   When I am using this network connection
   Select the network connection for which the synchronization settings apply.

   Synchronize the following checked items
   Select the items you want synchronized.

   When I log on to my computer
   Select this option to have synchronization take place when you log on.

   When I log off my computer
   Select this option to have synchronization take place when you log off.

   Ask me before synchronizing the items
   Select this option to have Windows 2000 prompt you to confirm the synchronization before it takes place.

4. Click the On Idle tab to configure synchronization during system idle time using the following list as a guide:

   When I am using this network connection
   Select the network connection for which the synchronization settings apply.

   Synchronize the following checked items
   Select the items you want synchronized.

   Synchronize the selected items while my computer is idle
   Select this option to turn on synchronization during idle time. Deselect the option to prevent synchronization during system idle time.

5. Click Advanced on the On Idle page to specify settings for how soon and how often on-idle synchronization takes place. You can specify how long the system must be idle before synchronization occurs, how often synchronization repeats, and prevent synchronization from occurring when the computer is running on batteries.

6. Click the Scheduled tab to configure specific times at which you want specific items synchronized.

7. Click Add and follow the wizard's prompts to configure an item or items for synchronization at a specified time. The options presented by the wizard are self-explanatory.

8. Close the Synchronization Manager.

3.9   How to browse for resources in the Active Directory

The Active Directory (AD) is the *directory service* included in Windows 2000 Server. In a nutshell, a directory service is a hierarchical namespace for naming and tracking resources. Nearly any object can be stored in the AD, but common objects include users, groups, printers, servers, and workstations.

Browse resources in the AD

You can browse for resources in the AD just like you can for local resources or resources shared on the LAN, provided your computer is a member of the domain or a trusted domain. You'll find the AD under My Network Places. Follow these steps to browse for resources in the Active Directory:

1. Open My Network Places from the desktop.

2. Open Entire Network and click Entire Contents.

3. Double-click the Directory icon. Items in the AD will appear under their respective icons.

CHAPTER 4

Configuring the Windows 2000 Interface

Perhaps no other topic arouses more interest than tweaking the user interface. Whether it's something as simple as making the wallpaper fit on the desktop or as complex as integrating live Internet content on the desktop, you'll find the answers to your interface configuration questions in this chapter. For example, you'll learn how to configure and use multiple monitors to extend your desktop area.

The Startup folder, which Windows 2000 uses to execute programs automatically at startup, is also covered in some detail in this chapter along with other methods for automatically starting programs. You can bypass the Startup folder when needed to prevent programs from executing, move the Startup folder to a different location, and modify the registry to control program execution.

Customization of the interface is another hot topic, and you'll find plenty of information in this chapter. Windows 2000 enables you to modify the Start menu, add and remove items from the taskbar, create your own floating toolbars, rearrange the Start menu items, add administrative and other common items to the Start menu, and much more. You'll also find quick fixes to annoying problems like a Start menu item such as the Control Panel expanding rather than opening when you click it.

In addition to the Start menu and taskbar, you'll find several solutions to customization issues with folders, the desktop, the Network and Dial-Up Connections folder, special desktop and menu effects, and other topics of interest to most users. You'll also learn a handful of ways to control the way applications start, how to use command-line switches for shortcuts, and how to start programs with *cmd.exe*.

4.1   Using multiple monitors

You're not limited to just two monitors; Windows 2000 supports up to ten. Because each monitor requires its own adapter, however, it's unlikely you'll be using more than two or three (though some adapters do support multiple outputs). Plus, except in rare circumstances, two or three is plenty.

But why use multiple monitors in the first place? The main reason is to gain more desktop space. Programming, web site development, data analysis, desktop publishing, financial analysis, and even working with large spreadsheets are prime situations for using multiple monitors. You might even use multiple monitors in a word processing task to view one reference document while working on another. And for those few games that support it, multiple monitors offer a nice advantage over single-monitor systems.

Each adapter must be either AGP or PCI. The adapters don't have to be the same model or even manufacturer. The computer's BIOS detects the adapters according to their slot order, or in some systems, based on a BIOS setting that enables you to specify the default VGA device. One adapter serves as the primary display, where the logon dialog appears and where most applications will open by default. Some BIOS will let only the AGP card be the primary display; others are configurable.

Setting up the displays in Windows 2000 is relatively easy. All configuration happens through the Display Control Panel object. Each adapter can have different resolution and color depth settings, and you have full control over the arrangement of the desktop on the monitors.

Add and configure multiple monitors

The first task, even before you install additional adapters, is to make sure the adapters are compatible with Windows 2000. Check the adapters' documentation to make sure, or check the manufacturer's web site for the latest Windows 2000 drivers. When you have everything you need, follow these steps to add and configure the additional adapter(s):

1. Shut down the system and install the new adapter(s).

2. Restart the system. Windows 2000 should automatically detect the new hardware and install the necessary drivers or prompt you to provide the driver disk. If it doesn't detect the new hardware, run the Add/Remove Hardware wizard in the Control Panel to install the adapters.

3. Open the Display object in the Control Panel or right-click the desktop and choose Properties to open the Display properties.

4. Click one of the numbered display icons or select an adapter from the Display list.

5. Adjust the settings for the selected adapter based on the following list:

   Display
   Select the display adapter whose properties you want to change.

   Colors
   Select the color depth for the selected adapter.

   Screen Area
   Specify the screen height and width (resolution) for the selected adapter.

   Use this device as the primary monitor
   Show the logon dialog box, desktop icons, and taskbar on the selected display.

   Identify
   Briefly show the monitor number on the display to help you identify it.

   Extend my Windows desktop onto this monitor
   Enable the selected display and include the desktop on it.

6. Repeat step 5 for the other adapters.

7. Click and drag the numbered monitor icons to arrange the displays according to your physical monitor layout.

4.2   Prevent a program from executing automatically at startup

On your computer, certain applications might launch when the system starts or when you log on. If you're troubleshooting a problem or simply don't want the program starting up automatically anymore, you're probably looking for a way to keep this from happening. How you do that depends on how the application is being started and involves the Startup folder, registry, and services. If you don't need the program anymore you can simply uninstall it. If you have problems uninstalling or want to keep the program but not have it start automatically, read on.

Check all Startup folders

The first step in disabling startup applications is to search the Startup folders for them. Windows 2000 maintains a separate Startup folder for each user in \Documents And Settings\user\Start Menu\Programs\Startup. In addition, Windows 2000 maintains a common Startup folder in \Documents And Settings\All Users\Start Menu\Programs\Startup that applies to all users. All applications or shortcuts in the Startup folders are executed after logon.

The Startup folders are located in *systemroot\Profiles\user\ Start Menu\Programs\Startup* if you upgraded from Windows NT.

You can bypass the Startup folders during logon by holding down the Shift key. Type your password, hold down the Shift key, then continue holding Shift until the logon process completes and the desktop appears. This method is useful when you want to bypass Startup on specific occasions and don't want to modify the contents of the Startup folders.

If you want to permanently disable an item in one of the Startup folders from starting at logon, you can remove the item from the appropriate Startup folder. Just browse to the folder, select the shortcut, and delete it (or move it to a different folder if you think you might want to restore the shortcut later).

Check the registry

In addition to running applications from the Startup folders, Windows 2000 also executes applications at logon based on the contents of the registry key HKEY_LOCAL_MACHINE\SOFTWARE\Microsoft\Windows\CurrentVersion\Run. Any applications specified in this key run automatically at logon. You can prevent those applications from running by removing their entries from the registry. Here's how:

1. Make sure you're careful using the registry editor, as an incorrect change to the registry could prevent your system from booting.

2. Choose Start → Run, and enter **regedit** in the Run dialog box.

3. In the Registry Editor, open the key HKEY_LOCAL_MACHINE\SOFT-WARE\Microsoft\Windows\CurrentVersion\Run.

4. Choose Registry → Export Registry File.

5. Type **run** in the File Name text box, select the option Selected Branch, and click Save to save a backup copy of the key. You can restore the key later if you have problems editing it. Just double-click on the file to restore the settings to the registry.

6. Find the registry entry for the application you want to remove, then select the key and press Del. Click Yes to delete the key.

Check services

Certain applications run in Windows 2000 as services. These can include third-party applications you install yourself or Windows 2000 components.

In either case, you can change the startup mode for the service to prevent it from starting automatically. You do so through the Services branch of the Computer Management console:

1. Right-click My Computer and choose Manage to open the Computer Management console.

2. Open the Services and Applications\Services branch.

3. Using the service name as a guide, locate the service that you want to modify, then double-click the service to open its properties.

4. Select Manual from the "Startup type" drop-down list.

5. Click Stop to stop the service.

6. Click OK to close the dialog box then close the Computer Management console.

4.3   Change the location of the Startup folders

The Startup folders (one for all users and one for the currently logged on user) are defined by settings in the registry. The Startup folder that applies to all users is located in *Documents and Settings\All Users\Start Menu\ Programs\Startup*. The current user's Startup folder is located in *Documents and Settings\user\Start Menu\Programs\Startup*, where *user* is the user's logon name.

 The Startup folders are located in *systemroot\Profiles\user\ Start Menu\Programs\Startup* if you upgraded from Windows NT.

You can change the location of the Startup folders if desired. For example, you might want to point the Startup folder for all users to a folder on a network server so all users have the same set of startup applications. Or you might need to move the Startup folder to a disk with more space. In either case, moving the Startup folder is simply a matter of changing the registry entry that defines it.

Edit the registry

You modify the location of the Startup folders by editing the appropriate value in the registry. In the case of the individual user Startup folder, the existing registry entry is *userprofile*\Start Menu\Programs\Startup. The replaceable variable *userprofile* points to the current user profile and describes the Startup folder in the context of the current user. In effect, *userprofile* points to the *Documents and Settings**user* folder. You can modify the part of the string after the variable to place the Startup folder at a different location within the *Documents and Settings**user* folder or replace the entire string to specify an absolute path.

The existing registry entry for the common Startup folder is *allusersprofile*\Start Menu\Programs\Startup. The *allusersprofile* variable points to the *Documents and Settings**All Users* folder. You can modify the value of HKEY_LOCAL_MACHINE\SOFTWARE\Microsoft\Windows\ CurrentVersion\Explorer\User Shell Folders\Common Startup if you want all users to have different common Startup folders.

Follow these steps to change the location of the Startup folder(s):

1. Choose Start → Run, enter **regedit**, and click OK to start the Registry Editor.

2. Open the key HKEY_LOCAL_MACHINE\SOFTWARE\Microsoft\ Windows\CurrentVersion\Explorer\User Shell Folders for the common Startup folder or HKEY_CURRENT_USER\SOFTWARE\Microsoft\ Windows\CurrentVersion\Explorer\User Shell Folders for the individual user's Startup folder.

3. Choose Registry → Export Registry File if you want to make a backup copy of the key in case you experience problems after editing it. Export the selected branch to a file of your choosing.

4. Double-click the value Common Startup (for the common folder) or Startup (for the user folder) to open the Edit String dialog box.

5. Change the path specified in the string to point to the desired folder and click OK.

6. Close the Registry Editor.

4.4 Customize the taskbar

The taskbar serves as a control center for the tasks you perform in Windows 2000. While it's useful as is, there are several things you can do to customize its appearance and function and make it even more useful. For example, you might add shortcuts to the Quick Launch toolbar for applications or documents you use frequently. You might also want to create other toolbars for other applications or common tasks.

Add or remove Quick Launch items

The taskbar by default includes one toolbar at the left edge of the taskbar just to the right of the Start button. This Quick Launch toolbar contains three items by default that open Internet Explorer, open Outlook Express, and minimize all windows to display the desktop. You can remove any of these items or add other items to help you quickly launch applications and documents.

The Quick Launch toolbar shows the contents of the folder *Documents And Settings\user\Application Data\Microsoft\Internet Explorer\Quick Launch*. On systems upgraded from Windows NT, the folder is located in *systemroot\ Profiles\user\Application Data\Microsoft\Internet Explorer\Quick Launch*. You can add or remove items in the Quick Launch toolbar by adding or removing objects from the folder. Or you can use the following procedure to modify the Quick Launch toolbar with drag and drop:

1. Open a folder that contains the application or document you want to add to the Quick Launch toolbar.

2. Right-drag the object to the Quick Launch toolbar, release it, and choose Create Shortcut(s) Here.

3. Right-click an existing icon on the Quick Launch toolbar and choose Delete to remove it from the toolbar.

 Drag My Documents to the Quick Launch toolbar to give yourself a quick way to access your documents from the task-bar. Also, you can copy existing shortcuts to the Quick Launch toolbar by right-dragging the shortcut to the toolbar, then choosing Copy from the context menu.

Add toolbars

You can easily add other toolbars to the taskbar to use in conjunction with or in place of the Quick Launch toolbar. For example, you might add a commonly used folder (such as My Documents) to the taskbar as a quick means of opening the folder.

1. Close running applications so you have plenty of space on the taskbar.

2. In Explorer, locate the folder you want to add to the taskbar as a toolbar.

3. Drag the folder to a blank area of the taskbar and release it.

You can also add an Internet address or network folder to the taskbar. In the case of an Internet address, the content of the specified URL appears on the taskbar in a scrollable window. Here's how to add Internet content to the taskbar:

1. Right-click a blank area of the taskbar and choose Toolbars → New Toolbar.

2. In the New Toolbar dialog box, select the folder you want to use or type the path to the folder or the Internet URL in the Folder text box.

3. Click OK.

4. Use the vertical bar at the left of the toolbar to resize it.

Move or resize the taskbar

While it isn't apparent from looking at it, the taskbar is movable and resizable. Just click on a blank area of the taskbar and drag it to one of the four edges of the desktop to relocate it. Click and drag the inside edge of the taskbar to resize it.

Auto-hide the taskbar or set it to appear always on top

You can configure properties for the taskbar so it always stays on top even when an application is open (this is the default behavior for the taskbar). Or, you can configure the taskbar to move behind the current window, giving you more space for the current window. You also can configure the taskbar to *auto-hide*, which means it automatically disappears when you aren't using it. It reappears when you move the mouse over the edge of the screen where the taskbar is hidden. Use the following steps to configure these properties:

1. Right-click the taskbar and choose Properties.

2. Select the option Always on Top if you want the taskbar to remain visible at all times, or deselect the option if you want the taskbar to move to the background when you select another window.

3. Select the option Auto Hide if you want the taskbar to disappear automatically when you're not using it.

4. Click OK to apply the changes.

4.5   Change or rearrange the contents of the Start menu

Setup creates a default Startup menu when you install Windows 2000, and applications typically modify the Start menu when you install them. Over time the Start menu can get a little crowded and out of order. Some items on the Start menu can't be changed, but fortunately, Windows 2000 makes it easy to modify the contents of the Programs menu and rearrange the order of items in it.

Add new menus and items

You can add new menus to the Start menu and add new items to existing menus using a couple of different methods. In the first method you use a wizard to add items:

1. Right-click the taskbar and choose Properties.

2. Click the Advanced tab then click Add.

3. The wizard prompts you for the item to add. Specify a folder, application executable, Internet URL, network share, or computer name, then click Next.

4. Specify the location on the Start menu for the new item and click Next.

5. Specify a name for the shortcut on the Start menu and click Finish.

You can also add menus and items manually simply by creating folders and shortcuts in the appropriate folder. By default the Start menu points to the contents of *Documents and Settings\\user\\Start Menu* (*systemroot\\Profiles\\ user\\Start Menu* on Windows NT upgrades). You can add additional menus to the Start menu by creating folders at any location under this folder. Add items to these menus by creating shortcuts in the folders.

A third method for adding items to the Start menu is to use drag and drop:

1. Locate in Explorer (or on the desktop) the item you want to add to the menu, then drag it on top of the Start menu.

2. Continue holding down the mouse button, then use the mouse to open the Start menu as you would normally, including opening cascading menus if necessary.

3. Place the cursor where you want to locate the new menu item and release the mouse button.

Remove menus and items

Occasionally you might want to remove items or entire menus from the Start menu. As when adding items, you have a couple of methods from which to choose. First, you can use the taskbar properties to remove items:

1. Right-click the taskbar and choose Properties.

2. Click the Advanced tab and click Remove.

3. Select the menu or menu item you want to remove and click Remove.

4. Remove other items as desired and click Close.

You also can remove items manually by browsing to the Start menu folder at *\Documents and Settings\user\Start Menu* or *systemroot\Profiles\user\Start Menu*. Delete the items you want to remove from the Start menu.

 You can left-click the Start menu to open it as normal, then right-click items to open a context menu that gives you several options, including deleting the item.

Show small icons on the Start menu

By default the Start menu shows the text "Windows 2000 Professional" or "Windows 2000 Server" and uses larger icons on the main Start menu than it does on subsequent menus such as the Programs menu. You can remove the Windows 2000 name and use smaller icons if you want to reduce the size of the Start menu (see Figure 4-1):

1. Right-click the taskbar and choose Properties.

2. On the General page select the option Show small icons in Start menu, then click OK.

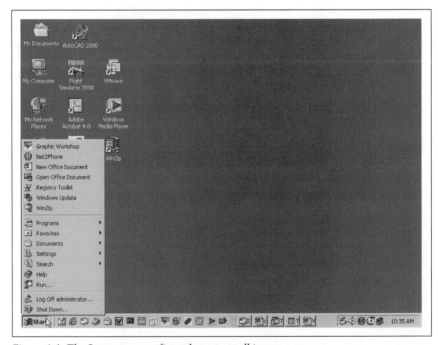

Figure 4-1. The Start menu configured to use small icons

4.6 The Start menu items are not in order

As you add new applications and add and remove items from the Start menu it tends to get out of order. Windows 2000 provides a couple of easy methods for sorting the menu.

Rearrange menu order

Here's an easy way to sort the Programs menu in alphabetical order:

1. Right-click the taskbar and choose Properties.

2. Click the Advanced tab then click Re-sort.

3. Click OK to close the property sheet.

You can also rearrange items in the Start menu manually. For example, using the Re-sort method just described doesn't always give you the results you want. So open the Start menu and simply drag menus and menu items around to rearrange them to suit your preferences.

4.7 Administrative Tools, Log Off, or Favorites are missing from the Start menu

On Windows 2000 Professional, Setup does not include the Administrative Tools folder on the Start menu by default. Although you can get to the folder through the Control Panel, it's much quicker to use the Start menu.

Also, your system might be configured so the Log Off option doesn't show up on the menu. If you log on and off your computer frequently, you'll probably want to add that option to the Start menu.

Finally, you can configure the Start menu to include or exclude the Favorites folder, which also appears under the Favorites menu in Internet Explorer.

Show additional options on the Start menu

It's a quick fix to add the Administrative Tools folder, Log Off option, or Favorites folder to the Start menu. Here's how:

1. Right-click the taskbar and choose Properties.

2. Click the Advanced tab, select the Display Administrative Tools option, Display Logoff, or Display Favorites options, and click OK.

4.8   A container on the Start menu expands instead of opening

You can configure certain items on the Start menu to expand rather than open when you click them. These items include the Control Panel, My Documents, Network and Dial-Up Connections, and Printers. When the Control Panel is configured to expand, for example, you click Start → Settings → Control Panel, and rather than the Control Panel folder opening, the contents of the Control Panel appear as items on the Start menu. This is a nice feature that helps you access objects more easily, but can be an annoyance if what you really want to do is open the folder rather than expand its contents.

Open instead of expand

While you could turn off expanding altogether (explained shortly), the number of times you want to open a folder rather than expand it is probably small. Windows 2000 provides a way around the problem through the menu item's context menu. To open a folder rather than expand it on the Start menu, simply right-click the menu item and choose Open from the context menu.

Turn off expanding

If you prefer that a specific item not expand by default when you click it in the Start menu, you can easily change its behavior to make it open instead:

1. Right-click the taskbar and choose Properties.

2. Click the Advanced tab, then deselect the appropriate Expand option in the Start Menu Settings list and click OK.

4.9   Turn off special menu and tooltip effects

Windows 2000 adds some new interface tweaks that offer special effects for menus and tooltips. For example, you can configure menus to fade out after you release them. While the effects add an interesting change to the Windows 2000 interface, they can also become annoying after a short time, slowing down performance a bit. So whether you want to use a different effect or turn them off altogether, you'll find the necessary options in the properties for the desktop.

Change or turn off special visual effects

You use the Effects page of the Display properties to configure the transition effect for menus and tooltips, including setting it to none:

1. Right-click the desktop and choose Properties or open the Display object in the Control Panel. Then click the Effects tab.

2. To select a transition effect, select the option "Use transition effects for menus and tooltips," then select the desired effect from the drop-down list. To turn off transition effects, deselect this option.

3. Click OK to close the Display properties.

4.10 Gain quick access to Control Panel and other folders

The Start menu includes four items that open to give you access to system settings, documents, favorite URLs, and printers: Control Panel, Network and Dial-Up Connections, My Documents, and Printers. By default each of these items opens its corresponding folder when you click the item in the Start menu. Wouldn't it be nice if you could have the folder expand right on the Start menu so you could access the needed object right from the menu rather than waiting for its folder to open? A quick fix in the taskbar properties makes that happen for you.

Expanding items on the Start menu

You can configure the Control Panel, My Documents, Favorites, or Printers folders to *expand* rather than open. When a folder is configured to expand, its contents appear in a cascading menu when you click the folder item on the Start menu. For example, you can see the contents of the Control Panel right on the Start menu rather than opening the Control Panel folder. Here's how to make that happen:

1. Right-click the taskbar and choose Properties.

2. Click the Advanced tab and select any of the following options depending on which folder(s) you want to expand rather than open:

   Expand Control Panel
   Expand My Documents
   Expand Network and Dial-Up Connections
   Expand Printers

3. Click OK.

4.11   Gain quick access to network resources

All your system's local volumes appear in My Computer along with any network shares that are mapped to local drive IDs. You can browse for shared network resources through My Network Places. Opening My Computer to access a volume doesn't take much time, but browsing for a network share can require several clicks and a sometimes lengthy wait for the interface to respond on a busy network.

You can get quicker access to local volumes, mapped or unmapped network shares, network printers, and remote computers by creating shortcuts to those resources right on the desktop, in the Quick Launch toolbar, or in another toolbar on the taskbar. You also can use UNC pathnames to quickly access network resources that are not mapped to local drive IDs.

Create shortcuts to local and network resources

You can create shortcuts on the desktop, in a folder, or on a toolbar to shared network resources to make it easier and quicker to access those resources than going through My Network Places. Creating a shortcut is an easy task:

1. Open My Network Places and browse to the location where the network resource resides.

2. Right-drag the resource (printer or shared folder) to the desktop or to a toolbar and choose Create Shortcut(s) Here. Alternatively, right-click the desktop or the target toolbar and choose New → Shortcut. In the Create Shortcut wizard specify the path to the resource using its UNC pathname (see the next section).

Use UNC pathnames

UNC stands for Universal Naming Convention. A UNC pathname specifies an absolute path to a network resource such as a shared folder or printer. A UNC pathname takes the form *server**share**subshares*, where *server* is the name of the computer sharing the resource, *share* is the name by which the resource is shared, and *subshares* represent additional levels in the remote folder structure. For example, assume that a computer named Barney shares a folder with the share name *Documents*. You could reference the folder with the UNC pathname *Barney**Documents*. You could also reference subfolders of the *Documents* share or documents on the UNC pathname, for example, *Barney**Documents**Letters**Resignation.doc*.

One advantage to using UNC pathnames to reference resources is that you don't have to map the resource to a local drive ID. This frequently saves time if you're using only a few resources from the remote computer and don't use the resources often enough to warrant mapping a drive letter. It's also handy when you know the server and share name but can't remember what drive ID is mapped to the share.

Following are some places where you might use a UNC pathname:

- In the Create Shortcut wizard, to specify a network resource without browsing to it

- In the Address bar in Explorer, to quickly browse to a specific share

- In the Open or Save dialog box of an application, to open a file from a network share or save to a network share without a mapped drive ID

Just type the UNC pathname to a resource any time you would otherwise specify a mapped drive ID or path to a network printer.

4.12   Change the folder associated with the My Documents icon

The My Documents icon on the desktop is associated with \Documents and Settings\user\My Documents by default. The My Documents folder and its integration with the desktop give you an easy means of organizing your documents and opening them quickly. In some cases, however, you might want to use a different folder as your primary document folder. For example, the drive containing the default My Documents folder might be filling up and you need to specify a different local drive. Or perhaps you want to point My Documents to a network share. In either case a quick change associates the My Documents object with the folder of your choice.

When you change the folder associated with My Documents the change applies across your local system for your user account. In addition to changing the folder that opens when you open the My Documents object on the desktop, the new folder also appears when you open the Documents folder on the Start menu or select My Documents in the common file Open and Save dialogs presented by Windows.

Changing My Documents properties

You can specify the folder associated with the My Documents object through the properties of the My Documents icon on the desktop:

1. Right-click My Documents on the desktop and choose Properties.

2. On the Target property page, click Move.

3. Browse to the location of the folder you want to use for your documents, select the folder, and click OK.

4. Click OK again. Windows prompts to ask if you want to move all files in the current My Documents folder to the new location. Click Yes to move the files or No to leave them where they are.

You can easily set the folder back to its default location in the future if needed. Just open the property sheet again and click Restore Default.

4.13   Add a new option to the Send To menu

The Send To menu appears on the common context menu for most items in the Windows 2000 interface (right-click an object to view its context menu). You can use the Send To menu to send the selected item to a floppy disk, email recipient, etc. Windows 2000 provides a handful of default choices on the Send To menu:

3 1/2 Floppy (A)
Send the selected item to the floppy disk.

Desktop
Place a shortcut to the item on the desktop.

Mail Recipient
Open a new email message with the selected object as an attachment to the message.

My Documents
Place a copy of the selected object in the My Documents folder.

You might want to add your own items to the Send To menu. For example, you might have a folder you use frequently and want to use the context menu to copy or move items to that folder. Or perhaps you want to add an item to the Send To folder that enables you to email an object directly to a specific person. Another reason to modify the Send To menu is to add Notepad or Wordpad to the menu, giving you a quick means of opening text-based documents that don't have a *.txt*, *.doc*, or other extension associated with these programs. And a really useful addition to the Send To menu is a shortcut to the printer you use most often, enabling you to send a document to the printer through the document's context menu.

Modify the Send To menu

The Send To menu works by reading the contents of the SendTo folder and displaying the contents of the folder as the contents of the Send To menu.

When you select an item from the Send To menu on an object's context menu (see Figure 4-2), you're actually directing the object to the selected shortcut.

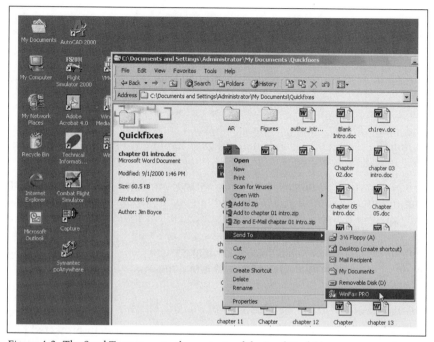

Figure 4-2. The Send To menu uses the contents of the Send To folder to generate the context menu

Adding an item to the SendTo folder is as simple as adding a shortcut to the folder. You can create shortcuts to folders, disks, printers, applications, and nearly any other object. Here's how:

1. Open Explorer and browse to *Documents and Settings\user*, where *user* is your username. On systems upgraded from Windows NT, browse to *systemroot\Profiles\user*.

2. Configure folder options to show hidden files.

3. Open the hidden SendTo folder.

4. Right-click in the folder and choose New → Shortcut.

5. Follow the prompts in the New Shortcut wizard to create a shortcut to the application, printer, or folder you want included on the Send To menu.

Another easy method for creating shortcuts in the SendTo folder is to simply right-drag the object from its current location to the SendTo folder and choose Create Shortcut(s) Here from the context menu. For example, you can right-drag a printer from the Printers folder to the SendTo folder to quickly create a shortcut to that printer.

4.14 Some files don't show up in folders

Windows 2000 by default doesn't display all folders or files. Any folders and files with the Hidden attribute set do not show up. In addition, certain system files are hidden. These system files include the boot files *boot.ini*, *ntldr*, and *ntdetect.com*. Windows 2000 also treats some other files as system files, hiding them from view. You can configure Explorer to show hidden files as well as system protected files if needed.

Before you configure Explorer to show system protected files, however, keep in mind that accidentally deleting, moving, or replacing these files can typically prevent the system from booting or cause other widespread havoc with the system. You should only enable display of system protected files when you absolutely need to access a particular system file. Turn off visibility of system protected files after you've performed the needed task on the file(s).

Show hidden and system protected files

You configure visibility of hidden folders and files and system protected files through the Folder Options dialog box:

1. Open any folder window (including My Computer) and choose Tools → Folder Options.

2. Click the View tab, then select the option "Show hidden files and folders." This makes hidden files and folders visible.

3. Deselect the option "Hide protected operating system files." This will make the system protected files visible in Explorer. Explorer prompts you to verify that you really want to turn on visibility of system protected files. Click Yes.

4. Click OK.

4.15 Customize the appearance of a specific folder

In Windows 2000 each folder can have a different background, which not only lets you customize the interface to your tastes but also gives you a visual clue as to the folder location. For example, you might apply a specific background to each drive folder so you can quickly identify the drive you're currently browsing. You can use graphics files in *.bmp*, *.jpg*, *.gif*, *.tif*, or *.dib* formats as the background.

In addition to specifying a background for a folder window, you can specify an HTML template to use to structure the appearance of a folder. Windows 2000 provides four sample HTML templates to customize the appearance of a folder that you can use as-is or modify. You can also create your own HTML files to use to define the folder appearance, though doing so naturally requires a strong understanding of HTML.

Finally, you can add a folder comment. This optional comment, structured in HTML, appears in the left pane of the folder window.

Customize folder appearance

Windows 2000 provides a wizard to step you through the process of setting folder appearance. Some of the potential tasks in customizing a folder—such as HTML programming—are outside the scope of this book. The following procedure explains where to go in the Windows 2000 interface to customize a folder:

1. Open the folder you want to customize and choose View → Customize This Folder to start the wizard, then click Next.

2. You can select any of three options that enable you to specify or edit an HTML template for the folder, specify a background image, and add the folder comment. Select the desired options and click Next.

3. Windows 2000 prompts you to select a template. After you select a template, you can select the option "I want to edit this template," and Windows 2000 will open the HTML code in a text editor so you can edit it. Click Next to continue.

4. The wizard next prompts you for an image to use for the background. Browse to the location containing the desired image and select it.

5. Specify the foreground and background colors for icon text using the Text and Background buttons, respectively, then click Next.

6. If you're specifying a folder comment, Windows 2000 provides a text box for you to type the HTML code for the comment.

7. Click Next, then Finish to complete the customization.

4.16   Determining which volumes and folders are compressed

Although Windows 2000 doesn't support compression for FAT or FAT32 volumes, it does support on-the-fly compression and decompression for NTFS volumes. By default Windows 2000 provides no visual indicator to differentiate folders or files that are compressed from those that are not compressed. In some situations it's useful to know at a glance which folders are compressed. For example, since compression and encryption are mutually exclusive, knowing which folders are compressed will tell which ones can or can't be used to store encrypted files.

Show compressed volumes and folders with a different color

You can configure Windows 2000 to show compressed folders and files using blue text for the folder or filename rather than the default color. The change means a quick trip to the Folder Options property sheet:

1. Open My Computer or any folder and choose Tools → Folder Options.

2. Click the View tab and select the option "Display compressed files and folders with alternate color."

3. Click OK, then verify that the compressed folders and files appear in a different color.

4.17   Double-clicking a document opens the wrong program

Windows 2000, like Windows 9x and Windows NT, uses document/application association properties to determine which application is used to view or edit a document when you double-click that document. The document properties also determine what action the application takes for different tasks such as play, open, edit, and print. With Microsoft Word installed, for example, files with a .doc extension open in Word. Text files with the .txt extension open in Notepad.

When you install applications their Setup programs typically register the application's document type to create the application/document association. If the application uses the same document extension or works with the same types of documents as another application, your current association could be overwritten. The next time you double-click that file type the new application opens instead of the old one.

Or perhaps you want to change the association to specify yourself what application Windows 2000 should use to open a given document. For example, maybe you prefer to use Wordpad to open *.txt* files rather than Notepad. If so, you need to change the application/document association for the file type.

Change application/document association

Document associations are stored in the registry. While you could modify the associations manually by editing the registry, you'd be inviting trouble. Plus, there is an easier way using the Folder Options property sheet in Explorer.

1. Open My Computer or any folder and choose Tools → Folder Options.

2. Click the File Types tab.

3. In the Registered File Types list, locate the document extension whose association you want to modify.

4. Select the extension from the list and click Change.

5. Browse through the application list and select the program that you want Windows 2000 to use to open the document. Click Other to browse for an application not included in the list.

6. Click OK on the Open With dialog box to return to the Folder Options sheet, and then click OK to close the Folder Options sheet.

Change advanced document settings

In addition to changing document association, you can use the Folder Options property sheet to change advanced settings that specify different actions for a document. This includes, for example, opening, printing, and editing a document. You also can determine what action your web browser takes for the document type after a download, specify that Explorer always show the document extension, and define other properties, all described in the following steps:

1. Open My Computer or any folder and choose Tools → Folder Options.

2. Click the File Types tab.

3. In the Registered File Types list, locate the document extension whose association you want to modify and click Advanced.

4. Configure options using the following controls:

   Change icon
   > Click to select a different icon to represent the document type in Explorer. You'll find lots of icons in *systemroot\System32\Shell32.dll*

Configuring the Interface

and *moricons.dll*. Executable files also often contain icons. You can select an executable (*.exe* or *.dll*) or icon file (*.ico*).

New

Click to specify a new action and a corresponding application. For example, you could use one program to view a document but another to edit or print it.

Edit

Select an existing action and click Edit to modify the settings for the selected action.

Remove

Select an existing action and click Remove to remove the action.

Set Default

Select an existing action and click Set Default to specify the default action for a document type, changing from Edit to View, for example. The default action is the one applied when you double-click the file.

Confirm open after download

Select this option to have Windows 2000 ask whether you want to open the document after downloading. Deselect the option if you want Windows 2000 to open the document automatically after download.

Always show extension

Select this option to specify that the document's file extension will always be visible in a folder even when other extensions are not displayed.

Browse in same window

Select this option to use the same window for browsing the document rather than opening a new one.

5. Click OK to close the Edit File Type dialog box, then click OK again to close the Folder Options sheet.

4.18   Keyboard navigation indicators are missing from menus and dialogs

Windows 2000 by default turns off keyboard navigation indicators in menus and dialog boxes. These indicators appear as underlined letters that specify which key to push to select the menu or control using the keyboard. While you probably use the mouse almost exclusively when working in Windows 2000, there are occasions when you need to use the keyboard to select a menu command or control in a dialog box.

In the default configuration the keyboard shortcuts are hidden but reappear as soon as you press the Alt key. In some situations you might need the navigation keys to appear all the time, such as when you're capturing screen shots for documentation. You can change the navigation indicators' behavior through the Display property sheet.

Turn on keyboard navigation indicators

Configure the behavior of the keyboard navigation indicators though the Effects page of the Display property sheet:

1. Right-click the desktop and choose Properties or open the Display object in the Control Panel.

2. Click the Effects tab and deselect the option "Hide keyboard navigation indicators until I use the Alt key."

3. Click OK to close the property sheet.

4.19   Change icons of common desktop objects

Windows 2000 uses a default set of icons for the desktop objects My Computer, My Network Places, Recycle Bin, and My Documents. You change the desktop icons through the properties for the desktop.

Restore or change desktop icons

The desktop properties include a set of controls you can use to specify the icon to use for the four primary desktop icons mentioned previously. You can reassign any icon you wish, pulling the icon from an executable file (*.exe* or *.dll*) or icon file (*.ico*). The files *systemroot\Sytem32\moricons.dll* and *systemroot\System32\shell32.dll* contain numerous icons you can use. Here's how to change the icon for one of these four objects manually:

1. Right-click the desktop and choose Properties or open the Display object in the Control Panel.

2. Click the Effects tab, select the item you want to change from the Desktop icons group, and click Change Icon.

3. Browse for and select the file containing the icon you want to use, then select the icon itself.

4. Click OK, repeat the process for any other objects you want to change, and close the Display property sheet.

4.20 Execute a program using command-line switches

Command-line switches modify the function of a command. For example, the switch /ogn when added to a *dir* command sorts the directory listing with directories first followed by files, all in alphanumeric order. You can open a console prompt and type **dir /ogn** to see how it works. Another example is Symantec's pcAnywhere, which supports several switches that control the way pcAnywhere starts. The /r switch, for example, hides the startup splash screen. Microsoft Word supports several switches including /m, which prevents any autoexec macros from executing. Many other applications, including most Windows 2000 console commands, also support command-line switches. You can incorporate these switches in a few different ways depending on what you're trying to accomplish.

 With most console commands you can execute the command followed by the /? switch to view a list of available switches and other command parameters, as well as the command syntax. For some Windows applications, executing the program with the /? switch opens the program's Help file focused on the page that references the program's startup switches.

Modify the shortcut's properties

Most likely you have a shortcut on the desktop, in a folder, or in the Start menu that points to an application with which you'd like to use command-line switches to modify the program's startup. You can add command switches simply by modifying the shortcut's target:

1. Right-click the shortcut and choose Properties.

2. Click in the Target text box and move the cursor to the end of the command line. The command is enclosed in quotes.

3. Outside of the last quote, add the desired switches.

4. Click OK to close the shortcut's property sheet, and then test the application.

If you try to add the switches inside the quotes, Windows 2000 interprets the switches as part of the path and generates an error. The switches must be added outside the quotes.

Start the program from a .cmd file

If for some reason you don't want to modify a shortcut or can't apply the switches through a shortcut, you can instead use a *.cmd* file to execute the application with the desired switches. Here's how:

1. Open Notepad.

2. Type the path and command you want to execute, such as:

   ```
   C:\Program Files\Office2000\Winword.exe /m
   ```

3. Save the file and give it the file extension *.bat* or *.cmd*.

4. Create a shortcut on the desktop, in a folder, or on the Start menu to the file you just created. Double-clicking the shortcut will execute the file, which executes the application contained in the file.

CHAPTER 5

Printing

Print services have come a long way from the early incarnations of DOS and Unix. Each new release of Microsoft's operating systems has improved on printing in one way or another, and Windows 2000 is no exception. Setting up and using a printer is easy in most situations. But there are a few special problems you might run across with some of the new printing features in Windows 2000, as well as tried-and-true features.

For example, Windows 2000 supports the Internet Printing Protocol, or IPP, which enables clients to print across the Internet or an intranet using TCP/IP and HTTP. Clients can browse and manage remote printers through a web browser. Although Windows 2000 Server automatically configures the computer to share its printer(s) via IPP, Windows 2000 Professional does not. You'll find quick steps in this chapter to make your Windows 2000 Professional computer an IPP server.

Juggling printer configurations for different paper trays or other settings is another source of frustration for many people. But, you don't need to reconfigure a printer each time you need different settings. Instead, you can use multiple printer instances and configure each one with the required settings, then just pick it from the printer list when you need that particular configuration. This chapter explains how.

You'll also find solutions in this chapter to problems with printer security, managing documents and the print queue, and separating print jobs from one another.

5.1   Can't print to an Internet printer

Windows 2000 adds support for the Internet Printing Protocol (IPP), which enables users to print to printers across the Internet or an intranet. Windows 2000 includes built-in support for IPP, enabling Windows 2000 clients to take full advantage of IPP to connect to, manage, and print to remote printers on the Internet. The Windows 2000 Server CD includes a Windows 9x IPP driver located in \Clients\Win9xipp.cli. There is no IPP client available currently for Windows NT.

You should be able to browse to a printer on the Internet, connect to it, install a driver from the server, manage the print queue, etc., all through your web browser. Just connect to *http://server/Printers*, where *server* is the IP address or server name of the server hosting the printer. Figure 5-1 shows an example of a client connected to a server's printer folder. Note that the */Printers* folder is the default location, but the server administrator could have changed the folder location. You also can connect directly to the printer's page if you know the URL. It typically takes the form *http://server/Printers/PrinterName*.

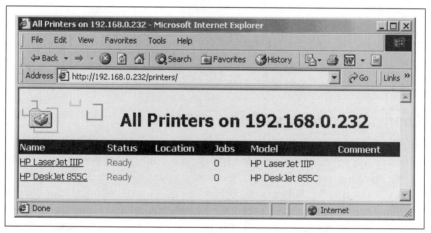

Figure 5-1. IPP enables you to browse and print to printers across the Internet or intranet

If you're having problems connecting to or using the printer, there are a couple of things you can check and change to overcome the problem.

Add a print driver for the printer

If the server doesn't contain the driver files for your printer (unlikely but possible) and you don't have the driver installed locally, you can install the printer driver locally. Depending on which driver is required you might or might not need the Windows 2000 installation CD. Here's how to install the printer driver:

1. Open the Printers folder in the Control Panel.
2. Run the Add Printer wizard.

3. Select the Network Printer option and click Next.

4. Select the Connect option to a printer on the Internet or on your intranet and specify the URL to the printer in the URL text box. You should be able to get this URL by browsing to the */Printers* virtual directory on the remote server. In general, the URL will be *http://server/Printers/ PrinterName*, where *server* is the name of the remote server and *PrinterName* is the name by which the printer is shared. Click Next and continue the installation process as you would for any other printer.

If Windows 2000 is unable to connect to the printer after you enter the URL and click Next, move back through the wizard and choose to install a local printer, configuring the printer for a local port. You can modify the port assignment through the printer's properties after you clear up the connectivity problem.

After the printer is installed and you have connectivity to the remote server, you can print to the printer just as you would any other network or local printer. The primary difference is that Windows 2000 uses HTTP to print rather than RPC as it would for a local or LAN printer.

Configure security settings

Another potential problem in printing to a remote printer is that you might not have the necessary permissions to do so. The remote server could have its permissions set such that it disallows anonymous access or prevents access from specific subnets or IP addresses. If you installed the correct printer driver but still have problems connecting to and using the printer, contact the system administrator for the remote server to troubleshoot the problem.

5.2 Make a printer available through the Internet or intranet

The mechanism that enables you to share your printer with other users on the Internet or an intranet is Internet Information Services (IIS). When you install IIS on Windows 2000 Server, Setup automatically creates the necessary virtual folder for printers and shares any currently shared printers through IIS. In the case of Windows 2000 Professional, installing IIS doesn't always configure the necessary Printers folder, so you have to do it manually. The following procedures will help you install IIS and configure your printers for sharing on the Internet or intranet.

Setup installs IIS by default when you install Windows 2000. You only need to reinstall IIS if it has been removed or was omitted as part of an unattended installation. The problem with Setup not configuring the Printers virtual folder under Windows 2000 Professional should not occur if you have installed all updates and Service Packs for Windows 2000, but you can still configure the folder manually, if needed.

Install IIS

As with other Windows 2000 components, you install IIS through the Add/ Remove Programs object in the Control Panel. If you're installing IIS under Windows 2000 Server, this should be the only thing you need to do to enable other users to access printers on the server from the Internet. If installing IIS on a Windows 2000 Professional computer you'll need to complete the other procedures in this section as well.

1. Install the drivers for the printers that are connected to or shared by the server using the Add Printer wizard in the Printers folder. When installing the printers, add drivers as needed for any other operating system clients that will be connecting to the server.

2. Open the Add/Remove Programs object in the Control Panel.

3. Click Add/Remove Windows Components.

4. Select Internet Information Services from the components list and click Details.

5. Select the IIS components you want to install. At a minimum you need the following to support IPP printing:

   — Common files

   — Internet Information Services Snap-In

   — World Wide Web Server

6. After selecting the desired components, click OK, and then click Next and follow the remaining prompts to install the software, providing the Windows 2000 CD when prompted.

Installing the IIS software is all you need to do on a Windows 2000 Server system to enable IPP sharing of the server's printers. On a Windows 2000 Professional computer you must manually configure the Printers virtual folder to enable clients to access through IPP any printers shared on the computer.

Create a Printers virtual folder

The second step in enabling IPP on a Windows 2000 Professional computer is creating the Printers virtual folder under the computer's default web site. You might also need to perform this procedure on a Windows 2000 Server computer if the Printers virtual folder has been removed. You use the IIS console to perform the task:

1. Right-click My Computer and choose Manage to open the Computer Management console.

2. Open the Services and Applications branch and then the Internet Information Services branch.

3. Expand the Default Web Site and verify that there is currently no Printers virtual folder. If there is, you should already be set up to allow printing to your printers through IPP.

4. Right-click Default Web Site and choose New → Virtual Directory, then click Next when the Virtual Directory Creation wizard starts.

5. Specify Printers as the alias for the virtual directory and click Next.

6. Type or browse to the folder *systemroot\Web\Printers* to specify the directory in the Directory text box (see Figure 5-2), and click Next.

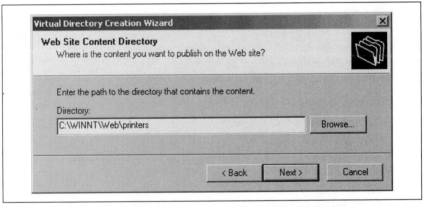

Figure 5-2. The default location for the Printers folder is \WINNT\Web\Printers

7. Set access permissions to include Read and Run Scripts, click Next, and then click Finish.

8. Right-click the virtual directory just created and choose Properties.

9. Click the Documents tab and select Enable Default Document.

10. Click Add, type **ipp_0001.asp**, and click OK. You can also use *page1.asp* as the default page.

11. Click OK to close the property sheet and then close the IIS console.

12. Attempt a test print from a network client to a shared printer through the Internet or intranet. If the client is unable to connect, use the IIS console to stop and restart the default web site.

Configure security and accounts

If the default web site and the Printers virtual folder are not configured to allow anonymous access, you'll have to specify a valid username and password to be able to print through IPP to a shared printer on that computer. You also can restrict access to the Printers folder to hosts in specific subnets or domains (not supported under IIS on Windows 2000 Professional). Follow these steps to configure security on the Printers virtual folder:

1. Right-click My Computer and choose Manage to open the Computer Management console. Open the Services and Applications\Internet Information Services branch.

2. Expand the Default Web Site, then right-click the Printers virtual folder and choose Properties.

3. Click the Edit button in the Anonymous Access and Authentication Control group.

4. Select options using the following list as a guide:

Anonymous access

Select this option to allow anonymous connections to the system's shared printers. Deselect to require users to have a valid account on the computer or in the domain in order to use the printers. When anonymous access is enabled, Windows 2000 uses the account IUSR_*ComputerName*, where *ComputerName* is the computer's host name, to authenticate anonymous access. You can click the Edit button in the Anonymous access group to specify a different account.

Basic authentication

Select this option to allow passwords to be sent in plain text for authenticated users. Click the associated Edit button to specify a default domain for those users who don't provide a domain during authentication.

Digest authentication for Windows domain servers

This option causes IIS to send a hash value across the network rather than the password, enabling authentication to work across proxy servers and firewalls. Digest authentication is less susceptible than clear text passwords to password interception. It is supported

Printing

only for domains with a Windows 2000 domain controller. Digest authentication requires a browser that supports HTTP 1.1.

Integrated Windows authentication
Choose this option to use Integrated Windows authentication, formerly known as Windows NT Challenge/Response. The server will attempt to authenticate the remote user with the user's current logon account and password, and failing that, will prompt for a user name and password.

5. Click OK to close the property sheet for the virtual folder.

5.3   A better method if you switch printer settings frequently

It's relatively easy to change printer settings such as portrait versus landscape, paper tray selection, spool settings, print quality, paper quality, etc. You open the Printers folder, open the properties for the printer, and make whatever changes are needed. Many of those changes, however, can take a lot of clicks to accomplish and waste time, particularly when there is an easier way. Just configure multiple instances of the same printer, each with its own group of settings.

Configure multiple printer instances

Windows 2000, like Windows NT and Windows 9x, can maintain a single copy of a printer driver but use multiple *instances* of the driver. Each instance has its own name and settings but uses the same print driver and physical printer. The advantage to using multiple instances is that you can configure each instance with its own group of settings for paper tray, page layout, etc. When you want to print using a particular group of settings, you simply select the printer by name from the printer list in the application. You save the time and trouble of opening the Printers folder, making changes, then printing. It's basically a one-click fix for frequent printer setting changes:

1. Open the Printers folder, right-click the existing instance of the printer, and choose Properties. Configure its settings as needed and change the name of the printer to something that will help you identify this instance's settings at a glance.

2. Close the property sheet for the current printer instance and run the Add Printer wizard.

3. Choose either Local or Network depending on the location of the printer, and select the appropriate port to match the settings for the current printer instance.

4. Select the same manufacturer and model number, and when prompted to either keep the existing driver or replace it, choose to keep the existing driver.

5. Specify a name for the printer that identifies the function of this instance.

6. After you add the new printer instance, right-click the printer and choose Properties. Configure its settings as desired.

7. Repeat steps 2 through 6 to add additional instances of the printer with their own settings as needed.

8. In your application, choose File → Print and select the printer instance from the Name drop-down list (see Figure 5-3). When you click OK, Windows 2000 will print the document using the settings assigned to that printer instance.

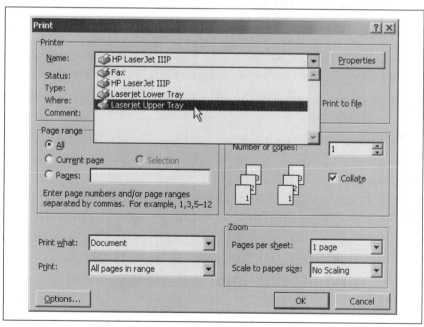

Figure 5-3. Three of these print selections point to the same physical printer, but with different configurations

5.4 People with other operating systems can't use your printer

The Add Printer wizard installs only the print driver for Windows 2000 when you add a printer. If you're sharing that printer, it's possible that other users on the network who have different operating systems (Windows 9x, for example) might want to print to your printer. If they don't have the necessary printer driver for their operating system, they won't be able to print. You can configure your system to include the printer drivers for those other operating systems, making them available for download and installation when another user connects to your printer for the first time. After the printer driver is installed on the remote computer it can print to your printer.

Although the Add Printer wizard doesn't give you the option of adding drivers for other operating systems when you first set up the printer, you can add them afterwards.

Add additional print drivers

You add printer drivers for other operating systems through the Sharing property page for the printer. You'll need the Windows 2000 Server CD or another source for the necessary printer drivers. The Windows 2000 Professional CD does not include printer drivers for other operating systems.

1. Right-click the printer for which you want to add other drivers and choose Properties.

2. Click the Sharing page, then click Additional Drivers.

3. Place a check beside each of the other operating systems you want to support and click OK.

4. Windows 2000 prompts you to insert the Windows 2000 Server CD. Insert the CD and click OK.

5.5 Simplify printer administration and provide load balancing

Windows 2000 provides a feature called *printer pooling* that lets you treat two identical local printers as a single printer for purposes of configuration and administration. Rather than configuring and managing the printers separately, you simply set up the pool and manage a single configuration that applies to all printers in the pool. In fact, you only deal with one printer driver instance. Instead of configuring the driver for a single port, however, you select multiple ports, one for each printer in the pool (see Figure 5-4).

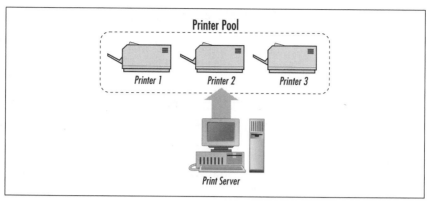

Figure 5-4. A printer pool enables several printers to be managed as a single logical unit for configuration

Printer pooling also provides *load balancing*, which means that Windows 2000 can parcel out print jobs to the printers according to which one is available or has the fewest pending print jobs. This relieves the load on a single printer and lets users get their printed documents back more quickly.

 Printers in a pool can be local or located across the network.

Set up a print pool

It's a simple matter to set up a print pool and really only requires a single option change in the print driver's properties. The following procedure explains how to add a print driver and configure it for print pooling. If you already have the driver installed and are simply adding other printers, skip to step 3.

1. Open the Printers folder and run the Add Printer wizard.

2. Add the first local printer, specifying one of the ports in the pool. Configure other settings in the wizard as desired such as name, etc.

3. After the printer has been added, right-click the printer in the Printers folder and choose Properties.

4. Click the Ports tab then select the option Enable Printer Pooling at the bottom of the page.

5. Select all ports to which this type of printer is connected.

6. Configure other properties for the printer driver as desired then click OK. Your pool is now set up and Windows 2000 will handle job allocation in the pool.

You'll find that the queue folder for the printer pool includes a Port column that indicates which port is being used to print a particular job. You can manage print jobs in a pool just as you would manage them for a single printer.

5.6   Restrict others' use of your printer at certain times

When you share your printer with other users you probably make it available most, if not all, of the time. However, you might need exclusive access to a printer at certain times of the day, such as when you print a group of daily reports. Or you might have a large print job come up unexpectedly and need to prevent others from printing to the printer while you're printing your job. A third possibility is that you don't want *anyone* to use the printer during a given period, including yourself. For example, you might want to restrict printing to business hours only.

You have two options for restricting access: configure the printer to allow access only during specific times, or completely remove the printer from sharing. Use the former when you want to prevent anyone from using the printer during certain hours and the latter when you want to have exclusive use of the printer.

Restrict printer access times

You can make a printer available all the time or only during certain hours. When a printer is available only during a certain period of time, print jobs are still accepted by the printer's queue but are not sent to the printer. The jobs remain in the queue until the printer becomes available again. You configure availability through the Advanced page of the printer's properties:

1. Open the Printers folder, right-click the printer, choose Properties, and click the Advanced tab.

2. Select the Available From option and use the two spin controls to select the start and stop time during which the printer will be available.

3. Click OK to close the printer's property sheet.

Remove a printer from sharing

When you want to have exclusive use of a printer and prevent other network users from printing to it, you need to remove the printer from sharing. When you no longer need exclusive access you can re-share the printer.

1. Open the Printers folder, right-click the printer, and choose Sharing.

2. On the Sharing page select the Not Shared option, then click OK.

3. When you want to re-share the printer, open the Sharing page again and select the Shared As option. Use the same share name as before to enable other users to access the printer without modifying their printer settings.

5.7   Printing is slow to start or complete

Windows 2000 provides *print spooling* to enable printing to occur in the background. An application prints a job, Windows 2000 intercepts it and sends it to the spool, and then Windows 2000 takes care of sending the job to the printer on behalf of the application. When you install and configure a printer, you can set it up to spool or to print directly to the printer, bypassing the spooler.

Using the spooler offers the advantage of giving you control of the application more quickly so you can continue working while Windows 2000 takes care of printing the document. If you find that your application waits until the print job is complete before giving you back control, it's a good sign that spooling is turned off for that printer.

If you have a long document that is being spooled but not printing right away, you probably have the printer configured to start printing after the last page is spooled. To make the document start printing right away, you can configure the spooler to start printing as soon as the first page is spooled, rather than the last.

Change spool properties

You configure the spool settings through a printer's property sheet. You can configure spool settings differently for each printer as needed.

1. Open the Printers folder, right-click the printer, and choose Properties.

2. On the Advanced page, select the option "Spool print documents so program finishes printing faster."

3. To have a document begin printing as soon as it starts spooling, select the option "Start printing immediately." To have a document start printing only after all pages have spooled, select the option "Start printing after last page is spooled."

4. Click OK to close the property sheet.

Printing

5.8   Keep documents in the queue for resubmission

By default Windows 2000 removes jobs from a printer's queue after the job finishes printing. In most cases you probably won't need to retain the documents in the queue, but you can configure the queue to retain the documents, if desired. This enables you to resubmit the print job if you find a problem with the completed job, such as the printer running out of toner in the middle of a long document.

Keeping printed documents in the queue

Retaining printed documents in the queue involves a quick change to a setting in the printer's properties.

1. Open the Printers folder, right-click the printer, and choose Properties to open its property sheet.

2. Click the Advanced tab.

3. Select the option "Keep printed documents" and click OK.

4. When you need to restart a document that has already printed, open the Printers folder and double-click on the printer to open the queue. Select the document and choose Document → Restart.

5.9   Separate your print job from someone else's

When you're the only person using your printer, you don't have to worry about other users' print jobs getting mixed in with your own. You can print like crazy and be fairly sure that the stack of paper in the printer's output tray is all yours.

When you share the printer with others, whether from a single computer or across the network, it's likely that print jobs from other users will be mixed in with your own. Separating the finished jobs could be a headache unless you use *separator pages*.

Use separator pages

A separator page is a simple page of data that Windows 2000 prints at the beginning of each print job to show the document owner and other pertinent information. Rather than search through a large stack of paper for the first page of each print job, you can instead search for separator pages, which are much easier to spot.

Windows 2000 includes four separator pages you can use as-is or modify. They include the following files, all located in the *systemroot\System32* folder:

pcl.sep
> Switches the printer to PCL mode and prints the separator page.

pscript.sep
> Switches the printer to PostScript mode but does not print a separator page.

sysprint.sep
> Switches the printer to PostScript mode and prints a separator page.

sysprtj.sep
> This separator is similar to *sysprint.sep* but uses Java.

Here's how to select a separator page for a printer:

1. Open the Printers folder, right-click the printer, and choose Properties.

2. On the Advanced tab, click Separator Page.

3. Type the script name or browse to the script, and then click Open.

4. Click OK to close the Separator Page dialog, then OK again to close the printer's property sheet.

5.10 Allow only certain people to use your printer

When you're sharing your printer with other users on the network, you might want to restrict access to specific individuals, or deny access to a group of individuals. In either case, only those users who have the necessary permissions can print to the printer. In addition, you can specify the actions that individuals or groups can take with a printer, which include the following:

Print
> The specified user or group can send documents to the printer's queue. Print permission is assigned by default to the Everyone group.

Manage Printers
> The specified user or group has full control over the printer and can pause and restart the printer, change spool settings, share the printer, change printer permissions, and change printer properties. Manage Printers is by default assigned to the Administrators and Power Users groups.

Manage Documents
> The specified user or group can pause, resume, restart, and cancel documents submitted by other users. This permission does not implicitly

give the user or group the right to print to the printer or manage the printer. Use the Print and Manage Printers permissions for that purpose.

Configure security options

You configure security for a printer through the Security page of the printer's property sheet. Here's how:

1. Open the Printers folder, right-click the printer, and choose Properties.

2. Click the Security tab.

3. Select a user or group from the Name list and select Allow or Deny for each of the three permissions as desired. Leave a permission deselected if you don't want to allow the permission but don't want to explicitly deny it, either. Denying Print permission for a specific user account would override allowing Print permission in one of the user's groups.

4. If the user or group for which you want to apply printer permissions doesn't appear in the list, click Add, select the user or group, click Add, and then click OK. Set the permissions as desired, then click OK on the printer's property sheet to close it and apply the change.

CHAPTER 6

The Command Console

New users typically don't realize that the personal computer operating system started as a user-hostile command console environment named DOS. While inexperienced users generally prefer the graphical user interface, many diehard users like the flexibility offered by a command console. This chapter provides answers to a range of questions about the Windows 2000 command console.

For example, this chapter covers basic command console issues such as how to get help for a particular command, change background and foreground colors, configure screen size, and use the command-line history.

This chapter also covers more complex command console topics. In some situations, for example, you might want a particular driver loaded for every command console you open. Or perhaps you only want that driver loaded for a specific console session. Both scenarios are explained in this chapter. Other advanced topics include using *runas* to change the user context of the command console, opening a console rooted in a specific folder, controlling console operation when started from a shortcut, and using autocomplete to automatically complete folder and filenames to save typing.

6.1   Get help for a command

Many applications support at least some command-line switches or parameters that determine how the application starts or functions. This is true for Windows applications as well as console commands. For example, Microsoft Word supports several switches, one of which is /m, which prevents Word from executing autoexec macros at startup. An example of a console command that supports several switches is *xcopy*.

Knowing the syntax and available switches and parameters for a command is essential to using it effectively. Unlike Windows applications that typically offer extensive online help through the Windows Help application, console commands typically embed information about the command and its options within the command executable. You can view syntax and parameter or switch information about nearly any console command.

Use the /? Switch

Almost all the console commands included with Windows 2000 support the /? switch to list the command's syntax, parameters, and optional switches. Third-party developers also typically add support for a /? switch to their command-line utilities as well. To view the syntax and options for a command, just type the command followed by the /? switch, as in the following example:

```
xcopy /?
```

Windows 2000 responds with a listing showing additional information about the command and how to use it.

Use help at the console prompt

Another way to get help on console commands is through the *help* command. When used by itself, *help* displays a list of available commands, including internal commands that are incorporated in the command interpreter rather than existing as separate executable files. You can type **help** *command*, where *command* is replaced by the command name, to get more information about individual commands.

Page help information with more

Some applications support only a handful of options while others support several. In some cases the help information doesn't fit on one screen. Since by default there isn't any way to scroll the screen, it's sometimes difficult or impossible to see the first page of a command's help information. In those situations you can use the *more* command to view the information one page at a time.

To use *more*, type the command that displays the required help information and *pipe* it to the *more* command with the | symbol. Piping redirects the output of the command to *more*, which processes it so you can see it a page at a time. Following are two examples:

```
help | more
xcopy /? | more
```

See Section 6.5, "Use more than 25 lines of text in a window," to learn how to show more than 25 lines at a time in a command console.

Redirecting help information to a text file for printing or viewing

While the *more* command is certainly useful, you might want to print a hard copy of a command's options or view it in Notepad or Wordpad. You can redirect the help output of the command to a text file using either the > or >> symbols. The > symbol redirects to a file, overwriting the file if it already exists. The >> symbol appends the output to the file. Following are two examples:

```
xcopy /? > xcopyhelp.txt
xcopy /? >> commands.txt
```

Getting Windows 2000 help on console commands

Windows 2000's general help file includes information on console commands if you prefer to get your help within the Windows 2000 GUI. To view the information, click Start → Help → Contents → Reference, and explore the MS-DOS Commands listing in the help file. All of the commands are listed grouped alphabetically. Click on the command for which you want more information.

6.2   Execute a particular program with all command consoles

In some cases you might want to have Windows 2000 automatically execute a particular application for each command console you open. For example, you might need to load a special-purpose driver for your consoles. Or perhaps you want to automatically issue a command that changes directories, echoes a message to the screen, writes a string to a log file, etc. You can use a setting in the registry to specify a program or command that Windows 2000 automatically executes for all command consoles.

Configure the console AutoRun setting

The registry key HKEY_LOCAL_MACHINE\SOFTWARE\Microsoft\Command Processor contains a handful of commands that globally affect command consoles. You can use the AutoRun setting to specify an internal command or path to an external command that Windows 2000 automatically executes when each console starts.

1. Click Start → Run, and enter **regedit** in the Run dialog box.

2. In the Registry Editor open the HKEY_LOCAL_MACHINE\SOFTWARE\Microsoft\Command Processor key.

3. Double-click the AutoRun value and set its value to the internal command or path to the executable file you want to execute. Include any required command parameters or switches.

6.3 Load a special driver or program for a specific console only

The previous section explained how to configure all command consoles to execute a command or program at startup. What if you want to execute a driver or program only for a specific console command or application? The easiest method is to create a shortcut to *cmd.exe* with the appropriate switch and command string needed to execute the program.

Create a shortcut to cmd.exe with switches

cmd.exe is the command interpreter responsible for what you see when you open a command console, just like *command.com* on DOS and Windows systems. *cmd* supports several parameters and switches that control the way it functions and enable you to start a specific application. Two of *cmd*'s switches that let you start an application are:

/c *string*
> Execute the command specified by *string* and terminate the console.

/k *string*
> Execute the command specified by *string* and remain.

Both switches give you a means of executing either an internal or external command. Follow these steps to create a shortcut to *cmd* that executes a program and remains (use /c if you want the console to terminate after executing the application):

1. Right-click the desktop or folder location where you want the shortcut created and choose New → Shortcut.

2. Type **cmd** /k *string*, where *string* is the command to execute. Include in the string any optional parameters or switches for the application.

3. Specify a name for the shortcut and click Finish.

4. Double-click the shortcut to test it.

6.4 Recall, modify, and re-execute a command previously used

Like Windows NT, Windows 2000 maintains a command buffer that keeps track of the commands you execute in a command console. Rather than retype a long command, you can select the command from the history to save typing time and avoid mistakes. Press the up and down arrows on the keyboard to move through the command history. Use the left and right arrows, Home, and End keys to move the cursor within a command. Use the Insert key when you need to insert text in a command.

Setting history options

Windows 2000 provides three options you can use to configure the command history for the console. You set these options through the property sheet for the console.

1. Click Start → Programs → Accessories, right-click Command Prompt, and choose Properties.

2. Click the Options tab.

3. Configure options in the Command History group using the following list as a guide:

    Buffer Size
    Specifies the number of commands maintained in the history list.

    Number of Buffers
    Specifies the number of processes that can have individual history buffers.

    Discard Old Duplicates
    Select this option to discard duplicate commands from the history, maintaining only one copy of each unique command string.

6.5 Use more than 25 lines of text in a window

By default Windows 2000 sets up the command console with an 80-column by 25-line display. For some tasks a 25-line display is fine, but when you're working with a long directory listing or want to see all the options for a command as the result of a /? switch, 25 lines just isn't enough. Or, perhaps you're working with an application that outputs more than 80 columns. Fortunately, you can change the screen size to provide more lines or columns, plus configure a screen buffer to give you a scrollable window, providing a history of screen output.

Command Console

Change buffer and screen size

You change screen buffer and size settings through the Layout page of the console's property sheet:

1. Click Start → Programs → Accessories, right-click Command Prompt, and choose Properties.

2. Click the Layout tab.

3. Configure settings according to the following list:

    Screen buffer size
    Use these two controls to specify the size of the buffer Windows 2000 uses to store the console's output. Increase the Height value to maintain a longer history of console output. Increase the Width value to accomodate a wider display.

    Window size
    Use these two controls to specify the number of columns and lines for the console window. For example, increase the Height value to increase the number of lines you can view at one time in the window. Increase the Width value to obtain a wider display.

    Window position
    Use these two options to specify the X and Y coordinates for the upper-left corner of the console window, controlling where it opens by default.

    Let system position window
    Select this option to let Windows 2000 automatically position the console window when it opens.

6.6 Quickly open a command prompt in a specific folder

A command console opens by default in the root folder of the boot drive. While you can use the *cd* command to change to the folder you want, it's nice to be able to go straight to the required folder without having to traverse several folders. You have two options that will make it possible to open a command console in a local folder. These options require add-on utilities from Microsoft. You can actually add this functionality by directly editing the registry, but it's much easier to use one of the methods that follows.

 Use the AutoRun setting described in Section 6.2, "Execute a particular program with all command consoles," to issue a *cd* command if you want to start all consoles in the same folder.

Use the Resource Kit CMD Prompt Here

The Windows 2000 Resource Kit includes a tool called CMD Prompt Here that adds a command to the context menu for folders that lets you quickly open a command console with the selected folder active. You right-click the folder, choose CMD Prompt Here, and Windows 2000 opens a command console in the selected folder.

Follow these steps to install CMD Prompt Here from the Resource Kit:

1. Open the folder where the Resource Kit is installed.

2. Right-click the file *cmdhere.inf* and choose Install.

3. After installation, right-click a folder and choose CMD Prompt Here to test the installation.

Use PowerToys

The Microsoft Windows 95 development team put together a collection of add-ons for Windows 95 called PowerToys that expanded functionality and made certain tasks easier. Some of the tools are compatible with Windows NT and Windows 2000. One of these is the Command Prompt Here tool, which lets you open a command console on the selected folder just like the Resource Kit utility CMD Prompt Here. You can use this tool if you don't have access to the Windows 2000 Resource Kit.

 The other PowerToys you should have no problems with under Windows 2000 are Find X, Send To X, and Shortcut Target Menu.

To obtain and use the Command Prompt Here tool, follow these steps:

1. Connect to Microsoft's web site at *http://www.microsoft.com/Windows95/ downloads/contents/WUToys/W95PwrToysSet/Default.asp* and download the PowerToys file.

2. Create a new folder to contain the PowerToys and move the downloaded file to the new folder.

3. Double-click the downloaded file to extract its contents to the folder.

4. Locate the file *doshere.inf*, right-click the file, and choose Install.

5. After installation, check operation of the tool. Right-click any folder and choose Command Prompt Here. Windows 2000 should open a command console in the selected folder.

6.7   Run tasks as Administrator when logged on as a user

It's a good idea to use a user account without administrator privileges as your primary account, particularly if your system is connected directly to the Internet or if you spend a lot of time online. Trojan horse applications and viruses (not to mention hackers) can do a lot more damage on a system that is logged on as Administrator than one logged on as a user. Plus, running as a user prevents you from accidentally making changes you might not intentionally want to perform.

In some cases, though, you might need to run an application or open a command console with administrator privileges. You can use the *runas.exe* utility to do just that.

 You can also hold down the Shift key, right-click a program or shortcut, and choose Run As from the context menu to start a program in a different user context. Windows 2000 prompts you for the user credentials.

Use runas

The *runas* command included with Windows 2000 enables a process to run in a specified user context. For example, you can use *runas* to start a command console or other application (including Windows applications) within the security context of the Administrator account. This allows the application (or you, in the case of a command console) administrative access to the system.

Use the following steps to create a shortcut that opens a command console within the security context of the Administrator account:

1. Right-click where you want the shortcut created and choose New → Shortcut.

2. For the command line, type `runas.exe /user:administrator cmd.exe` and click Next.

3. Give the shortcut an appropriate name such as "Admin Console" and click Finish.

4. Double-click the shortcut and when prompted enter the password for the Administrator account.

 You can use the shortcut creation method to start an application or console within the context of any user account. Just specify the desired account name in place of Administrator.

To start a Windows application within a specific security context, replace *cmd.exe* in the command with the executable for the Windows application. You can also click Start → Run, and type **runas** to execute an application in a given security context without creating a shortcut.

6.8   Change the colors used by command consoles

The Windows 2000 command console defaults to white text on a black background. However, you might prefer a different color scheme. You have two ways to change the colors: through the properties for the command console or using the *color* command. The former changes the color scheme for all consoles, and the latter changes it only for the current console.

Changing color for all consoles

You can change the color scheme for all command consoles by changing the properties for the Command Prompt shortcut:

1. Click Start → Programs → Accessories, right-click Command Prompt, and choose Properties.

2. Click the Colors tab.

3. Use the controls on the Colors page to configure the default colors for all consoles.

Changing color for the current console

In addition to changing color for command consoles globally, you also can specify colors for the current console only. You do so using the *color* command from the command prompt:

1. Open a command console.

2. Type **color** *bf* and press Enter, where *b* is the background color and *f* is the foreground color. Use the values listed in Table 6-1 for *b* and *f*.

Table 6-1. Background and foreground color values

b & f color values	b & f color values
0 = Black	1 = Blue
2 = Green	3 = Aqua
4 = Red	5 = Purple
6 = Yellow	7 = White
8 = Gray	9 = Light Blue

Command Console

Table 6-1. *Background and foreground color values (continued)*

b & f color values	b & f color values
A = Light Green	B = Light Aqua
C = Light Red	D = Light Purple
E = Light Yellow	F = Bright White

Enter **color** without any parameters to switch back to the default color settings.

 You can use the command cmd /t:*fg*, where *f* and *g* are foreground and background colors, in a shortcut or the Run dialog box to start a console with the specified color settings. Use the values in Table 6-1 for *f* and *g*.

You can also change color for the current console alone through the console's properties. Click the console's control menu and choose Properties. Click the Colors tab and set colors as desired. Click OK, and when prompted, select the option "Apply properties to current window only."

6.9   Execute a command from a shortcut but have the window remain open

When you execute a shortcut associated with a console command (*xcopy*, *dir*, etc.) the command executes and the console windows closes on completion. This means you can't see the results of the command. In many cases you probably will want to keep the window open, if for no other reason than to verify that the command performed its intended function without errors.

Run the application using a shortcut to cmd /k

Rather than execute the command from a shortcut to its own executable, create a shortcut to *cmd.exe* with the /k switch that will keep the window open when the command completes execution.

1. Right-click where you want the shortcut created and choose New → Shortcut.

2. Type **cmd.exe /k** *string*, where *string* is the command you want to execute, then click Next.

3. Give the shortcut an appropriate name and click Finish.

6.10   Use an autocomplete function for folder and filenames in command consoles

If you've used Internet Explorer 5 much, you've probably run across the AutoComplete feature, which completes text entry for you automatically. It's a handy feature that can save a lot of typing, particularly for commonly used text.

You can enable a form of AutoComplete in command consoles, enabling you to automatically complete folder and filenames without typing them. This feature is called *file and directory name completion*. By default this feature is turned off, but it's a quick fix to turn it on.

Turn on file and directory name completion

You use the following commands to turn on and off file and directory name completion, respectively:

```
cmd /f:on
cmd /f:off
```

You can execute *cmd* with the appropriate switch using one of the following methods:

From a shortcut

Create a shortcut with the command **cmd /f:on** as the command string, and include any other parameters as needed (such as a parameter to run another application).

In an open command console

Within an open command console, enter **cmd /f:on** to start a new console with completion turned on.

With completion turned on, press Ctrl-D to complete folder names and Ctrl-F to complete filenames. Windows 2000 cycles through the folder names or filenames as you continue pressing Ctrl-D or Ctrl-F. You can specify a different character for either by modifying the following registry keys:

*   HKEY_LOCAL_MACHINE\Software\Microsoft\Command Processor\ CompletionChar

*   HKEY_LOCAL_MACHINE\Software\Microsoft\Command Processor\ PathCompletionChar

Specify the hex value for the character as the value of the setting. For example, use 0x4 for Ctrl-D and 0x6 for Ctrl-F.

CHAPTER 7

Network Configuration

While the average user is comfortable with the applications he or she uses on a regular basis, network configuration is another story. Unless you've had a reason to go digging through your computer's network settings, you might have little experience or understanding of how to configure a network interface and what to do when problems occur.

This chapter provides answers to specific questions about network configuration and troubleshooting. You'll learn how to configure a protocol, enable and disable network interfaces, unbind a protocol from a client or service, and change the order in which Windows 2000 uses various network providers.

You'll also discover how to move between workgroups and domains, change computer names, install multiple network adapters, and disable protocols without removing them. Security is covered in detail as well, with solutions that will help you filter traffic coming to and from your computer, enforce the use of strong passwords, force users to change their passwords regularly, hide your logon name, and display special logon messages.

7.1   Change settings for a network adapter

In Windows 9x and Windows NT, network configuration was easy to find. You right-clicked Network Neighborhood, chose Properties, and there it was. In Windows 2000 it's actually a little easier, even though it might seem like there is an extra step involved. The benefit in Windows 2000 is that network properties for each interface are separate, an advantage on multihomed systems.

Find your network settings

The Network and Dial-Up Connections folder contains the settings for each of your computer's network interfaces. In a multihomed system with multiple network adapters, for example, you'll find an icon for each adapter. Also appearing in the folder are dial-up connections (modem, VPN, etc.) and an icon for incoming connections if your computer is configured as a dial-up server.

Click Start → Settings → Network and Dial-Up Connections to open the folder, or right-click My Network Places and choose Properties. Following are common tasks you might perform in the Network and Dial-Up Connections folder:

- Right-click an interface and choose Properties to configure its settings (protocols, IP address, client, etc.).

- Run the Make New Connection wizard to create a new dial-up or VPN connection.

- Double-click an interface icon to view the interface's status (connection duration, speed, packets sent/received) or disable the interface.

- Right-click an interface and choose Rename to change the name by which it appears in the folder.

Configure network adapter settings

Most new network adapters support plug-and-play, and Windows 2000 can automatically configure these adapters. For those that don't support plug-and-play, or in cases where another device might conflict with the automatically assigned resources, you might need to reconfigure network adapter settings. You do so through the properties for the network interface:

1. Open the Network and Dial-Up Connections folder, right-click the interface you want to change, and choose Properties.

2. Click Configure.

3. Use the General page to enable or disable the adapter, the Advanced page to specify individual settings that vary by adapter, the Driver page to reinstall or update drivers for the adapter, and the Resources page to configure IRQ, I/O base address, and memory range.

Configure, add, or remove a protocol

When you open the properties for a network interface, the protocols associated with that interface appear in the General page for the connection. To configure a protocol, select the protocol and click Properties. The available properties vary according to the selected protocol. The Properties button is dimmed if the protocol has no configurable properties.

Configuring TCP/IP is covered in Chapter 9, *Using and Troubleshooting TCP/IP*.

You can easily add a new protocol by clicking the Install button. Click Protocol, then Add, and follow the prompts provided by the wizard to select and install the selected protocol. To remove a protocol, select the protocol from the Components list and click Uninstall.

7.2   Unbind a protocol from a client or service

When you add a protocol to a network interface, Windows 2000 automatically *binds* the protocol to all the installed clients and services. Likewise, when you add a client or service, Windows 2000 binds all existing protocols to it. Binding associates the protocol with the client or service, enabling that client or service to use the bound protocol. You can bind more than one protocol to any particular client or service.

In some situations you won't want all protocols bound to a particular client or service. For example, you probably don't want the File and Printer Sharing service bound to the TCP/IP protocol if your computer is hardwired to the Internet or you spend a lot of time online through a dial-up connection. Having the TCP/IP protocol bound to File and Printer Sharing not only makes your computer's shares visible to users on the Internet but also makes them susceptible to hacking and virus or worm attacks. So you should *unbind* that protocol from the File and Printer Sharing service.

Unbind a protocol from a client or service

You change protocol bindings through the Advanced properties for the network interface. It's a simple matter of deselecting a checkbox:

1. Open the Network and Dial-Up Connections folder and click Advanced → Advanced Settings to display the Adapters and Bindings page (see Figure 7-1).

2. From the Connections list on the Adapters and Bindings page, select the interface whose bindings you want to change.

3. In the Bindings list, deselect the protocol you want to unbind.

4. Click OK to apply the change.

When TCP/IP needs to be bound to File and Printer Sharing

If TCP/IP is your only network protocol, you can't unbind it from the File and Printer Sharing service and still enable other users on the LAN to access your shared resources. With no protocol bound to the service, the service is essentially "mute," with no language to communicate with other computers. If you don't need to share your local resources with other users, you can ignore the problem or remove the File and Printer Sharing service altogether.

However, if TCP/IP is your only protocol and you do need to share your resources, you should consider two options: add a protocol for LAN sharing or implement a firewall to restrict incoming connections (or a combination of the two for best security). Since NetBEUI is not a routable protocol, remote users on the Internet can't use it to gain access to your system. So consider adding NetBEUI, binding it to your File and Printer Sharing service on all computers on the LAN, and unbinding TCP/IP. This will enable users to access shared resources on the LAN and continue to use the Internet, but will prevent direct access to network shares.

For a detailed discussion of firewalls and Internet security, see *Basic Computer Security* and *Building Internet Firewalls*, both from O'Reilly & Associates.

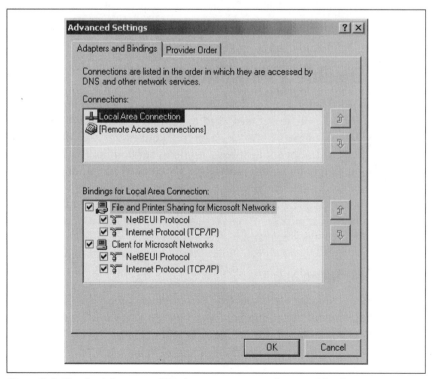

Figure 7-1. Use the Adapters and Bindings page to control protocol bindings

7.3 Change the order in which network clients or services are used

When a system has more than one client or service installed, Windows 2000 uses them in a specific order. For example, you might have both the Client for Microsoft Networks and the Client for NetWare Networks installed to support both Windows-based and NetWare-based servers. If most of your servers use a specific client, you can improve network browsing by setting that client first in the order.

Change provider order

As with most other network changes, you modify provider order through the Network and Dial-Up Connections folder. Provider order is defined in the Advanced Settings property sheet:

1. Open the Network and Dial-Up Connections folder.

2. Click Advanced → Advanced Settings and click the Provider Order tab.

3. Click a provider and use the up and down arrow buttons on the property page to change the provider's position. Click OK to close the property sheet.

7.4 Disable a network interface

In a system with multiple network interfaces (which usually means more than one adapter), you sometimes need to disable a network interface. For example, you might have a network adapter in your notebook's docking station and a PC Card network adapter for when your computer isn't docked. While you can create hardware profiles for the docked and undocked situations and enable/disable adapters accordingly, you might prefer to manually disable an interface. Or perhaps your situation warrants a manual method rather than hardware profile. Whatever the case, disabling a network interface is nearly a one-click operation.

Disable an interface

You disable an interface through the Network and Dial-Up Connections folder, using one of two methods. Both are described in the following procedure:

1. Open the Network and Dial-Up Connections folder.

2. Double-click the interface you want to disable and click Disable. Or right-click the interface's icon and choose Disable.

3. To re-enable the interface, simply double-click its icon or right-click the icon and choose Enable.

 You can configure Windows 2000 to display a status icon on the tray for a network interface, giving you a visual indicator of the interface's status. To display the tray icon, open the properties for the interface and select the option "Show icon in taskbar when connected."

7.5   Change workgroup or domain

Workgroups and domains provide a means of logically grouping computers and other network resources such as printers. Domains add the benefit of centralized authentication and security management. Although you specify the workgroup or domain for your computer during Setup, you can change the workgroup or domain at any time. You can join any existing domain (subject to restrictions) or workgroup or create a new workgroup by becoming its first member.

Change workgroups

Changing workgroups is easy. You simply specify the workgroup name, and if it exists, your computer is added to that workgroup. If the workgroup doesn't exist, Windows 2000 creates a new workgroup and your computer becomes its first member. You can access your workgroup/domain identification through either My Computer or the Network and Dial-Up Connections folder:

1. Right-click My Computer, choose Properties, and click the Network Identification tab. Or, in the Network and Dial-Up Connections folder, choose Advanced → Network Identification.

2. Click Properties to open the Identification Changes dialog box.

3. Highlight the existing workgroup name in the Workgroup text box, type the new workgroup name, and click OK.

4. Click OK to close the system properties, and then restart the computer for the change to take effect.

Change domains

You can change domain membership for your computer if it has an existing account in the domain or if you have a username and password in that domain that has the right to create computer accounts in the domain. You make the changes through the Network Identification page of the System Properties sheet:

1. Right-click My Computer, choose Properties, and click the Network Identification tab. Or, in the Network and Dial-Up Connections folder, choose Advanced → Network Identification.

2. Click Properties to open the Identification Changes dialog box.

3. In the Domain text box, type the name of the domain you want to join and click OK.

4. Windows 2000 prompts you for an account with permission to join the domain. Enter the appropriate username and password and click OK.

5. If all goes well, Windows 2000 welcomes you to the new domain. Restart the computer for the domain change to take effect.

7.6   Modify your computer's name

Setup automatically assigns a computer name during Windows 2000 installation. This is the name by which the computer is recognized on the network. When other users browse the network for shared folders, for example, they see the computer name in the browse list.

Setup assigns a fairly cryptic name if you let it. In most cases, you'll want to assign a different name that is easier to remember for those users who want to connect to your computer's resources through a UNC pathname.

Change computer names

You change computer names through the Network Identification page of the System Properties sheet. You must be logged on as Administrator to change the name:

1. Right-click My Computer, choose Properties, and click the Network Identification tab.

2. Click Properties to display the Identification Changes dialog box.

3. Type the new name in the Computer name text box and click OK.

4. Click OK to close the System Properties sheet.

Following are some additional notes on renaming a computer:

• If you are currently logged on to a secure Windows 2000 domain, the computer account is automatically updated in the domain to reflect the name change.

- If TCP/IP is not installed, the name is limited to 15 characters.

- If TCP/IP is installed, the name can be up to 63 characters long, but names longer than 15 characters could prevent other users from seeing your computer on the network. Names can be mixed case when TCP/IP is installed.

- The domain administrator must enable registration of DNS names that are 16 bytes or longer so that names longer than 15 characters will be recognized by the Active Directory.

- For computers that are members of a workgroup, where TCP/IP is not installed, or where no networking is installed, the name is limited to 15 characters and must be all uppercase.

7.7   Use two network adapters with different protocols on each one

When you install a second network adapter, it automatically takes on the protocols that are already installed for the existing adapter. In some cases you'll want the same protocols on each one, but in other cases you'll want to separate the protocols onto the different adapters. For example, you might have one adapter for a direct Internet connection (requiring TCP/IP) and another adapter for local network traffic (typical on a multihomed server).

If the LAN side uses NetBEUI, you might need to remove TCP/IP from the LAN side. What's more, you can only have NetBEUI on one adapter, so you need to remove it from the Internet side. The following section explains how to disable a protocol without removing it from your system.

7.8   Disable a protocol without removing it

When you're troubleshooting or testing a system it's sometimes necessary to turn off a protocol for one or more adapters. Or perhaps you need to turn off a protocol for security or performance reasons or because of a conflict. In either case, you probably want to retain the protocol so you don't have to reinstall it later. Or you might need to retain the protocol for use on a second interface.

You have two options for preventing an interface from using an installed protocol: uninstall the protocol or disable it for either a selected adapter or all adapters. Uninstalling a protocol removes it from the system completely. Disabling it simply turns it off for the selected adapter(s).

Disable a protocol

Disabling a protocol is easy: you simply deselect it in the interface's list of installed components. Here's how:

1. Open the Network and Dial-Up Connections folder, right-click the interface, and choose Properties.

2. In the Components list, deselect the protocol you want to disable and click OK (see Figure 7-2). To re-enable the protocol later, open the properties again and simply select the protocol in the Components list.

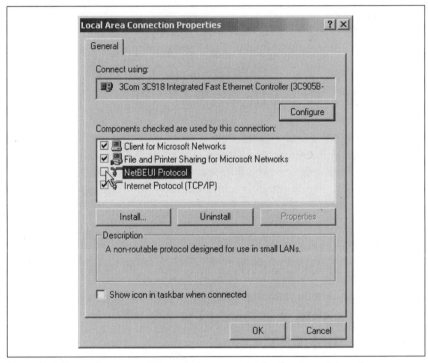

Figure 7-2. Turn off a protocol through the properties for the network interface

7.9 Restrict traffic through your PC without a firewall

A firewall is one of the best lines of defense against unauthorized or unwanted network traffic coming from the Internet or your local intranet. But firewalls can be expensive and difficult to set up. While the security options for TCP/IP included with Windows 2000 can't take the place of a dedicated firewall, they can go a long way toward protecting a system from all but the most concerted attacks.

Use simple IP filters

Windows 2000 lets you configure IP filters that determine the type of traffic that reaches your computer. You can configure filters to restrict traffic for specific TCP ports, UDP ports, or IP protocols. IP filters apply to all adapters in the computer, filtering traffic on a global basis. You configure filters individually on an inclusive basis. In other words, you either permit all traffic of the specified type or allow only those ports you've explicitly specified.

Setting filters effectively requires that you know which ports you want to allow in to the computer. If you enable filtering but forget to include a required port, network functions supported by that port won't work until you add the port to the filter list. To view a complete port list, connect to Microsoft's web site at *http://windows.microsoft.com/windows2000/reskit/ webresources*.

To configure IP filters, follow these steps:

1. Open the Network and Dial-Up Connections folder, right-click the interface in question, and choose Properties.

2. Double-click the TCP/IP protocol in the Components list, or select the protocol and click Properties.

3. Click Advanced, and then click the Options tab.

4. Select TCP/IP Filtering in the Optional Settings list and click Properties.

5. Select the option Enable TCP/IP Filtering (see Figure 7-3).

6. For each filter type (TCP, UDP, IP Protocols) you want to apply, select Permit Only, then click Add to add the port or protocol number for traffic to be allowed into your computer.

7. Click OK, then close the property sheet for the interface.

8. Check operation of the computer to make sure all functions work. If you experience a problem with any function, temporarily turn off filtering to determine if filtering is the source of the problem. To turn off filtering, deselect the Enable TCP/IP Filtering option on the TCP/IP Filtering dialog box.

Use IPSec policies

Your second option for applying IP security is IPSec, which stands for IP Security. IPSec provides several features for securing traffic coming to and from your computer. IPSec is a very complex topic that requires the better part of a book by itself to explain in detail. This section gives you a quick primer on where to configure IPSec policies.

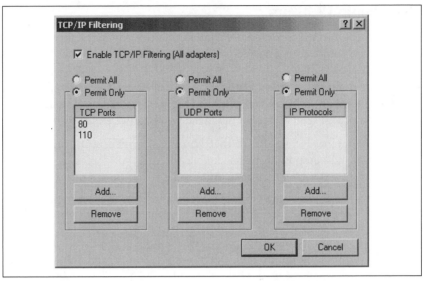

Figure 7-3. IP filters let you control the traffic that comes to and from your computer on a port-by-port basis

 IPSec policies can be defined at the domain security policy level or at the local computer level. This example assumes you're configuring IPSec policies at the local level.

1. Open the Local Security Policy console from the Administrative Tools folder in the Control Panel.

2. Open the IP Security Policies branch.

3. View the properties for the existing policies to determine if they fit your needs. If not, right-click in the right pane and choose Create IP Security Policy. Follow the wizard's prompts to create a new policy, including choosing between Kerberos (default Windows 2000 authentication) and a certificate for authentication.

4. Double-click the policy you want to use to open its property sheet.

5. On the Rules page, click Add to add any other required security rules.

6. Make any other changes to the policy as needed and close the Local Security Policy console.

7. In the Network and Dial-Up Connections folder, open the properties for the interface where you want to apply IPSec.

8. Double-click the TCP/IP protocol to open its properties, and then click Advanced.

9. Click the Options tab, select IP Security, and click Properties.

10. Select the option "Use this IP security policy," then select the desired policy from the associated drop-down list (see Figure 7-4).

11. Click OK, then close the interface's property sheet.

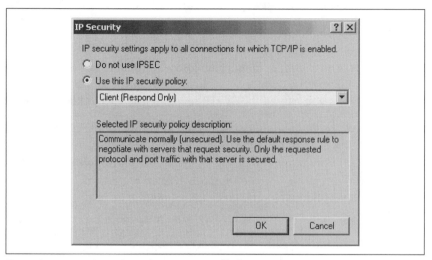

Figure 7-4. Use IPSec to provide secure IP traffic between systems

7.10 Assign IP addresses automatically without a DHCP server

Automatic IP address assignment takes the headache out of IP address management. When adding systems you don't have to worry about finding an unused address but can simply hook up the computer, boot it, and let it take its address lease automatically.

While automatic address assignment becomes more important as network size increases, it still can be an important tool even on small networks. It often isn't practical on a small network to install a DHCP server because of server hardware and software costs. Fortunately, with Windows 2000 you can take advantage of automatic address assignment without the presence of a DHCP server.

Use automatic address assignment

Windows 2000 supports Automatic Private IP Addressing, or APIPA. When a Windows 2000 computer that is configured for dynamic addressing boots and can't locate a DHCP server, Windows 2000 automatically assigns an IP address in the range 169.254.*n.n* with a subnet mask of 255.255.0.0. This means that all computers on the LAN can automatically assign themselves a nonconflicting IP address in the same range, providing connectivity between them.

Windows 98 clients also support automatic address assignment through APIPA.

Each computer polls the network every five minutes for the presence of a DHCP server, and if one is found, the computer obtains an address lease from the DHCP server in whatever address scope(s) the DHCP server handles. This means you can add a DHCP server at any time without making any changes to your network clients' configurations.

There is nothing special you need to do to configure a client to use APIPA other than configure it for dynamic address assignment:

1. Open the properties for the interface from the Network and Dial-Up Connections folder.

2. Double-click the TCP/IP protocol to open its property sheet.

3. On the General property page, select the option Obtain an IP address automatically.

4. Specify the IP address for the DNS server(s) you want the client to use.

5. Click OK and close the interface's property sheet.

7.11   A duplicate name exists on the network

This error is caused by two adapters on the same computer using the Net-BEUI protocol. NetBEUI can be used on only one adapter on a given network segment. Each computer using NetBEUI must use a unique NETBIOS name (taken from the computer name in the system properties). Because there is no means of assigning a unique name to each adapter, enabling Net-BEUI on more than one causes a naming conflict.

Disable NetBEUI on all but one interface

The solution to this error is to enable NetBEUI on only one network interface. You can simply disable NetBEUI on the additional interfaces.

You don't need to disable NetBEUI on dial-up adapters or VPN connections because the protocol is encapsulated and doesn't cause a naming conflict.

1. Open the Network and Dial-Up Connections folder, and then open the properties for the interface where you want to disable NetBEUI.

2. Deselect the NetBEUI protocol in the Components list and click OK.

3. Repeat the process for any other interfaces on which you need to disable NetBEUI.

7.12   Log on automatically at startup

For increased security, Windows 2000 presents a logon dialog box at startup and requires that you have a valid user account on the computer or domain in order to log on to the computer. While you can't get around the requirement for a valid user account, you can configure Windows 2000 to automatically log on at startup. If you always use the same logon account and are not concerned with your system logging on automatically at startup, automatic logon will save you the extra few steps of pressing Ctrl-Alt-Del and typing your username and password to log on.

Specify an automatic logon account

It's easy to configure the system for automatic logon through the Users and Passwords object in the Control Panel:

1. Open the Users and Passwords object in the Control Panel.

2. Deselect the option "Users must enter a username and password to use this computer," and click OK.

3. Windows 2000 prompts you to specify the username and password for the account that will be used to log on automatically at startup.

If you later want to reconfigure the system to require manual logon, just open the Users and Passwords object again and select the option "Users must enter a username and password to use this computer."

7.13   Shut down without having to log on

It's a hassle to have to log on when what you really want to do is shut down the computer, particularly if you're installing software or doing testing that requires frequent restarts. If you don't have access to the Shutdown button on the Log On to Windows dialog box that appears when you press Ctrl-Alt-Del, you can easily enable it. Then when you need to shutdown, you can just click Shutdown on the dialog box without logging on.

Add Shutdown to the logon dialog

You configure the system to allow shutdown without logon through the security policy for the computer. This policy can be configured in the domain security policy or at the local security policy level. If it's defined in both policies, the domain policy takes precedence.

Use the following steps to enable the Shutdown button on the Log On to Windows dialog box:

1. Open the Local Security Policy console from the Administrative Tools folder in the Control Panel.

2. Open the Local Policies\Security Options branch.

3. Double-click the policy "Allow system to be shut down without having to log on."

4. Set the policy to Enabled and click OK.

5. Close the Local Security Policy console. The next time you log on you should be able to click Options to expand the dialog box and then click Shutdown to shut down the computer.

7.14 Force users to change passwords

Each user account includes several options that define security parameters for the account. One of these determines whether Windows 2000 ages the users' passwords, eventually expiring the password and requiring the user to specify a new one. Using password expiration guards against a user keeping the same password for a long period of time, making it more susceptible to being stolen or discovered and thereby compromising the user's account.

Configuring accounts for password expiration requires two steps. You first configure the user accounts for password expiration and then define the expiration period through the password policy.

Configure user accounts

The first step in enforcing password expiration is to configure each user account's properties to enable expiration. You configure expiration for local accounts through the Local Users and Groups branch of the Computer Management console. You configure expiration for domain accounts through the Active Directory Users and Computers console. This section assumes you're configuring the properties for local accounts. The steps are similar for domain accounts:

1. Open the Computer Management console and then the Local Users and Groups branch, or open the Local Users and Groups console.

2. Open the Users branch and double-click the user whose settings you want to change.

3. Deselect the option "Password never expires" and click OK.

4. Configure other accounts for expiration as desired and close the management console.

Configure the password policy

The second step in configuring password expiration is to configure the password policy. You do so either through the local security policy or through the domain security policy. If both are defined, the domain security policy takes precedence. Here's how to configure password policy at the local level:

1. Open the Local Security Policy console from the Administrative Tools folder.

2. Open the Account Policies\Password Policy branch.

3. Set the following two options:

   Maximum password age
   Specify the maximum number of days a user can have the same password. When this period is reached, Windows 2000 expires the password and requires the user to specify a new password.

   Minimum password age
   Specify the minimum amount of time a user must keep a password after changing it. Leave this value at 0 to allow the user to change the password immediately.

 You can also enable the policy "Enforce password history" to prevent a user from reusing a password.

7.15   Enforce strong passwords

Windows 2000 by default doesn't require any specific password properties, which means a user can select a very simple password or even no password at all. In networks where security isn't a big concern, this lack of strong password enforcement doesn't pose a problem. Where security is a concern, however, enforcing strong passwords can help prevent brute force hack attacks on user accounts.

You can configure Windows 2000 to require a minimum password complexity. By default this means the password must not contain the username and must contain at least three of the following: English uppercase letters, English lowercase letters, Westernized Arabic numerals, and nonalphanumeric characters (!, @, #, and so on). With strong password enforcement turned on, Windows 2000 prevents users from specifying passwords that don't meet this criteria.

Configure a password policy

You configure Windows 2000 to enforce strong passwords through the security policy settings. You can define these settings through the local security policy or the domain security policy. If both are defined, the domain security policy takes precedence.

 Consider implementing password aging and history along with strong passwords for optimum security.

Use the following steps to enforce strong passwords through the local security policy:

1. Open the Local Security Policy console from the Administrative Tools folder.

2. Open the Account Policies\Password Policy branch.

3. Double-click the policy "Passwords must meet complexity requirements" and set it to Enabled.

4. Click OK and close the Local Security Policy console.

Use a custom password filter

The *password filter* in use determines the criteria for a strong password. The default password filter is defined by the file *scecli.dll* in *systemroot\System32*. You can define different or more stringent criteria for password complexity by providing a custom *scecli.dll* file, either by creating one yourself (which requires programming ability) or by acquiring one from a third-party vendor.

7.16 Don't have your username appear automatically in the logon dialog

By default Windows 2000 keeps track of the last account used to log on and automatically enters the username for that account in the logon dialog box at startup or when you log off. Knowing a valid username is half the challenge of breaking into a system so keeping your account name secret (at least as much as possible) can go a long way toward preventing brute force break-ins or other security compromises. Hiding the username from the logon dialog is one step in keeping your account secure.

Don't save last logon name

You configure Windows 2000 to not display the last username in the logon dialog box through the security policy, either at the local level or at the domain level. If both are defined, the domain security policy takes precedence.

The following steps assume you are configuring the setting through the local security policy:

1. Open the Local Security Policy console and open the Local Policies\ Security Options branch.

2. Double-click the setting "Do not display last username in logon screen."

3. Configure the setting as Enabled, click OK, and close the Local Security Policy console.

The next time Windows 2000 displays the logon dialog box, the username field will be blank.

7.17   Display a special logon message

In today's litigious business world, legal technicalities often overshadow good sense. For example, you have to give reasonable notice to potential thieves and hackers that your system is off limits—something that a reasonable person would assume from the start—or you might not succeed in prosecuting them. For this reason, you might want to display a custom message during logon that warns the person logging on that the system is restricted and that there are legal consequences for unauthorized access. Or perhaps you simply want to broadcast a message of the day or other information at logon. You can do so by defining a group policy setting. This message appears in a dialog box before the user is prompted for her username and password.

Create a custom logon message

You define a custom logon message through either the local security policy or the domain security policy. When both are defined the domain security policy takes precedence. Here's how to set up a custom logon message through the local security policy:

1. Open the Local Security Policy console from the Administrative Tools folder in the Control Panel.

2. Open the branch Local Policies\Security Options.

3. Set the following policy settings:

   Message text for users attempting to log on
   Specify the text that you want to appear in the body of the dialog box as the message to the user.

   Message title for users attempting to log on
   Specify the title text that you want to appear in the title bar of the dialog box.

4. Close the Local Security Policy console, then log off and log back in to view or check the message.

CHAPTER 8

Sharing and Accessing Network Resources

The primary purpose for a network is to enable users to share their resources and data, whether those resources are files, printers, email, or other data. Windows 2000 makes it easy to share resources and access shared resources across the network, giving you various levels of security to protect those resources as needed. For example, you can use two different levels of access control to restrict user access to your shared resources: share permissions and NTFS permissions. As you'll learn in this chapter, these two types of permissions help you fine-tune the access you want others to have to your shared folders and files.

You'll also learn in this chapter about *hidden shares*, which are accessible just like a regular share but don't show up when users browse the network for shared resources. Windows 2000 uses hidden shares for administrative purposes, and you'll learn how to take advantage of these shares as well as hide shared resources from browsing.

Security goes hand-in-hand with resource sharing, and this chapter provides solutions for sharing-related security issues. You'll discover how to determine which users are connected to your computer at any given time and what resources those users are accessing. You'll also learn how to control access and turn off file sharing altogether if needed. Another important security-related topic explained in this chapter is *user rights*, which define the types of tasks a user can perform.

General networking topics are covered as well, including how to change workgroup or domain, network your home computers, automatically connect resources as logon, and use a *roaming profile*, which enables you to have the same working environment regardless of your logon location.

8.1   Restrict access to a folder you're sharing

When you share a folder you actually have two lines of defense to protect the folder's contents. The first line of defense is the folder's *share permissions*. These are the permissions you access through the folder's Sharing property page when you create the share. The default share permissions include Full Control, Change, and Read. These are called *standard permissions* because they are a standard set of combined permissions. Although you can allow or deny any of these three standard permissions to any user or group, they don't offer a lot of flexibility of access control. Share permissions apply only to users who access the folder from the LAN—they have no effect on local users.

The key to enjoying tighter control over shared folders and files is using *NTFS permissions*. These object permissions that you can set on folders and files in NTFS volumes give you much finer control over who can access a resource and the level of access they have. Plus, NTFS permissions enable you to assign permissions to individual files, unlike share permissions that apply only to the shared folder (called the *share point*).

 NTFS permissions are available only on NTFS volumes. You can't set NTFS permissions on FAT or FAT32 volumes. Share permissions are your only line of defense on these types of volumes.

Use NTFS object permissions instead of share permissions

In a way, you can think of share permissions as the lock on an office door. If you don't lock the file cabinets inside the office, your files are at risk to anyone who can open the door. NTFS permissions are like the locks on those file cabinets, providing an extra layer of security. You can use share permissions to control who gets in the office and then use NTFS permissions to control what they can do once they're inside.

You set NTFS permissions on a folder or file through the object's property sheet:

1. After you share the folder and set the desired share permissions on the folder, right-click the folder (or a sub-folder) and choose Properties.

2. Click the Security tab. If there is no Security tab, you're working with a FAT/FAT32 volume.

3. Set permissions as you would when setting share permissions, but note that you have additional permissions you can use. Click Advanced to set

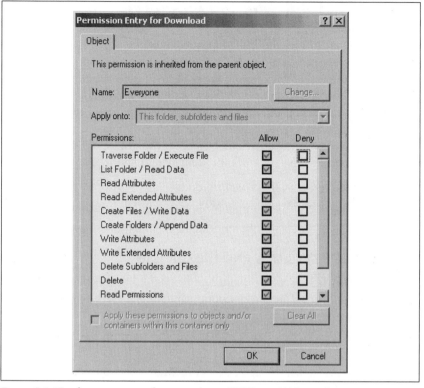

Figure 8-1. You have very granular control over NTFS permissions

permissions other than the standard NTFS permissions shown in the Permissions list (see Figure 8-1).

4. If you don't want NTFS permissions for the current object to be inherited from the parent (such as a parent folder), deselect the option "Allow inheritable permissions from parent to propagate to this object."

5. Close the property sheet and test the permissions.

NTFS permissions offer the additional advantage of protecting folders and files during local access. So if you share your computer with others, NTFS permissions give you the ability to secure your folders and files. FAT/FAT32 partitions can be accessed with full control by anyone with physical access to the computer.

Use the *convert* command from a console prompt to convert a FAT/FAT32 partition to NTFS. Open a console and type `convert d: /fs:ntfs`, where d: is the drive letter of the volume you want to convert. Bear in mind that if your system dual-boots to other operating systems, the other operating systems won't be able to access the NTFS volume.

8.2 Find out who is connected to your computer

Although it's more often necessary to know who is connected to a server, it can still be important to know who is accessing your computer even if you're using it as a workstation. Windows 2000 Professional supports up to ten concurrent connections, so you might have as many as ten other users accessing your computer at a given time. Perhaps you need to shut down your system but want to warn others first so they can close open files. Or maybe you just want to keep track for security reasons.

In Windows NT you use the Server object in the Control Panel to determine connections and files in use. In Windows 2000 you use the Computer Management console.

View current sessions and files in use

You can view which users are connected to your computer as well as which files they have open. You can disconnect individual users or disconnect all users, which is useful when you need to shut down your system or want to disconnect unauthorized users. Likewise, you can close individual files as well as all open files:

1. Right-click My Computer and choose Manage to open the Computer Management console.

2. Open the Shared Folders branch and then the Sessions node, which shows current connections.

3. Select the connection you want to terminate and choose Action → Close Session, or simply right-click the connection and choose Close Session from the context menu.

4. To close all connections, choose Action → Disconnect All Sessions or right-click in the right pane and choose Disconnect All Sessions from the context menu.

5. To manage open files, click the Open Files node in the left pane. As with connections, you can select a file to close or close them all.

8.3 Share a folder but hide it from network browsing

Windows 2000 provides great security options for protecting your local resources from unauthorized access by other users on the network, so you generally don't have to worry about someone getting access to folders or files they shouldn't have. But what if you make a mistake that compromises your security when you set up permissions for a share? Or perhaps you simply have some resources you don't want everyone to see, but need to give access to a select few. The solution is to hide the share.

Hide a shared resource

When you browse the network in My Network Places you see icons for each shared resource. What you don't see are *hidden shares*, which can be accessed just like any visible share, subject to its share permissions and underlying NTFS permissions, if any. A user who knows a hidden share is available can specify the path to the share in an Address bar or any other place where you can enter a UNC path (such as when mapping a drive letter to the shared folder).

You hide a share by adding a $ character at the end of the share name— that's all there is to it. The share works like any other resource except that it doesn't show up in the network browse list. Here's how to set it up:

1. Configure the NTFS options on the folder to be shared as needed to secure the contents.

2. Right-click the folder you want to share and hide, and choose Sharing.

3. Select the option "Share this folder."

4. In the Share Name text box, type the name by which you want the folder shared, including a $ as the last character.

5. Click Permissions to set share permissions for the shared folder.

6. Close the Sharing page to begin sharing the folder.

8.4   All drives are shared with a $ sign

Windows 2000, like Windows NT, automatically creates *administrative shares*. These administrative shares are used by the operating system and are useful for remote administration. Windows 2000 sets the permissions automatically for the administrative shares so that only members of the Administrators group can access them. Administrative shares have a $ as the last character to make them hidden from browsing.

There is typically no reason to try to modify or remove administrative shares. Since they are hidden, they don't clutter the browse list, and their inherent security settings prevent anyone but an administrator from accessing them.

Manage administrative shares

You can't modify permissions for an administrative share, but you can temporarily remove it. The administrative share comes back automatically when
you restart the computer. Follow these steps to remove an administrative
share:

1. Right-click the shared folder and choose Sharing.

2. On the Sharing page, select the administrative share from the Share
Name drop-down list (see Figure 8-2).

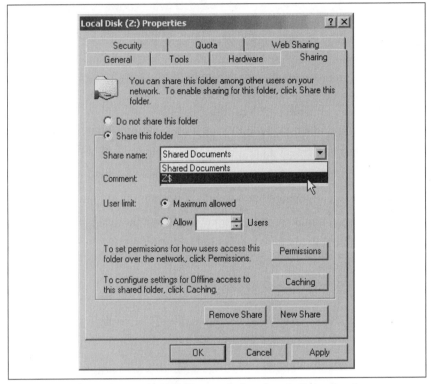

Figure 8-2. The Sharing page lists all shares including the administrative share

3. Click Remove Share and click OK.

You can create a visible share for a volume that already has an administrative share and assign permissions to the new share as needed. Keep in mind
that sharing the root folder of a volume shares the entire contents of the volume and can be a security risk if you don't carefully configure and monitor
share and NTFS permissions to protect the share's contents.

8.5 Limit the number of users who can access a folder or file at one time

There are a handful of reasons to limit access to a shared folder. You might have a slow computer and need to keep an eye on performance. Or perhaps the number of users is simply overwhelming your computer's bandwidth. Maybe you need to apply restrictions for licensing purposes. Whatever the reason, reducing the number of users who can connect to a shared resource is fairly easy.

Set access restrictions on shares

Windows 2000 Professional allows a maximum of ten concurrent connections. Windows 2000 Server allows an unlimited number of connections. With both platforms you can explicitly specify the number of users who can access a shared folder at one time. Here's how:

1. Right-click the shared folder and click Sharing to open its Sharing page.

2. Select the Allow option and use the spin control to select the maximum number of concurrent users.

3. Click OK to close the Sharing page.

8.6 Quickly open a shared network folder

Whether you work with network folders all the time or very seldom, you probably want to be able to access those shared folders quickly. While you can browse through My Network Places each time to get to the folder, that isn't a very efficient use of your time. You can take advantage of a few quicker methods to speed up access to those network resources.

Map a drive letter to the folder

You can map a local drive (volume) letter to any shared network folder. The folder then shows up in My Computer with the folder as the root of the volume. You can choose to have Windows 2000 map the drive letter to the folder each time you log on and, if needed, connect with a username other than your current logon name. Here's how to map a drive letter to a shared folder:

1. Browse the network and locate the share you want to map, then right-click the share and choose Map Network Drive. Or, right-click My Network Places and choose Connect Network Drive.

2. Specify the UNC path to the folder in the Folder text box. If you opened the Map Network Drive dialog box by right-clicking a share point, the folder path is already filled in for you.

3. Select "Reconnect at logon" if you want Windows 2000 to automatically reconnect the drive to the share each time you log on. Deselect this option if you want a one-time mapping.

4. Click "Different user name" if you want to connect to the share using a user account other than the current logon account (such as the administrator account on the remote computer).

5. Click Finish.

Create network shortcuts

Shortcuts are a great way to get quick access to remote computers and their shared folders and eliminate the need to map drive letters to the remote shares. You simply double-click the shortcut icon and the folder opens, just as it does for a shortcut to a local folder. You don't have to spend any time at all browsing through My Network Places to find what you need.

Creating a shortcut is easy. Open My Network Places, find the shared folder you want to use, then right-drag the folder to the desktop or a local folder and choose Create Shortcut(s) Here from the context menu.

Use UNC pathnames when browsing or opening files

Mapped drives and shortcuts are great when you know ahead of time that you're going to want to use a specific shared folder, but what about times when you want quick access to a folder you don't use often? In those cases you can use a UNC (Uniform Naming Convention) pathname.

UNC pathnames take the form *server**share*, where *server* is the name of the computer sharing the folder and *share* is the name of the shared folder. In Windows 2000, you can further define the path by including subfolders, such as *server2**public**documents**excel*.

When you need to open a file from a shared folder, just choose File → Open and enter the UNC path to the shared folder in the File Name text box of the Open dialog.

8.7   A network computer doesn't show up in My Network Places

My Network Places by default shows recently accessed computers on the network. You can open Computer Near Me to show the computers that belong in the same workgroup or domain as your own. Open the Entire Network object when you want to browse for computers in other workgroups or domains.

In some cases you won't find the computer for which you're searching. If you've browsed your own workgroup and the Entire Network object and still can't find it, there are a couple of additional things to try to locate the computer.

Use Search for Computers

If you're certain of the remote computer's name, or at least a portion of the name (such as the first few letters), use Windows 2000's search capability to locate the remote computer:

1. Right-click My Network Places and choose Search for Computers.

2. In the Computer Name text box of the Search for Computers window, type the name of the missing computer or use wildcards when you're not sure of the name. (For example, type **RA*** to find all computers whose names start with RA—RAY, RAZZLE, etc.)

3. Click Search Now. Windows 2000 searches the network and displays icons in the right pane for any computers whose names match the specified criteria.

Check protocol settings

If you still can't find the computer you want on the network, it could be that your computer and the missing computer don't have the same network protocols. Open the properties for your network interface and check the protocols in use to make sure you have at least one protocol in common with the other computer. Add the necessary protocol to your computer or to the remote computer. See Chapter 7, *Network Configuration*, for more information on installing protocols.

8.8   Wrong workgroup or domain

If you specified the wrong workgroup or domain when you installed Windows 2000, or if you simply want to change your workgroup or domain after the fact, it's an easy process. Changing workgroups has no real security impact and simply changes where in My Network Places your computer shows up. Changing domains, however, does have security ramifications because it places your computer in a different security context. Before you change domains, check with your network administrator to make sure you're taking the right approach.

Change workgroup or domain

Whether you're changing workgroup or domain, the process is much the same. You use the System Properties sheet for your computer to make the change:

1. Right-click My Computer and choose Properties.

2. Click the Network Identification tab.

3. Click Properties and in the Member Of group, select either Domain or Workgroup, depending on which type of entity you want to join.

4. In the associated text box, type the name for the workgroup or domain you want to join. If joining a domain, the domain must already exist. You can specify a new workgroup name to create and become the first member of that workgroup.

5. Click OK to apply the change.

You can also use the Network ID button on the Network Identification page to start the Network Identification Wizard, which will step you through the process of changing your domain or workgroup.

 When changing domain, keep in mind that you must either already have a computer account in the domain or have the name and password for an account that has the necessary rights to add computers to the domain.

8.9   Network your home computers

Networking your home computers is a fairly simple task, particularly if you're comfortable opening your computer and installing adapters. Even if you've never opened your computer, however, it's still a task you can accomplish with a little foresight and care.

There are two phases to networking your home computers, starting with choosing the type of network hardware you'll use.

Choose network hardware

Each computer to be added to the network needs a *network interface card*, or NIC. The most common is one that installs in your computer just like a display or sound card. If your computers include USB ports, a nice choice that can simplify the process and eliminate the need to open your computer is a USB network adapter. These external devices plug into your computer's USB port and are almost effortless to install.

Unless you choose a wireless solution, you also need the appropriate cable to connect together your computers. You have two main options: twisted pair cable or coax cable. Twisted pair looks like a thick phone cable and has a connector that is similar to a phone connector but has eight wires instead of four. Coax cable looks like the cable used for cable TV but is a little different size. A third option uses the electrical wiring in your house for the network cable, but this option requires a special network kit designed specifically for that purpose.

 Wireless solutions are typically more expensive than hard-wired solutions but are much easier to implement because they don't require any wiring.

The easiest option is to choose a home network kit that includes everything you need to hook up two computers. 3COM Corporation (*http://www.3com.com*) has networking kits, as do Intel (*http://www.intel.com*) and other manufacturers. Check the Internet or your favorite computer hardware store for availability.

 Before you buy any network adapters or a home network kit, check with the vendor or manufacturer to make sure it is Windows 2000 compatible.

Select protocols

After you install the hardware, you need to decide what protocols to use. Although you really only need one protocol, it might be a good idea to use two if your computers connect to the Internet. Use TCP/IP for your Internet connection and NetBEUI for sharing files and folders. Disable file and printer sharing for the TCP/IP protocol to prevent users on the Internet from gaining access to your folders and files. (NetBEUI isn't routable and can't be used by someone outside your local network to get access to your computers.) See Chapter 7 for detailed information on configuring protocols and unbinding TCP/IP from the File and Printer Sharing service.

8.10   Turn off sharing altogether

If you don't need to share your local folders or files with other users on the network, you can turn off sharing altogether. Doing so helps secure your computer from other users and saves a bit of memory by letting you unload the File and Printer Sharing service. After you disable the File and Printer Sharing service, you can still access shared folders and files on other computers. Disabling the service only prevents other users from accessing your computer.

Disable sharing

It's an easy task to disable sharing. You accomplish the task through the properties for the network connection:

1. Open the Network and Dial-Up Connections folder (click Start → Settings → Network and Dial-Up Connections).

2. Right-click the network interface you want to modify and choose Properties to open its property sheet.

3. In the Components list, deselect the File and Printer Sharing service, then click OK (see Figure 8-3).

 You can also remove the File and Printer Sharing service by selecting the service and clicking Uninstall. Just disabling it lets you re-enable it later if needed without having to reinstall it.

8.11   Automatically connect a drive letter to a network share at logon

If you use the same network shares all the time, you probably want to automatically map a local drive letter to those shares each time you log on. You have two options for doing so: use the Reconnect at Logon option, or map the drives through a logon script.

 You can map a drive through the Home Folder group of a user profile. Open the Local Users and Groups object in the Computer Management console to configure the user profile.

Use Reconnect at Logon

If you log on from the same computer all the time, the easiest way to configure a network share for automatic connection when you log on is to use the Reconnect at Logon option when you map the drive.

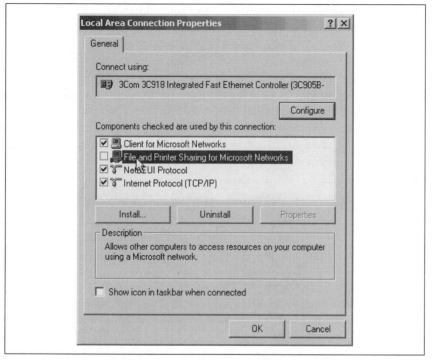

Figure 8-3. Deselect the File and Printer Sharing service to disable it for an interface

1. Right-click My Network Places and choose Map Network Drive.

2. Select the drive letter and folder to map, then select the option Reconnect at Logon. If you deselect this option, the mapping applies only for the current logon session.

3. Click OK.

Map network drives with a logon script

A logon script is a good option if you log on from different computers on the network and need to map multiple drive letters to network shares. Because the logon script can follow you around the network (see the following section on roaming profiles), the script maps your drives for you no matter where you log on:

1. If you already have a logon script, you can modify it to add the commands required to map the network drives. Otherwise, create a new logon script using Notepad and give it a *.bat* or *.cmd* file extension.

2. Open the logon script in Notepad and add as many *net use* commands as needed to map all of the drives to local drive IDs. The following

example maps three local drive IDs to three different shares on the network:

```
net use m: \\mailserv\boxes\jboyce
net use r: \\appserv1\apps
net use z: \\docserv\word\docs
```

3. Add the logon script to the user profile. To do so, open the Local Users and Groups node of the Computer Management console. Click on the Profile tab and enter the path to the logon script in the Logon Script text box (see Figure 8-4). In a domain, you'll have to use the Active Directory Users and Computers console to configure the logon script.

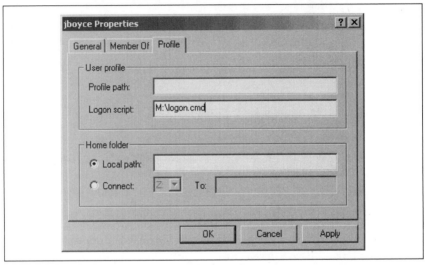

Figure 8-4. Specify the logon script in the user profile properties

8.12 Use the same settings from different computers

If you log on from different computers on the network, you probably want to have the same working environment no matter where you go. The trick is to use a *roaming profile*, which gets applied each time you log on. In addition to registry settings that define such things as desktop color and other working environment properties, the profile includes common folders such as Application Data, My Documents, Favorites, Desktop, and Start Menu.

When considering whether to use a roaming profile, bear in mind that the profile folders and their contents are actually copied across the network to the current computer. If your folders (such as My Documents) contain a large number of files or very large files, it can take a while and generate a lot of network traffic to copy the data across the network when you log on.

Check the amount of data contained in the user profile before deciding whether or not to use profiles. The following procedure explains how to check the size of a user profile.

Set up and use a roaming profile

Setting up a roaming profile is fairly easy but there are a few steps to the process. You copy the current local profile to a network server then specify in the user account settings where the profile is stored. You specify a UNC path to the user's profile in the account settings to ensure a relative path that is valid regardless where the user logs on:

1. Set up a network share where the user profile will be stored. Assign the necessary permissions to the folder to allow the user to access it from across the network. You don't have to specifically share the user's profile folder as long as you share a parent folder. For example, assume you've shared \\server\users and given the user jboyce access (through share permissions) to that shared folder. You can create a folder under \\server\ users named *jboyce* and use it to store the profile without actually sharing *jboyce*.

2. Open the Active Directory Users and Computers console and open the properties for the user for whom you're configuring a roaming profile.

3. Click the Profile tab and use a UNC path to specify the user's profile folder on the server. Using the example in step 1, you'd enter **\\server\ users\jboyce**.

4. Log on to a computer where the current profile already exists. Right-click My Computer and choose Properties.

5. Click the User Profiles tab and locate the user profile in the list. Note that the list shows the current size of the user profile to help you determine if you really want it to roam or not.

6. Select the profile and click Copy To.

7. Type the UNC path to the user's profile folder on the server or browse to the shared folder. Click OK to copy the profile and close the System Properties sheet.

8. Log off then log on at a different computer to test the roaming profile.

8.13 You don't have the necessary right to perform a task

While permissions determine the actions you can take with folders, files, and printers, *rights* determine the types of tasks you can perform in general within Windows 2000. For example, the Log on Locally right determines whether or not you can log on to a computer. If you attempt to log on at a computer where you don't have that right, Windows 2000 displays an error message and prevents your logon.

Other rights determine your ability to perform other tasks. The right Remove Computer from Docking Station determines, as you might guess, whether you can undock a computer. The right Shut Down the System determines if you can shut down your computer. Other rights control other tasks.

If you attempt to perform a task and receive an error message that you don't have the necessary rights to perform the task, you can grant the right to your account or a group in which your account is a member (assuming you have the necessary permissions to do so).

Change rights assignments

You assign rights through the local security policy or through group policies at the domain level. If both are configured, the domain settings take precedence over the local security settings. The following procedure assumes you're using the Local Security Policy console to assign rights:

1. Open the Local Security Policy console from the Administrative Tools folder of the Control Panel.

2. Open the branch Local Policies\User Rights Assignment.

3. Locate and double-click the right you want to assign.

4. If your account or a group in which you have membership isn't listed, click Add.

5. Select your account or a group in which you are a member, click Add, and click OK.

6. Click OK to close the dialog box for the right then modify other rights assignments as needed.

7. Close the Local Security Settings console when you're finished.

CHAPTER 9

Using and Troubleshooting TCP/IP

TCP/IP

With the increasing popularity of the Internet, TCP/IP has rapidly become the network protocol of choice. TCP/IP is more difficult to configure than other protocols, however, leading to potential configuration errors and conflicts. Fortunately, Windows 2000 provides a relatively easy means of configuring TCP/IP as well as several utilities you can use to troubleshoot TCP/IP connections.

This chapter covers both configuration and troubleshooting for TCP/IP, starting with a look at automatic IP addressing. Windows 2000 offers two options, DHCP and APIPA, and both are explained in this chapter. You'll learn how to configure your computer to receive its IP address dynamically, as well as turn off automatic addressing for situations that don't require it.

Dynamic DNS, or DDNS, is a new feature of Windows 2000. It enables client name-to-address mappings to be updated in a Windows 2000 DNS server automatically when the client's host name or IP address changes. For example, keeping host names properly mapped to IP addresses is a nightmare for DHCP clients with DDNS. This chapter explains DDNS and helps you configure your computer to take advantage of it. You'll also find other DNS-related solutions for configuring and using DNS.

Troubleshooting is a major focus of this chapter as well. You'll find solutions that will help you quickly identify the cause of specific problems and fix them. You'll also learn how to use several of the TCP/IP troubleshooting and configuration tools included with Windows 2000.

9.1   Configure TCP/IP automatically

No other network protocol is as complex as TCP/IP in terms of configuration. Errors in configuration can cause problems ranging from inconsistent connections to complete lack of connectivity. Fortunately, you can simplify

TCP/IP configuration by enabling the computer to obtain its configuration automatically. Not only does this eliminate the need to configure each client individually, but it also simplifies administration. Whenever you need to make a change in network configuration across the entire network, you simply change it at the server and restart the computers, which obtain the new settings.

You have two options for automatic TCP/IP configuration: DHCP and APIPA. The former requires a special server; the second does not but offers much less flexibility.

Become a DHCP client

Dynamic Host Control Protocol (DHCP) defines a standard that enables network clients to receive all aspects of their TCP/IP configuration from a DHCP server, including IP address, DNS server addresses, default gateway, and so on. The DHCP server can also be configured to assign a wide range of other properties to the, client. The server maintains one or more DHCP *scopes* that maintain the information associated with the address ranges managed by the server. When a TCP/IP client configured for automatic address assignment starts up, it broadcasts a request. The DHCP server responds with an *address lease* that includes the IP address and other configuration data and gives the computer the right to use the assigned address for a given period of time (the *lease duration*, defined by the address scope).

This book doesn't detail the server-side issues for DHCP, instead focusing on how to configure a Windows 2000 computer for DHCP. You do so through the properties for the TCP/IP protocol:

1. Open the Network and Dial-Up Connections folder, right-click the network interface, and choose Properties.

2. Double-click the TCP/IP protocol in the list of installed network components.

3. Select the option Obtain an IP address automatically.

4. If your DHCP server doesn't assign DNS server addresses (which is unlikely), select the option "Use the following DNS server addresses," then enter the IP addresses of your primary and secondary DNS servers. Otherwise, choose "Obtain DNS server address automatically" to receive DNS server address assignment from the DHCP server.

5. Click Advanced to display the Advanced TCP/IP Settings property sheet.

6. Click the IP Settings tab. If your DHCP server doesn't automatically assign gateway addresses (again, unlikely), click Add under the Default

Gateways section to add the IP address of the default gateway. If the DHCP server does assign gateway addresses, don't make any changes on the IP Settings page.

7. Click OK to close the TCP/IP property sheet.

There are several other properties you can configure for DNS, IP Security, etc. However, none of these directly relates to DHCP.

Use automatic address assignment without DHCP

If you don't have a DHCP server on your network (as may be the case with a small business or home network), you can still use automatic address assignment to simplify IP configuration. Windows 2000 supports Automatic Private IP Addressing (APIPA), which enables Windows 2000 computers to automatically assign themselves a nonconflicting IP address when no DHCP server is present. The computer attempts assignment through DHCP, and failing that, automatically assigns itself an address in the class B address range 169.254.*n.n* (subnet mask 255.255.0.0). The computer continues to check every five minutes for a DHCP server, and if it finds one, it takes an address lease from the server.

 Windows 98 also supports APIPA, enabling these clients to automatically assign themselves addresses, just like Windows 2000 clients.

There is nothing special you need to do to configure a Windows 2000 computer for APIPA. Just configure the TCP/IP protocol to obtain an IP address automatically, as you would for DHCP (see the previous section).

9.2   Turn APIPA off

In some cases, you might not want Windows 2000 to use APIPA to automatically assign an address. For example, where DHCP services are available, automatic address assignment can temporarily mask connectivity problems because the computer assigns itself an address rather than generating an error. Whatever your reason for wanting to disable APIPA, you disable it through a simple registry change.

Disable APIPA through the registry

You must create a setting in the registry to disable APIPA. You can disable it for a single adapter or for all network interfaces:

1. Run *regedt32* or *regedit* to modify the registry.

2. Expand the following key:

   HKEY_LOCAL_MACHINE\SYSTEM\CurrentControlSet\
   Services\Tcpip\Parameters\Interfaces*adapter_name*

   where *adapter_name* is the name of the interface for which you want to disable APIPA.

3. Create a DWORD value named IPAutoconfigurationEnabled and set its value to 0. (If you later need to re-enable APIPA set this value to 1.)

4. If multiple adapters are installed in the system and you want to disable APIPA for all interfaces, expand the following key:

   HKEY_LOCAL_MACHINE\SYSTEM\CurrentControlSet\
   Services\Tcpip\Parameters

5. Create a DWORD value named IPAutoconfigurationEnabled and set it to 0. As with individual interfaces, you can later set this value to 1 if you need to re-enable APIPA.

9.3   Receive a set of special TCP/IP settings just for your computer

Normally, a computer configured for DHCP receives whatever settings are defined globally for the address scope(s) managed by the server. The configuration is assigned without regard to the client's location on the network, hardware configuration, or other criteria. In some situations, however, you might want DHCP to assign specific settings to specific computers. For example, you might want to assign shorter lease durations for notebook computers because they leave the network more frequently than desktop systems.

You can use a new feature of Windows 2000 called *user classes* to uniquely identify a computer to the DHCP server, enabling the server to respond with settings specifically for that client or client type. The client provides a user class ID to the server when it requests an address lease. The DHCP server provides all of the default options defined for the scope not otherwise defined for the class ID. This means you can assign most settings through the default scope settings and use a user class only for assigning any special settings required.

Configure the server for class IDs

The first step in putting user classes to work is to define the user classes on the DHCP server. You then assign settings as needed to the user class. Here's how to do it:

1. Open the DHCP console from the Administrative Tools folder in the Control Panel.

2. In the left pane of the console, right-click the server where you want to create the user class and choose Define User Classes.

3. Click Add, then in the New Class dialog box (see Figure 9-1), provide the following information:

   Display Name

   > This friendly name appears in the DHCP console to identify the user class.

   Description

   > This optional description appears in the DHCP console to help you identify the purpose of a user class.

   ID

   > Click in the ASCII column and type the user class string, or click in the Binary column and enter the value in binary.

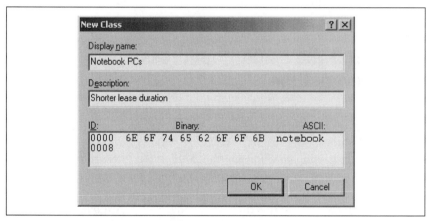

Figure 9-1. Create user classes on the server for assigning TCP/IP configuration properties on a per-client or client class basis

4. Click OK to close the dialog box.

5. In the DHCP console, right-click Scope Options and choose Configure Options, then click the Advanced tab.

6. From the User Class drop-down list, select the user class you just created.

7. Use the Available Options group to configure custom settings that you want applied for all clients that use the specified user class. You can rely on the standard options for all other settings.

8. Click OK then close the DHCP console.

Configure the client's class ID

The next step in assigning TCP/IP properties through user classes is to assign a user class to each client for which the user class applies. You assign a user class through the *ipconfig* command:

1. Open a command console.

2. At the command prompt type the following:

   ```
   ipconfig /setclassid adapter classid
   ```

   where *adapter* is the name of the network interface and *classid* is the class ID string. For example, you would use the following command to assign "notebook" as the class ID on the "Local Area Connection" interface:

   ```
   ipconfig /setclassid "local area connection" notebook
   ```

3. Repeat step 2 to assign additional user classes as needed.

4. Issue the following command to renew the IP address lease for the target adapter (replace *adapter* with the appropriate adapter name):

   ```
   ipconfig /renew adapter
   ```

9.4   Get the same IP address every time

In most cases it doesn't matter what IP address DHCP assigns a workstation. Unless you're hosting IP-identified resources such as web or FTP sites on the workstation, other clients won't care what IP address your computer uses. If you are hosting sites for your intranet or the Internet, or you're running special client or server software that requires your computer have a specific address, you can configure the computer to request the same address each time it starts. You do this through an address *reservation*.

An IP address reservation allocates a specific address based on the client's MAC address (the physical address of the network adapter). When the client requests an address lease, the DHCP server notes the MAC address and assigns the reserved address to the client.

Configure a DHCP reservation

Before you create a DHCP reservation you need to know the MAC address of the client's network interface that needs the reserved IP. You determine the MAC address using the *ipconfig* command on the client:

1. On the client computer, open a command console and type the following:

   ```
   ipconfig /all
   ```

2. Note the value for Physical Address.

3. On the DHCP server, open the DHCP console from the Administrative Tools folder in the Control Panel.

4. Expand the scope where you want the reservation created, right-click Reservations, and choose New Reservation.

5. Fill in the information in the New Reservation dialog box (see Figure 9-2) using the following list as a guide, then click Add and close the DHCP console:

Reservation name

This is the name by which the reservation appears in the DHCP console and is purely for identification purposes.

IP address

Type the IP address to be assigned to the client.

MAC address

Type the MAC address determined in step 2.

Description

Specify an optional description to help identify the reservation's purpose.

Supported types

Select the type of client allowed to use the address lease. Leave the default of Both if you're not sure.

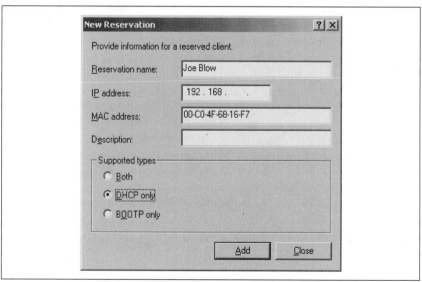

Figure 9-2. Use reservations to allocate specific IP addresses to specific MAC addresses

Configure the client to request a specific address

There is nothing you need to configure per se to enable a client to request a specific IP address through a DHCP reservation. Simply configure the client to obtain an IP address automatically and the DHCP server applies the reservation based on the client's MAC address.

Using DDNS instead of reservations

If your primary reason for using address reservations is to keep name-to-address DNS mappings current (such as mapping *www.somedomain.com* to a specific IP address), you should consider Dynamic DNS, or DDNS, as an alternative. DDNS enables Windows 2000 DHCP clients to request updates of their host (A) records when their host names or addresses change. A Windows 2000 DHCP server can also request an update of each client's pointer (PTR) record, and can even act as a proxy for non-Windows 2000 clients that need to have their host and pointer records updated but which don't support DDNS. See Section 9.8, "Register your computer with DNS and a dynamic IP address," for information on how to configure DDNS.

9.5 Can't connect to other computers on the local network

If you're having problems connecting to other computers on the network, there are a handful of troubleshooting steps you can take to identify and fix the problem. You should start by checking your hardware.

Check your hardware

The first thing you should check when you can't seem to connect to other computers on the network is the obvious: is the hardware working? Here are a few steps to help you check your network hardware:

1. Verify that the cable is securely connected to the computer's network adapter.

2. Look for a link light on the adapter. It should be lit if the adapter and cable are working properly.

3. Check the connection of the your network drop cable to the wall receptacle (if any).

4. Check the hub to make sure your connection shows a link light.

If you've checked all connections and still don't have a link light at the hub and network adapter, either the adapter or the cable might be bad. Replace the cable and/or adapter to see if the problem disappears.

Check local configuration

If the hardware seems to check out and you're getting link lights at both the hub and adapter, you should check the configuration for the adapter. Open the Network and Dial-Up Connections folder and use the following steps to check the configuration:

1. Check the network interface's icon. If it is dimmed, the connection is disabled. Right-click the connection and choose Enabled.

2. Right-click the connection and choose Properties. Make sure of the following:

   — The connection has a network client installed and the client is selected (such as Client for Microsoft Networks).

   — The connection has the same network protocol enabled as other clients on the network.

3. If TCP/IP is your primary LAN protocol, check the properties for TCP/IP to verify that the IP address, subnet mask, and default gateway are correct.

4. Open a command console and type `ipconfig /all` to view TCP/IP properties. Verify that your computer's address is in the correct subnet and the correct gateway is listed. If any settings are incorrect and you're not using DHCP, check the properties for the TCP/IP protocol and correct the settings. If you are using DHCP, check with the system administrator to determine why you're getting assigned the wrong settings.

Test connectivity to other hosts

If you're not seeing other computers in My Network Places, but you feel your network properties are correct, try connecting to another computer through a UNC path rather than browsing. Right-click My Network Places and choose Map Network Drive. Specify the UNC path to a known network share. If you can connect successfully but still don't see anything in My Network Places, verify that your computer is a member of the correct the workgroup or domain. See Section 8.8, "Wrong workgroup or domain," for instructions on how to change workgroup or domain.

TCP/IP

9.6   Can't connect to the Internet

TCP/IP is complex to set up, so problems with configuration often lead to the inability to connect to the Internet. And even when your computer is correctly configured, you may encounter problems with network hardware or remote sites. Understanding some basic troubleshooting steps will help you identify and fix your connectivity problems. The place to start is your local computer's configuration.

Test local configuration

The first step in testing Internet connectivity is to check your computer's network configuration. How you do that depends on whether your computer is hardwired to the Internet or you connect through a dial-up connection. For a hardwired connection, right-click the connection in the Network and Dial-Up Connections folder, double-click the TCP/IP protocol, and check for the following:

- Correct IP address and subnet mask. If your computer uses DHCP, open a console prompt and issue the command `ipconfig /all` to check address and subnet mask settings.

- Correct default gateway assignment. If your network includes more than one gateway, make sure you add all gateways to the Default gateways section on the IP Settings page of the Advanced TCP/IP Settings property sheet.

When you're confident your settings are correct, open a command console and ping your own computer with the following command:

```
ping localhost
```

If you don't get four replies, it's likely that your network adapter is not configured properly or has failed.

Test local connectivity

After you have successfully pinged your own computer to verify that the TCP/IP stack is working properly, try pinging other computers on your local network. First try to ping by IP address a known address on the network (pick a computer you know is on). The command takes the form:

```
ping n.n.n.n
```

where *n.n.n.n* is the IP address of the remote computer. If you can ping your own computer but you're unable to ping any other local computers, you probably have a problem with your network hardware or cabling or your TCP/IP configuration.

If you're not sure of a valid address, ping using the host and domain name, as in the following command:

```
ping host.somedomain.com
```

replacing *host.somedomain.com* with the host name of the remote computer. If you receive the message Unknown Host, either the host name is incorrect or name resolution isn't working on your computer. Check your DNS settings and try again. Also try pinging your DNS servers to check connectivity to them.

Test connection to the router

After you've successfully pinged at least one other computer on the network, try pinging the router by its IP address. If you're not sure of the router's address, open your computer's TCP/IP properties, click Advanced, and check the setting for default gateway on the IP Settings page of the Advanced TCP/IP Settings property sheet. The default gateway is the router address. If you have more than one gateway, try pinging each. Successful pinging of one but not another points to a problem with the router.

Test connections past the router

If you can successfully ping the router(s), try pinging computers past the router. You can ping by IP address or host name. If you don't know the IP address of any computers past your router, ping several web sites by their site names. Be aware, however, that some servers are configured to reject ICMP packets, which will cause the ping to fail. If you can ping by IP address but not by host name, you have a problem with your DNS configuration or with your DNS servers.

9.7   Can't connect to certain sites on the Internet

The ability to connect to some sites but not to others generally indicates a problem on the Internet backbone, heavily trafficked sites, or simply a site that is down for some reason. However, local factors could prevent you from reaching certain sites. The first step is to try to determine where the problem is occurring.

Trace the route to determine the point of failure

You can use the *tracert* command to test connectivity to a remote site. *tracert* sends out test packets with steadily incrementing time-to-live (ttl)

TCP/IP

values. Each gateway decrements the ttl value by 1. When the packet's ttl reaches zero, the remote router returns an ICMP Time Exceeded packet back to your computer. Subsequent packets make it one hop further before being timed out. The result is a table showing each hop. When the packets stop returning, you've identified the router where the problem exists.

You use *tracert* in much the same way you use ping, either with an IP address or host name, such as:

```
tracert www.cnn.com
```

Check for proxy or firewall blocks

If you are able to connect to and use certain sites but not others, and a *tracert* to the sites fails at your local network, the problem could be the way your firewall or proxy server is configured—certain traffic might not be allowed. Check with your system administrator to help resolve the problem.

9.8   Register your computer with DNS and a dynamic IP address

DNS enables your computer's host name to be mapped to its IP address, but only if a host record exists in the DNS namespace for your computer. For example, if your computer's host name is fred and your domain is somedomain.com, having a host record in the DNS zone for somedomain.com would enable other users to resolve fred.somedomain.com into your computer's address. This is useful when you're hosting one or more sites for an intranet or using other network applications that require name resolution.

When your computer's IP address changes because you receive your IP address through DHCP, however, your name-to-address mapping becomes a sort of "moving target." A new feature of Windows 2000, Dynamic DNS (DDNS), solves that problem by enabling automatic updates to the DNS namespace. If your host name or address changes, that change can be reflected in your zone's DNS records automatically. Setting up and using DDNS requires configuration at both the client and the DNS server.

Configure your system for DDNS

You configure your computer to support DDNS through the TCP/IP properties for the network interface in question. Here's how:

1. Open the Network and Dial-Up Connections folder, right-click the network interface, and choose Properties.

2. Double-click the TCP/IP protocol in the list of installed components.

3. Click Advanced and click the DNS tab.

4. Configure settings on the DNS page using the following list as a guide:

   Register this connection's addresses in DNS
   Select this option to have Windows 2000 attempt to update the host record using the Fully Qualified Domain Name (FQDN) specified on the Network Identification page in the computer's properties (right-click My Computer and choose Properties).

   Use this connection's DNS suffix in DNS registration
   Select this option to have Windows 2000 attempt to update the host record using the concatenation of the computer's host name (defined on the Network Identification page) and the DNS suffix for the connection. See the following setting for more details.

   DNS suffix for this connection
   Specify a DNS suffix for this connection. This suffix is appended to the host name specified on the Network Identification page to create the FQDN for the connection. Specifying a suffix here overrides the suffix assigned by the DHCP server (if any).

Server settings for DDNS

Most of the configuration for DDNS occurs on the client side, but there are a few details to handle on the server side. You enable dynamic updates on a zone-by-zone basis. The types of updates allowed depend on whether the zone is stored in the Active Directory. With AD-integrated zones you have the option of allowing only secured updates, which uses the access control list for the zone to determine who can perform an update. Standard zones outside the AD support only unsecured updates (or no updates at all).

You configure a zone's dynamic update behavior through the zone properties:

1. Open the DNS console from the Administrative Tools folder in the Control Panel.

2. Right-click the zone for which you want to configure DDNS and choose Properties (see Figure 9-3).

3. In the Allow Dynamic Updates drop-down list, select Yes to allow unsecure updates or Only Secure Updates to allow only secure updates.

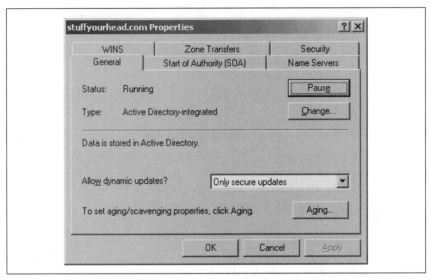

Figure 9-3. Configure DDNS security through the properties for the zone

9.9   Automatic update of your host name in the DNS server isn't working

There are a couple of items to check if your computer is configured for dynamic DNS but the computer's host record isn't being updated in your DNS zone when your host name or IP address changes. The problem could be a lack of connectivity to the DNS server or security restrictions.

Check connectivity

You should first verify that you have connectivity to the DNS server where your host record is stored. You can check connectivity easily by pinging the server:

    ping ns.domain.com

where *ns.domain.com* is replaced by the host name or IP address of the primary DNS server for your zone. If the server is configured to reject ICMP traffic, which will cause the ping to fail, you can test connectivity by configuring the server as your only DNS server, then attempting to resolve a name:

1. Open the TCP/IP properties for the connection.

2. In the Primary DNS Server address field, specify the IP address of the server where your host record is stored.

3. Make note of the current Alternate DNS Server entry, then clear it and click OK.

4. Try resolving a host name using *ping* or *tracert* or by connecting to a web site. If the name resolves, you have connectivity to the DNS server and should check for security issues on the server (see the next section). If the name doesn't resolve, begin troubleshooting the connection to the DNS server.

You also can check connectivity using the *nslookup* command:

1. Open a command console and enter **nslookup**.

2. At the prompt, type **SERVER** *ns.domain.com*, where *ns.domain.com* is the FQDN or IP address of your DNS server.

3. Type **LS** *domain.com*, replacing *domain.com* with your domain name. If you have connectivity to your DNS server you should see a list of records from the zone.

Check security settings

By default, Windows 2000 clients first attempt to perform an unsecured host record update and, failing that, attempt a secured update. If the DNS server is configured to only allow secure updates, registration of the host name will fail. If the DNS server is located in a different domain, you might have problems enabling clients outside the domain to update their host records. You need to establish a trust relationship between the domains or configure the zone to allow unsecured updates.

9.10 Enter only the host name and no domain for local searches

If you have an intranet or you frequently access local network resources through a web browser or other application that requires you to enter host names, you might prefer not to type the domain name each time. For example, assume your intranet includes the site *www.mydomain.com* (where *mydomain.com* is your local domain). Rather than type **www.mydomain.com** to browse the site, you want to type just **www** in the address bar of your browser. You can configure your computer to automatically append your local domain for unqualified host names, saving you the trouble of typing it.

Append domain names for local DNS searches

The DNS properties for the TCP/IP protocol on your computer determine how Windows 2000 handles unqualified host names for lookup. You can configure Windows 2000 to append your global and connection-specific domain names, or append a selected set of domain names:

1. Open the Network and Dial-Up Connections folder, right-click the connection, and choose Properties.

2. Click Advanced and click the DNS tab.

3. Select options using the following list as a guide:

Append primary and connection specific DNS suffixes
Select this option to have Windows 2000 append the primary DNS suffix (defined through the Network Identification tab—right-click My Computer and choose Properties) and the connection-specific DNS suffix (defined on the DNS tab) to unqualified host names prior to resolving them.

Append parent suffixes of the primary DNS suffix
Select this option to query the parent domain as well as your current domain. For example, if your domain is *support.somedomain. com*, pinging *www* would resolve *www.support.somedomain.com* and *www.somedomain.com*.

Append these DNS suffixes (in order)
Select this option to limit search of unqualified hosts to a specific set of domains. Click Add to add the domain suffixes you want appended to unqualified names prior to resolution.

9.11 Specify more than two DNS servers or change their order

The General page of the TCP/IP properties enables you to specify two DNS servers. In most cases two is sufficient, but if your DNS servers are heavily loaded or are available sporadically, you might want to specify more than two or change the order in which the servers are attempted for resolution. You can change these properties through the advanced TCP/IP properties for the connection.

Use advanced DNS properties

Use the Advanced properties page to configure advanced DNS settings, such as changing DNS server order. Here's how to configure advanced settings:

1. Open the Network and Dial-Up Connections folder, right-click the connection, and choose Properties.

2. Double-click the TCP/IP protocol.

3. On the General page, click Advanced, then click the DNS tab.

4. To change server order, select a server and click the up or down arrow on the property page.

5. Click Add to add other DNS servers, or select a server and click Edit to change the IP address of the server.

CHAPTER 10

Using and Sharing Dial-Up Networking Connections

Like Windows NT and Windows 9x, Windows 2000 provides dial-up (remote access) connectivity features that enable you to dial out from a Windows 2000 computer as well as have your computer function as a dial-up server. This chapter covers several aspects of remote access that apply to both client- and server-side issues.

Security is a critical issue to consider when your computer is connected to a public network such as the Internet, and this chapter addresses those security issues. You'll learn how to use encryption and certificate-based authentication to secure a connection, prevent others from browsing your computer while you're online, and establish a secure virtual private network (VPN) connection to a remote network, enabling you to use that remote network as if it were local.

Windows 2000 provides a handful of new features that improve remote access performance and enable you to share a single connection among multiple users. Multilink support lets you combine multiple dial-up connections to achieve a higher aggregate bandwidth for better throughput. Internet Connection Sharing (ICS) lets multiple users on your LAN share a single dial-up connection to the Internet, saving on hardware and connection costs.

Other topics covered in this chapter include using a credit card for outbound calls, configuring the computer as a dial-up server, using callback to save on toll charges, and allowing clients to request a specific IP address for a dial-up connection.

10.1 Use the best possible security for a dial-up connection

If you're working from home or another location away from your main office, and you're working with sensitive data, you probably want the best possible security for the connection. This means preventing hackers from intercepting your account or password data, ensuring that someone else can't get in if they do compromise your account, or perhaps even preventing specific types of traffic through the connection.

Windows 2000 offers some excellent features for ensuring high security for dial-up connections. You can use various levels of encryption or use certificates to ensure secure and digitally verified authentication. Smart cards offer another means of preventing unauthorized logon from stolen accounts. Another feature, IPSec (IP Security), lets you secure the traffic coming to and from your computer, making it less susceptible to interception.

Use encrypted authentication

To ensure security you should not use unsecured (plain text) password transmission. Windows 2000 provides support for a handful of authentication protocols that support encryption, which prevents hackers from intercepting and compromising your account. You can specify which authentication protocol to use, or you can let Windows 2000 determine which protocol to use based on which ones are offered by the server. Follow these steps to configure your connection to require encrypted authentication:

1. Open the Network and Dial-Up Connections folder, right-click the connection's icon, and choose Properties.

2. Click the Security tab.

3. From the "Validate my identify as follows" drop-down list, select "Require secure password."

4. Use the following list as a guide to select additional options:

   Automatically use my Windows logon name and password (and domain if any)
      Select this option to have the connection automatically use your current logon name, password, and domain for logon to the remote server.

   Require data encryption (disconnect if none)
      Select this option to force data encryption for the connection and disconnect if the server doesn't offer a supported encryption method. This option ensures that encryption is used.

Alternatively, you can specify the authentication protocol to be used. Follow these steps to select a protocol:

1. On the Security tab for the connection, click Advanced (custom settings), and click Settings.

2. From the Data encryption drop-down list (see Figure 10-1), select "Require encryption (disconnect if server declines)." This option ensures that the connection uses encryption for authentication and disconnects if encryption is unavailable.

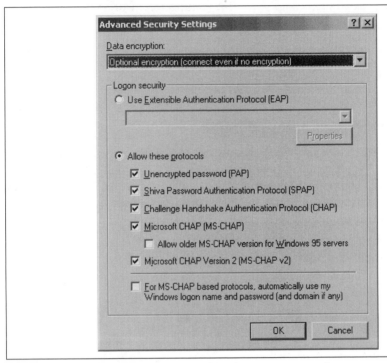

Figure 10-1. Windows 2000 supports several authentication protocols

3. Select "Allow these protocols" and place a check beside each authentication protocol you want to use. The connection will actually only use one. Your selections here determine which ones the client will attempt and accept from the remote server.

4. If you're using MS-CHAP–based protocols, you can select the option at the bottom of the dialog box to have the connection automatically use your Windows logon name, password, and domain to authenticate the connection.

5. Click OK, then close the connection property sheet and test the connection. If you're unable to connect, verify that the remote server supports the authentication protocols you've selected and also supports encryption.

Use certificate-based authentication through Extensible Authentication Protocol (EAP)

You can use certificate-based authentication to further protect your account during authentication. Using a certificate also helps ensure against someone else using your account and password to log on, as they must have the appropriate certificate in addition to your account information. You must acquire and install the certificate on your system before you can connect and authenticate. Here's how to configure EAP on your system:

1. Obtain a computer (machine) certificate from a Certification Authority (CA) in your domain or request a certificate from your system administrator. Check with the administrator if you're unsure of how to obtain the certificate yourself from the CA.

2. Use the Certificates MMC console to install on the client computer the certificate obtained in step 1.

3. Open the Network and Dial-Up Connections folder, right-click the connection, and choose Properties.

4. Click the Security tab, select Advanced, and click Settings.

5. Under Logon Security, select Use Extensible Authentication Protocol (EAP).

6. Select "Smart Card or other Certificate" from the drop-down list.

7. Click Properties and set additional options as needed based on the following list:

   Validate server certificate
   Select this option to have your computer verify that the certificate provided by the server has not expired. Deselect the option to have the client accept the server's certificate without validating it.

   Connect only if server name ends with
   Use this option to limit connections to servers that reside in a specified domain. For example, enter **foofang.com** if you only want to connect to servers in the *foofang.com* domain.

   Trusted root certificate authority
   Select the trusted root certificate authority for your server.

   Use a different user name for the connection
   Select this option if the username stored in the smart card or associated with the certificate you're using is not the same as the username you need to use to log on in the remote domain.

Use a smart card for authentication

While it's unlikely that your certificate will be compromised along with your account, it is possible. For that reason, a smart card in combination with encrypted authentication offers the best security for your connection. The smart card is a tangible item that someone would have to steal in order to compromise your account, making it very unlikely that your account would be compromised. Here's how to use a smart card for authentication:

1. Connect a smart card reader to your Windows 2000 computer and install the necessary drivers for it (Windows 2000 should automatically detect the reader and install the software).

2. Obtain the smart card from your system administrator. The smart card contains the data necessary for you to authenticate, including the certificate. (The administrator will also have to configure the remote access server to accept smart card authentication. Because that is a server-side issue, it isn't covered in this book.)

3. Open the Network and Dial-Up Connections folder, and then open the properties for your dial-up connection.

4. Click the Security tab, select Advanced, and click Settings.

5. From the Data encryption drop-down list, select "Require encryption."

6. Select Use Extensible Authentication Protocol (EAP), select "Smart Card or other Certificate (encryption enabled)," then click Properties.

7. From the Smart Card or other Certificate Properties dialog, select "Use my smart card."

8. Specify additional options using the list in the previous section as a guide.

Use IPSec

An additional feature you can use in conjunction with any of the authentication methods described in the previous sections is IP Security, or IPSec. You can use IPSec to control the type of traffic coming to and from your computer.

IPSec is a very complex topic that requires a good understanding of authentication and encryption to implement effectively. This section shows you where to go to configure IPSec but doesn't cover the technology in detail. If you're not familiar with IPSec or authentication and encryption, check with your system administrator for help in configuring IPSec on your system.

1. If you don't already have the necessary IPSec policy configured on your computer, open the IPSec console and create it. To do so, run the MMC and add the IPSec snap-in to a custom console, then create the policy. Close the IPSec console when you're finished configuring the policy.

2. Open the Network and Dial-Up Connections folder and open the properties for the dial-up connection.

3. Double-click the TCP/IP protocol to open its properties and click Advanced.

4. Click the Options tab, select IP Security, and click Properties.

5. Select the option "Use this IP security policy."

6. From the drop-down list, select the policy to apply to the connection.

7. Click OK four times to close all the property sheets and dialog boxes.

8. Test the connection to make sure you can connect and authenticate.

10.2   Hide shared resources when you're online

Just connecting to the Internet poses some security risk for your system, but having your shared resources (folders and printers) visible on the Internet can be a major security problem. Hackers and intrusion programs can take advantage of your shared resources to gain access to your data and wreak havoc with your system. Making your shared resources invisible to the Internet is therefore an important step in securing your system from intrusion and damage.

Remove File and Printer Sharing service from a dial-up connection

If you're connecting to the Internet through an Internet service provider (ISP), you probably don't need the File and Printer Sharing service enabled under the dial-up connection. You can disable it for the dial-up connection. Here's how:

1. Open the Network and Dial-Up Connections folder, right-click the dial-up connection, and choose Properties.

2. Click the Networking tab and deselect the File and Printer Sharing check box in the Components list.

3. Click OK to save the changes. If you are currently online, you'll need to disconnect and reconnect for the change to take effect.

Unbind TCP/IP from File and Printer Sharing

In some situations you might need to retain the File and Printer Sharing service for a dial-up connection but still need to unbind it from TCP/IP. For
example, perhaps you connect to your office LAN and need to use File and
Printer Sharing to enable others on the LAN to access files on your local system, but you also use TCP/IP to connect to the Internet through the same
dial-up connection (the office LAN has a direct Internet connection).

In this situation you need to unbind TCP/IP from the File and Printer Sharing service. Here's how to do that:

1. Open the Network and Dial-Up Connections folder.

2. Click Advanced → Advanced Settings.

3. Deselect TCP/IP in the File and Printer Sharing branch and click OK.

When TCP/IP needs to be bound to File and Printer Sharing

If TCP/IP is your computer's only protocol and you're connected to a local
area network, you'll have to have TCP/IP bound to File and Printer Sharing
to enable other users to access your local resources. You can unbind TCP/IP
if you're not sharing any of your folders or printers, however, or even deselect
the File and Printer Sharing service in the property sheet for your LAN connection, which turns it off altogether. Turning off File and Printer Sharing
doesn't affect your ability to access other users' computers or servers on the
LAN—it only affects other users' ability to connect to your computer.

You can opt for another solution if you need to share your resources but are
concerned about intrusion from the Internet: add and use the NetBEUI protocol for all LAN traffic and use TCP/IP only for Internet traffic. Bind Net-
BEUI to the File and Printer Sharing service and unbind TCP/IP from it. Any
other computers on your LAN that need access to your system will also need
to have NetBEUI enabled for their LAN connections and bound to their network client (such as Client for Microsoft Networks). Because NetBEUI is not
a routable protocol, NetBEUI traffic can't get past your Internet gateway, preventing users outside your LAN from seeing or using your shared resources.

Finally, if you must use TCP/IP as your only protocol and still need to share
your local resources, make sure there is some kind of firewall or proxy server
between your LAN and the Internet that will help prevent intrusions to your
LAN.

10.3   Use multiple connections at one time to improve performance

If you've ever used a direct Internet connection, you know how nice a fast connection can be. Trying to download a large file or remotely manage another computer over a dial-up connection can be a real pain because of the relatively slow connection (even at 56K). Windows 2000 offers an option called *multilink* that can help you boost your connection speed. A multilink connection combines two or more individual connections to provide an aggregate speed equal to the total of all individual connections. If you have two dial-up connections that each connect at 50Kbps, for example, your overall throughput will be 100Kbps. Add another connection and you get 150Kbps, and so on.

Use multilink to combine connections

Assuming you are using modems to dial your connection, the following is a list of the items you'll need in order to use multilink:

- A modem for each connection.

- A phone line for each connection.

- An ISP or dial-up server that supports multilink. Many services allow multiple connections with a single account and track utilization based on total connection time for all logons for the specified account.

- Phone numbers to dial. Some services require that you dial separate numbers for multilink, while others let you dial the same number for all connections (typical of an ISP).

Use the following procedure to configure multilink for a connection:

1. Install the additional modems so they are recognized by Windows 2000.

2. Open the Network and Dial-Up Connections folder, right-click the connection's icon, and choose Properties.

3. On the General page, select all the modems in the Connect Using list that you want to use for the connection.

4. If you can use the same phone number for all connections, select "All devices call the same numbers," then enter the phone number in the Phone Number field.

5. If you have to use different numbers for each connection, deselect the option "All devices call the same numbers." Click a modem in the Connect Using list, then type the phone number for that connection in the

Phone Number field. Click on the next modem and type its phone number. Repeat the process for each modem.

6. Click OK to close the dialog box and then test the connection.

Use BAP to manage multilink connections dynamically

If the service you're calling supports Bandwidth Allocation Protocol (BAP), you can configure your computer to use BAP to more efficiently use multilink. BAP enables your computer to dial an additional line when bandwidth needs require it and drop a line when bandwidth requirements decrease. For example, if you're downloading large files you're probably using most of your bandwidth. If you're just reading email, you're probably only using a fraction of the available bandwidth. BAP can potentially save you some money or reduce your use of allocated hours by dialing multiple connections only when needed and dropping connections when not needed.

You configure BAP through the properties for the dial-up connection:

1. Open the Network and Dial-Up Connections folder then open the properties for the connection.

2. Click the Options tab.

3. In the Multiple Devices group, select "Dial devices only as needed" from the drop-down list, then click Configure.

4. Use the following list as a guide to configure settings on the Automatic Dialing and Hanging Up dialog box:

   Activity at least

   Select the threshold bandwidth utilization that, when reached, causes another connection to be dialed.

   Duration at least

   Specify the duration that the bandwidth utilization defined by "Activity at least" must be maintained before another connection is dialed.

   Activity no more than

   Specify the percent of bandwidth utilization at which connections will be dropped.

   Duration at least

   Specify the duration that the bandwidth utilization must be at or below that defined by "Activity no more than" before a connection is dropped.

10.4   Share a single dial-up Internet connection with other users on the LAN

Windows 2000 offers a very useful feature called Internet Connection Sharing, or ICS, that lets you share a single Internet connection with other users on the network. This is particularly useful in a small office or home office environment where you need to share a single dial-up account among several users. Sharing the account can save you the cost of a direct connection or multiple dial-up connections when the bandwidth provided by a single connection is sufficient for your network's needs.

Configure ICS

Configuring a dial-up connection to use ICS is easy, but there are a few critical steps to ensure that the other systems can use the dial-up connection. The first part of the puzzle is to configure ICS on the computer where the connection exists. Windows 2000 automatically assigns the IP address 192.168.0.1 (subnet 255.255.255.0) to your computer when you share a connection. See the next section, "Set LAN client settings," to learn how to avoid connection problems caused by this address change.

Follow these steps to share a dial-up connection:

1. Open the Network and Dial-Up Connections folder. Create and test the dial-up connection to make sure your computer can dial and connect properly.

2. Open the properties for the dial-up connection and click the Sharing tab.

3. Select the option "Enable Internet Connection Sharing for this connection."

4. If you want the computer to automatically dial the connection when another user attempts to connect to the Internet (by opening Internet Explorer, for example), select "Enable on-demand dialing."

5. Click OK to begin sharing the connection.

Set LAN client settings

Because ICS changes the IP address of the sharing computer to 192.168.0.1, the other clients on the network that will be using the share connection also need to have IP addresses in that same subnet. You can achieve that by either of two methods: configure the clients for dynamic IP address assignment, or give them static IP addresses in that subnet. If you choose dynamic assignment you don't need to install a DHCP server. ICS enables the computer sharing the connection to act like a DHCP server, allocating addresses in the appropriate subnet.

Follow these steps to configure each client to use the shared connection:

1. Open the Network and Dial-Up Connections folder, right-click the LAN connection, and choose Properties.

2. Double-click the TCP/IP protocol to open its property sheet.

3. Select the option "Obtain an IP address automatically."

4. Select "Use the following DNS server addresses," and specify the appropriate DNS server addresses in the Preferred and Alternate boxes.

5. Close the TCP/IP dialog box, then close the connection's property sheet.

6. Right-click the Internet Explorer icon on the desktop and choose Properties.

7. Click the Connections tab and click Setup to start the Internet Connection Wizard.

8. Select the option "I want to set up my Internet connection manually," then click Next.

9. Select "I connect through a local area network (LAN)" and click Next.

10. Complete the wizard as you would for a LAN connection.

Configure dialing properties

One final step you should take is to configure the dial-up connection to automatically disconnect after a given period of idle time. This enables your computer to disconnect from the Internet when no one is using the connection.

1. Open the Network and Dial-Up Connections folder, and then open the properties for the dial-up connection.

2. Click the Options tab, then select the desired idle time from the drop-down list labeled "Idle time before hanging up." If the connection is idle for longer than the specified time, Windows 2000 disconnects.

3. Click OK to close the property sheet.

4. Open a connection on a client, let the computer autodial, then close the browser on the client and wait the specified period of time to make sure Windows 2000 disconnects when the idle timeout is reached. If not, something on your computer (like your email program) or on another client computer is generating Internet traffic, which is preventing the

connection from being idle for the specified time. See the next section for tips on resolving the problem.

10.5   Disconnect automatically when sharing an Internet connection

ICS is a great way to share an Internet connection with other users, but it can lead to a lot of unexpected online time if you don't configure the connection properly or other users generate a lot of unnecessary Internet traffic. If your connection isn't disconnecting when you think it should, there are a few potential problems to investigate.

Check idle time

First, you should verify that the connection is configured to disconnect after a specified idle time. See "Configure dialing properties" in the previous section to configure the connection to disconnect after a specified idle period. Decrease the idle time and see if the problem is resolved.

Check clients for unnecessary Internet traffic

Another possible reason your connection isn't disconnecting even though you've specified a short idle time is that other clients on the network are generating unnecessary Internet traffic. For example, one or more users might have their email clients configured to automatically check for mail more frequently than your connection's timeout period. If your connection's timeout period is 30 minutes but a client might has his email program configured to check for new mail every 10 minutes, your connection will never reach the 30-minute idle period.

Also, check for users who have configured their computers to use an active desktop that constantly downloads updates from the Internet. In general, you won't want other users generating excessive traffic because you probably won't want the connection to stay active all the time. Even if you have an unlimited access account, it's courteous to disconnect and make a line available to others who use the same Internet service when you don't need a connection.

10.6   Create a secure remote connection to your LAN

Here's a common scenario: you're going out of town but still need to be able to connect to your computer at the office or to the office LAN to continue working while you're away. Or, perhaps you want to do a little work from home on your off hours or even telecommute for an extended period. Whatever the case, you no doubt want a secure connection. You could achieve a secure connection by dialing straight into your computer or to a remote access server on the LAN, but when the office is a toll call or the computer or LAN doesn't offer direct dial-up connections, your local Internet connection is a good alternative.

You can create a secure connection to your office LAN or computer through a *virtual private network*, or VPN. The VPN connection encapsulates your network traffic in normal Internet IP traffic. In addition, the VPN can provide encryption to ensure that others can't intercept and use the data moving to and from your computer. Windows 2000 offers two protocols for VPN: PPTP and L2TP. The former is the easiest to set up, but the latter provides better security.

Set up the VPN server

You can configure either Windows 2000 Professional or Windows 2000 Server to act as a VPN remote access server. This section provides the steps to configure Windows 2000 Server to function as a VPN server. It assumes you have some background in Server, routing, etc., and primarily need to know where to go in Server to configure incoming VPN connections.

 See 10.7, "Allow other users to dial into your computer to access local resources," to learn how to configure a Windows 2000 Professional computer to accept incoming connections, including VPN connections.

The following steps assume you have not yet enabled RRAS on the server:

1. Open the Routing and Remote Access console from the Administrative Tools folder in the Control Panel.

2. Click the server in the left pane and choose Action → Configure and then Enable Routing and Remote Access. Click Next when the RRAS Setup wizard starts.

3. Select the option "Virtual private network (VPN) server" and click Next.

4. Verify that the protocols the clients will need are listed in the Protocols list. Select Yes if they are or No if you need to add the protocols, and then click Next.

5. If you selected No in the previous step, the wizard prompts you to select and install the required protocols.

6. On the Internet Connection page, select the network interface through which the clients will access the server (the interface that connects the server to the Internet), and then click Next.

 The server requires two connections to enable VPN support. One is the server's local LAN connection and the other is used for the VPN. If the server currently contains only one interface you'll need to install a second to accommodate VPN.

7. Specify how you want the VPN server to assign IP addresses to remote VPN clients. If a DHCP server is available or you want the VPN server to allocate addresses on its own without DHCP, choose Automatically. Otherwise, choose the option "From a specified range of addresses." Click Next, and if you selected the latter option, the wizard prompts you to enter the address to be assigned for allocation to VPN clients.

8. The wizard next prompts to determine if you're using RADIUS for authentication and accounting. If so, select Yes and provide the requested information for addresses of the RADIUS authentication and accounting servers. If you're going to use either local accounts or accounts in the domain for authentication, choose No. Click Next and then click Finish to complete the installation.

Next you need to decide if you're going to use L2TP for increased security for your VPN connections. If so, follow these additional steps to complete the server configuration, which include configuring IPSec filters to restrict all but L2TP traffic:

1. If you intend to use L2TP you'll also need to obtain and install a computer certificate on the server for that purpose. Open the Certificate console on the VPN server and use it to request a computer certificate from a CA on your network. Or connect to *http://server/certsrv* through your web browser, where *server* is the name or IP address of the computer providing certificate services. Follow the prompts provided by the wizard or certificate web site to obtain and install the certificate on the VPN server.

2. Open the RRAS console, open the IP Routing branch, and click General.

3. Right-click the interface on which you want to configure IPSec filters and choose Properties.

4. Click Input Filters to display the Input Filters dialog box and then click Add to display the Add IP Filter dialog box (see Figure 10-2).

5. Select Destination Network, then in the IP Address field enter the address of the VPN server's Internet connection. Specify a subnet mask of 255.255.255.255.

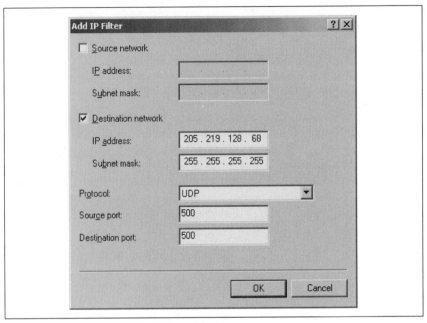

Figure 10-2. You must configure input filters for L2TP

6. Select UDP from the Protocol drop-down list, enter 500 in both the Source Port and Destination Port fields, and click OK.

7. Click Add on the Input Filters dialog box. Add another Destination Network entry for the same IP address and subnet mask as in step 5, but this time use UDP port 1701 for both Source Port and Destination Port fields. Click OK.

8. Back in the Input Filters dialog box, select "Drop all packets except those that meet the criteria below," then click OK.

9. On the General page of the interface's property sheet, click Output Filters. Add two filters as you did for incoming filters, specifying UDP port 500 for one and UDP port 1701 for the second.

10. Close the property sheet and the RRAS console, and then test the VPN connection from a L2TP-ready client.

After installing and configuring the server through the wizard, you can modify the configuration to add more ports, change authentication settings, and make other changes through the RRAS console. Also, verify that you have configured individual user accounts to allow remote access, or configure a remote access policy either at the local level or domain level if you want to control remote access on a group or global basis.

You'll find that using the wizard to configure RRAS for VPN connections creates 128 PPTP ports and 128 L2TP ports. You can use the Ports branch of the RRAS console to add, remove, or configure ports or other VPN settings.

Configure Windows 2000 Professional for incoming VPN connections

A Windows 2000 Professional computer can allow remote clients to connect and establish VPN connections to it. For example, assume that your workstation at the office has a direct connection to the Internet. You want to be able to establish a VPN connection to it through your local ISP so you can securely access files or other resources. Enabling VPN connections requires just one configuration change:

1. Configure the computer for incoming connections. See 10.7, "Allow other users to dial into your computer to access local resources," if you're not sure how to enable incoming connections.

2. In the Network and Dial-Up Connections folder, right-click Incoming Connections and choose Properties.

3. On the General tab, select the option "Allow others to make private connections to my computer by tunneling through the Internet or other network."

4. Click OK.

Set up a VPN client with PPTP

The easiest client configuration for VPN uses Point-to-Point Tunneling Protocol, or PPTP. While it doesn't offer the same level of security as L2TP (discussed next), PPTP is still a good option if you're not concerned with someone intercepting traffic between your client computer and the server, and it's easier to set up and configure.

1. On the client computer, open the Network and Dial-Up Connections folder and start the Make New Connection wizard.

2. Click Next, select "Connect to a private network through the Internet," then click Next again.

3. If you need Windows 2000 to dial a connection (such as your ISP) before dialing the VPN connection, select "Automatically dial this initial connection," then select the appropriate connection from the drop-down list (see Figure 10-3). Click Next.

4. Type the host name or the IP address of the VPN server and click Next.

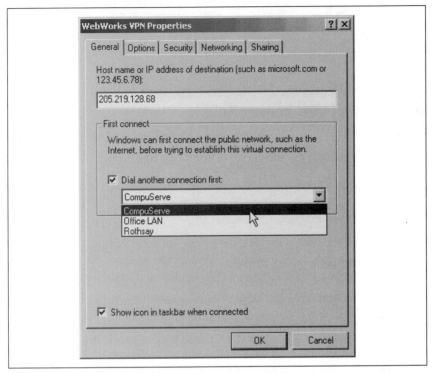

Figure 10-3. You can configure the VPN connection to dial your Internet connection before attempting the VPN connection

5. If you want all users to be able to access the VPN connection, select "For all users." Otherwise, select "Only for myself" to limit the connection to your use only. Click Next.

6. Specify a name for the connection (or accept the default) then click Finish.

After you create the connection, you can change the configuration as you would for any other dial-up connection. Open the Network and Dial-Up Connections folder, right-click the connection's icon, and choose Properties. The properties in the resulting property sheet are essentially the same as for a regular dial-up connection.

Set up a VPN with L2TP

Setting up a VPN connection to use L2TP requires a little more work because L2TP requires a certificate to provide encryption services. The system administrator needs to install a computer certificate on the server, and you need to install a computer certificate on your local computer as well.

The following steps assume the system administrator has already installed the necessary certificate on the server:

1. Obtain and install a computer certificate from your Certificate Authority (CA) either through the Certificates console on your computer or by connecting to the CA through a web browser at *http://server/certsrv*, where *server* is the IP address or name of the CA computer. Follow the prompts provided by the wizard or web site to obtain and install the computer certificate. If your system has a computer certificate from your CA already installed, you don't need to acquire a new one.

2. Run the Make New Connection wizard and create a VPN connection as you would for PPTP. Windows 2000 VPN clients automatically attempt L2TP connections before attempting PPTP connections, and since the server is configured for L2TP, that's the type of connection the client should create when you dial.

10.7 Allow other users to dial into your computer to access local resources

While you'll usually find a Windows 2000 Server computer acting as a dial-up server, there are situations where a Windows 2000 Professional computer is also handy as a dial-up server. For example, you might have a small office with no server per se, and other users need to connect to your computer to use files either on your computer or on the LAN. Or perhaps you want to set up your office computer so you can dial into it from home to work after hours. In either case, it's easy to configure Windows 2000 for incoming connections.

Configure your system as a dial-up server for local resources only

Windows 2000 Professional treats all incoming connections through a single icon in the Network and Dial-Up Connections folder. It's easy to configure the system as a dial-up server since Windows 2000 provides a wizard to help automate the task:

1. Install the modem or other device that remote callers will use to connect to your system. If you're setting up a VPN connection to enable remote clients to connect to your computer through the Internet, make sure your Internet connection is in place. Whatever device you're using, make sure it's installed and working before moving to the next step.

2. Start the Make New Connection wizard in the Network and Dial-Up Connections folder and click Next.

3. Select the option "Accept incoming connections" and click Next.

4. Select the device(s) you want to use for the incoming connections. You can select and use more than one. For example, you might have more than one modem connected to your computer and want to enable each for incoming calls. Click Next.

5. The wizard prompts to determine if you want to support VPN connections. Select "Allow" if you want to enable VPN connections or "Do not allow" if you don't. Typically, you'll only enable VPN when accepting incoming connections through a direct Internet connection. Calls directly to a modem are typically secure by nature and don't really require VPN.

6. Next select the users to whom you want to give remote access capabilities. You can use the Allowed Users page to add, remove, and configure accounts for remote access. Click Next when you're satisfied with the accounts.

7. The wizard next prompts you to select the network components to enable for incoming connections. If the remote caller needs NetBEUI to access shared resources, for example, make sure you select NetBEUI. You can use the controls on the Networking Components page to install components if they are not already present. Click Next when you're ready to continue.

8. The final page of the wizard would normally let you change the name, but for incoming connections you have to accept the default name. Click Finish to complete the wizard.

9. In the Network and Dial-Up Connections folder, right-click Incoming Connections and choose Properties.

10. Click the Networking tab, then double-click the protocol the remote clients are using to access shared resources.

11. If you're using TCP/IP, choose the option to assign address automatically or specify a range of predefined IP address that will be assigned to remote users.

12. Deselect the option Allow callers to access my local area network, then close the property sheet.

13. Dial in from a remote client to verify that you can connect to and access resources on your computer.

As with dial-out connections, you can modify the properties for incoming connections through the Network and Dial-Up Connections folder. Just right-click the Incoming Connections icon, choose Properties, and use the property sheet to enable/disable devices and VPN, configure components, and allow or deny access to users.

10.8 Allow other users to dial into your computer to access network resources

You can configure your computer to allow incoming callers to access just your local resources (folders and printers shared on your computer), or you can allow them to also access the LAN and resources located there. The only difference in terms of how you configure the connection is a single check box in the connection's properties. Enable incoming connections as explained in the previous section, omitting steps 9–11, which disable access to the LAN and limit connections only to your computer. By default Windows 2000 allows pass-through access to LAN resources for incoming connections.

10.9 Other users can't dial in to your PC

While configuring a Windows 2000 Professional computer for dial-in access is relatively easy, there are a couple of problems that might crop up. Problems are generally caused by overlooking a step in the configuration, such as not giving specific user accounts the right to connect. Differences in protocols can also be a problem.

Configure accounts for dial-in access

As part of the wizard that configures your computer for dial-up access, Windows 2000 prompts you to select the users who should have the right to dial into your computer. If you forget to enable a given user, that user won't be able to dial in. Or, you might add a user later and need to grant that user dial-in access. In either case, it's easy to grant a user dial-in access. Here's how:

1. Open the Network and Dial-Up Connections folder, right-click Incoming Connections, and choose Properties.

2. Click the Users tab.

3. If the user for whom you want to allow dial-in access is already shown, select the checkbox next to that user's name. If the user isn't shown, click New and add the user.

Check configuration

If you've enabled dial-in access for a user and he still can't connect, first verify that the user is attempting to connect with the proper user account and password and is entering the password with the proper case. If that looks good, check the configuration to make sure there are no configuration problems:

1. Open the Network and Dial-Up Connections folder, right-click Incoming Connections, and choose Properties.

2. Click the Networking tab.

3. Verify that the protocol the remote user needs is installed and selected for the connection. If not, install and/or select it.

4. Verify that the File and Printer Sharing service is installed and selected for the connection.

5. Click OK then retest.

10.10 Using a credit card for dialing

You might expect that configuring Windows 2000 to dial using a credit card would be easy, but that isn't always the case. When you throw in the fact that there are lots of different credit cards, each with its own access number, the task gets a little more difficult.

Set up and use a credit card for dialing

Setting up a dialing card isn't too tough, but there are a few steps to follow. You make the necessary changes through the properties for the dial-up connection. Since you might be dialing the same connection locally as well as from remote locations, the following steps assume you want to create a location specifically for using a credit card:

1. Open the Network and Dial-Up Connections folder, right-click the dial-up connection, and choose Properties.

2. On the General page, select the option "Use dialing rules," then click Rules to open the Dialing Rules property sheet.

3. Click New and type Credit Card in the Location name field (or use a name of your choice).

4. In the Area code field, type the area code from which you'll be dialing. Don't worry if you dial from different area codes. Windows 2000 uses this value to determine whether or not to treat the call as long distance.

5. If you need to dial a number to get an outside line, such as dialing 8 in a hotel prior to dialing out, enter the number in the "To access an outside line for long-distance calls, dial:" field.

6. Click the Calling Card tab and look in the Card Types list for the type of calling card you're using. If the card is listed, select it and enter your calling card number in the Account number field and your PIN (if any) in the Personal ID Number (PIN) field. See step 7 for configuration changes, if needed. Otherwise, click OK, select the Credit Card option from the Locations list, and click OK. You're ready to try a connection.

   If your card isn't listed in the Card Types list, add it. Click New on the Calling Card tab. Enter a name for the card in the Calling card name field, then enter the account number and PIN for the card in the fields provided. Click OK to close the property sheet.

7. You might need to fine-tune your card settings even if your card is one of the ones predefined in the card list. On the Calling Card tab, select your card and click Edit. Use the Long Distance (see Figure 10-4), International, and Local Calls tabs to specify the step-by-step tasks Windows 2000 should perform when dialing with the calling card for each of the three types of calls. To determine how to configure the settings, first dial the connection manually, noting the steps you need to take and numbers to dial to establish the connection.

10.11 Reverse the connection and have the server call you to save toll charges

When you're working away from the office and need to dial in to access files, email, or other resources, the toll charges can sometimes be high, particularly if you're connected for an extended period. You can avoid incurring the charges for the call by having the server call you back. This has the added benefit of security if you always call from the same number, since your account can be configured at the server to always call you back at the same number. This eliminates the possibility for someone else to use your account to dial the server.

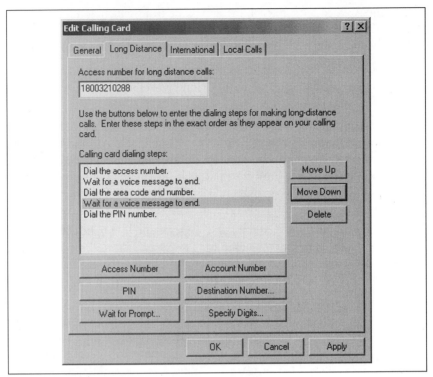

Figure 10-4. You might need to fine-tune your dialing card settings

Set callback options on the server

The first step in enabling callback is to configure your account on the server for callback. You can configure the account to deny callback, allow you to specify the callback number, or always use the same callback number. The steps are much the same whether you're configuring callback on a Windows 2000 Server or Professional computer. The only real difference is how you get to the appropriate dialog box:

1. Under Windows 2000 Server, open the Active Directory Users and Computers console, double-click the user account in the Users branch, and click the Dial-in tab.

   Under Windows 2000 Professional, open the Network and Dial-Up Connections folder, right-click the Incoming Connections icon, and choose Properties. Click the Users tab, double-click the user account, and click the Callback tab.

2. Select one of the following options (listed as they appear under Server/Professional):

No callback/Do not allow callback
> Select this option to explicitly deny callback for the user.

Set by Caller/Allow the caller to set the callback number
> Select this option to allow the caller to set the callback number when he dials in. You'd use this option when the callback number changes.

Always Callback to/Always use the following callback number
> Select this option to always use the same callback number.

3. Repeat the process for each of the other users for whom you need to configure callback.

Configure your client for callback

The next step in using callback is to configure your dial-up computer's connection for callback:

1. Open the Network and Dial-Up Connections folder and choose Advanced → Dial-Up Preferences. Click the Callback tab.

2. If you need to have callback at different numbers, select the option "Ask me during dialing when the server offers." After the initial connection, the server will prompt you for a callback number, your system will disconnect, and the server will call you back at that number.

3. If you want to use the same callback number for all sessions, select the option "Always call me back at the number(s) below." Select the modem whose callback number you want to modify, click Edit, and enter the callback number, complete with any prefixes or area codes the server might need to complete the call. Repeat the process for other modems, if installed.

10.12 Have the same IP address each time you connect

In most cases you won't need the same IP address for each connection, particularly if you're mainly doing web browsing, email, or accessing remote LAN resources. But in some situations, such as when you use TCP/IP applications that rely on a fixed IP address, you might need the same address each time you connect.

The process for enabling clients to request a specific IP address depends on whether the dial-up server is running Windows 2000 Server or Windows 2000 Professional.

Configure a Windows 2000 Server computer for IP requests

Enabling users to request a specific IP for dial-up connections under Windows 2000 Server is a two-phase process. You first configure a remote access policy to allow specific users or groups that ability, then you specify the IP address in each user's account properties. The following procedure assumes you're going to create a new policy to handle request for predefined IP addresses:

1. Open the Routing and Remote Access console from the Administrative Tools folder, then click the Remote Access Policies branch.

2. Right-click in the right pane and choose New Remote Access Policy.

3. Enter the friendly name Allow Predefined IP Address (or a name of your choosing) and click Next.

4. Click Add then select the type of attribute to use as the criteria for allowing predefined IP addresses. This example assumes you'll allow that privilege through group membership, so select Windows-Groups and click Add.

5. Click Add, select the group, click Add, and click OK.

6. Add any other groups and click OK in the Groups dialog box.

7. Click Next, select "Grant remote access permission," and click Next.

8. Click Edit Profile and click the IP tab.

9. Select the option "Client may request an IP address," and then click OK.

10. Click Finish.

Next you need to configure each user's account for the appropriate IP address. On a domain controller you do so through the Active Directory Users and Computers console. On a standalone server you use the Local Users and Groups branch of the Computer Management console. The following procedure assumes you're in a domain:

1. Open the Active Directory Users and Computers console and then open the properties for a target user.

2. Open the properties for the user and click the Dial-In tab.

3. Select the option Assign a Static IP Address, then enter the IP address in the associated text box.

4. Modify any other dial-in properties as needed and click OK.

5. Repeat the process for any other accounts that need a predefined IP address.

Configure a Windows 2000 Professional computer for IP requests

Configuring a Windows 2000 Professional computer to allow clients to request predefined IP addresses is a little easier than with Server:

1. Open the Network and Dial-Up Connections folder, right-click Incoming Connections, and choose Properties.

2. Click the Networking tab and then double-click the TCP/IP protocol.

3. Select the option "Allow calling computer to specify its own IP address" and click OK.

4. Click OK to close the property sheet.

Request a specific IP address

The last step in enabling clients to request a predefined IP address is to configure the client for that address. Here's how:

1. Open the Network and Dial-Up Connections folder, right-click the connection, and choose Properties.

2. Click the Networking tab and double-click the TCP/IP protocol.

3. Select the option "Use the following IP address," then enter the required IP address in the provided field.

4. Close the connection's properties and test the connection.

Dial-Up
Connections

CHAPTER 11

Web Services and Security

Windows 2000 Server offers a great set of tools in Internet Information Services (IIS) you can use to create a Windows 2000-based web server for web sites, file transfer, email, and newsgroups. You can use most of these same features on a Windows 2000 Professional computer, with a few limits, to enable the computer to function as a web server on an intranet or even the Internet. (Windows 2000 Server is the best choice for an Internet server because of connection restrictions in Windows 2000 Professional.)

This chapter provides several solutions to web-related issues, including how to configure the computer to host a web site, how to host multiple sites on one computer with a single IP address, and how to develop a directory structure for a web site that spans multiple computers.

You'll also find coverage directed at the File Transfer Protocol, or FTP. This chapter explains how to set up an FTP server, incorporate hidden folders in the FTP filesystem structure, control FTP connections, and have users automatically placed in a specific folder at logon.

Other, more advanced topics are covered in this chapter as well. If you're having problems getting Secure Sockets Layer (SSL) to work on a web site, you'll find the solution to the problem here. You'll also learn how to manage a computer remotely through the Telnet service, manage a web server remotely, configure site error messages, and install and configure FrontPage Extensions to support publishing web sites through Microsoft FrontPage.

11.1   Host a web site on your computer

If your computer has a direct connection to the Internet, you might want to host a web site on it. Or, perhaps you want to host a site on your local intranet. In either case, Windows 2000 includes everything you need to set up and manage a web site, along with FTP sites for file transfer and services for mail forwarding and newsgroups (the latter supported only on Windows 2000 Server).

When Setup installed Windows 2000 on your computer it probably also installed Internet Information Services (IIS), the Windows 2000 component that enables you to set up and manage web resources. The first step in setting up a site is to verify that IIS is installed, and if not, install it.

Install IIS

As you do with most other Windows 2000 components, you install IIS through the Add/Remove Software object in the Control Panel:

1. Open the Control Panel and open the Add/Remove Programs object.

2. Click Add/Remove Windows Components.

3. Select the check box beside Internet Information Services to select all components, then click Details.

4. Deselect any IIS components you don't want installed. If you won't be using the SMTP service to route email through your computer, for example, you can deselect it.

5. Click OK, click Next, and follow the remaining prompts to install IIS.

Create a web site in IIS

When you install IIS the setup program automatically creates a default web site (explained in more detail in the next section) for administration and supporting Internet printing through the Internet Printing Protocol (IPP). You can use the existing default site to host your web site or create a new site. Windows 2000 Professional only supports a single site, while Windows 2000 Server lets you create an unlimited number of sites.

The following procedure provides a quick run through the most common steps for setting up a new web site in Windows 2000 Server:

1. Open the Internet Services Manager from the Administrative Tools folder.

2. Right-click on the server and choose New → Web Site.

3. Click Next and enter the following information in the wizard:

    Description
    This is the description for the web site as it appears in the IIS console. It is not displayed to remote browsers.

    IP address
    Select the IP address to associate with the site or choose All Unassigned to have the site respond to all IP addresses that are bound to the computer but not assigned to other web sites.

TCP port
> Specify the TCP port on which the site will respond. The default port is 80. Unless you specifically direct users to a nondefault port through a link on an existing page, remote users must know and enter the port number as part of the URL (such as *http://www. stuffyourhead.com:8080* to go to port 8080 on the specified site).

Host header
> You can use the host header to host multiple sites on the same IP address. The host header is the site name portion of the URL, such as *www.stuffyourhead.com*.

SSL port
> Specify the port to be used for Secure Socket Layer communication, if applicable. The default is port 443.

Home directory
> Enter or browse to the directory that contains the home page for the site.

Allow anonymous access
> Select this option to allow all users access to the site. Deselect to protect the site using Windows 2000 user accounts.

Access permissions
> Select the level of permissions users will need for the site depending on what tasks they need to perform.

After the wizard completes setup of the new site, you'll probably want to make a few configuration changes as explained in the next section.

Configure the Default Web Site

Whether you are setting up a new web site under Windows 2000 Server or need to tweak the configuration of the Default Web Site under Windows 2000 Professional, the process is the same. The following procedure explains how to make the most commonly needed changes to a web site:

1. Right-click the site in the IIS console and choose Properties, then click the Documents tab.

2. If your default (main) document isn't named *default.htm* or *default.asp*, click Add, type the name of the document, and click OK. Select the newly added document and then click the Up arrow on the property sheet to move it to the top of the document list.

3. If you did not enable anonymous access, you need to configure directory security to specify which users can access the site. Click the Directory Security tab, then click Edit in the "Anonymous access and

authentication" control group. Select options to define authentication methods using the following list as a guide (see Figure 11-1), then click OK:

Basic authentication

Select this option to allow usernames and passwords to be sent as clear text without encryption (not recommended unless neither of the other two options are applicable).

Select a default domain

Click Edit to select a default domain other than the current domain. IIS will attempt to authenticate users against the specified domain if they don't explicitly provide a domain during authentication.

Digest authentication for Windows domain servers

This option sends a hash value across the network rather than the password and works across proxy servers and firewalls. The hashed value is difficult to decrypt and therefore more secure from interception. Digest authentication is supported only for domains with a Windows 2000 domain controller. It also requires a browser that supports HTTP 1.1 or higher.

Integrated Windows authentication

This option was formerly known as Windows NT Challenge/ Response, or NTLM authentication. It provides for secure authentication but does not work across proxy connections and requires a browser that supports this type of authentication (IE 2.0 or higher).

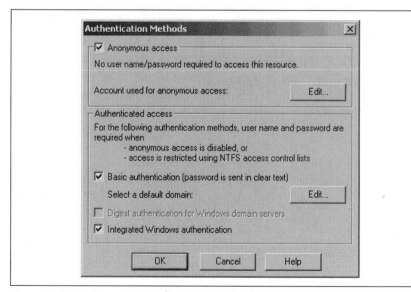

Figure 11-1. Configure access and authentication options for the site

4. Back on the Directory Security page, click Edit in the "IP address and domain name restrictions" group. By default all users are granted access subject to their account permissions, if applicable. You can deny access based on IP address, subnet (IP address range), or client's domain name (see Figure 11-2). Configure settings accordingly and click OK.

5. Click OK on the site's property sheet to apply the changes.

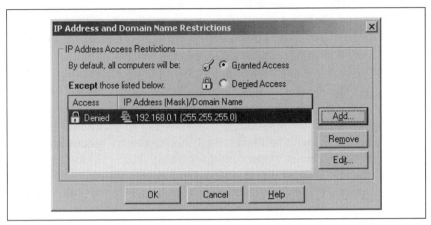

Figure 11-2. Deny access to specific IP addresses, subnets, or domains

There are numerous other settings you can configure for a web site in addition to those described previously. The ones already covered apply in the vast majority of situations. Others are covered under other topics in this chapter. Some fall outside the scope of this book.

11.2   Host multiple sites on one IP address

Perhaps you're setting up a Windows 2000 Server computer to use as a web server, and need to know how to host multiple sites with just one IP address. With IP addresses at a premium, this type of problem is common. You can use one of two methods to host multiple sites on a single IP address: use host headers or use varying TCP ports.

Unfortunately, Windows 2000 Professional only supports the single default site—you can't host multiple sites under Windows 2000 Professional. (But you can simulate it, as explained later, in the section "What about Windows 2000 Professional?").

Use host headers

Each site has three properties that help locate the site: IP address, host header, and TCP port. On a given server, at least one of these three must be unique. The other two can be the same from one site to another. The host header is the domain portion of the URL, such as *www.stuffyourhead.com*. The browser passes the host header to the server, which in turn can determine which site to serve up based on that host header.

So you can host multiple sites on the same server using a single IP address as long as the host headers are unique. Browsers that support HTTP 1.1 support host headers, which means that most browsers in use today do support host headers (including Internet Explorer 3.0 and Netscape 2.0 and later).

Here's how to configure a site's host header:

1. Open the IIS console from the Administrative Tools folder, right-click the site, and choose Properties.

2. On the Web Site tab, click Advanced to open the Advanced Multiple Website Configuration dialog box.

3. Double-click the IP address currently assigned to the site and enter the host header name in the Host Header Name text box (see Figure 11-3), then click OK.

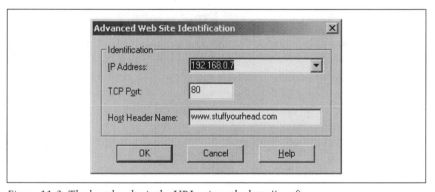

Figure 11-3. The host header is the URL minus the http:// prefix

4. Close the property sheet for the web site and repeat the process for any other sites you want to host on the server.

If you try to set up a new site using the same three properties (address, host header, and TCP port) as an existing site on the server, IIS generates an error message and does not start the site. You can change one of the properties for the site through the site's property sheet, then start the site.

You can't use host headers on a site that uses SSL because the host header gets encrypted.

Use different TCP ports

Another option that lets you host multiple sites on a single IP address is varying the TCP port for each site. This isn't the ideal solution since remote users will need to know the port number ahead of time and specify it in the URL, or you'll have to create a default page that provides links to the individual sites (embedding the port numbers in the links' URLs). However, it can be useful in situations where host headers aren't practical or you can adequately address the port/URL issue using one of the methods mentioned.

You configure the TCP port when you create the site. You also can change the port after the fact:

1. Open the IIS console from the Administrative Tools folder, right-click the site, and choose Properties.

2. On the Web Site page, click in the TCP Port text box and assign the desired port number.

3. Close the site properties and test the site using the new port number.

What about Windows 2000 Professional?

Windows 2000 Professional only supports a single site, the Default Web Site, and doesn't enable you to create other sites. If you are hosting multiple sites on the Internet or in a larger enterprise, you really should be using Server anyway because of performance and the 10-connection limit of Professional. However, in some situations you might want to maintain apparently separate sites even on your intranet.

You can achieve a result similar to hosting separate sites by simply using different virtual folders, one for each "site." Rather than connect to a given site URL, the users connect to each as a folder under the same domain. Because each folder can have different permissions, you can allow or deny access on a folder-by-folder basis, if needed. To simplify access you can create a home page under the default web site that contains links to each of the other main pages in the virtual folders.

Here's how to set this up:

1. Create the folders to be used to contain the files for each site and place the files in their appropriate folders.

2. Open the IIS console and create each of the virtual directories under the default web site (see the following section if you're unsure how to create the virtual directories).

3. Right-click one of the virtual directories created in step 2, choose Properties, and click the Documents tab.

4. If the name of the home page document for the selected virtual directory isn't listed, click Add and add the document name to the list. Then click OK.

5. Set other properties for security, etc. in the property sheet for the virtual directory, then close the property sheet.

6. Repeat steps 3 through 5 for the other virtual directories.

7. Test the sites by entering the URL *http://localhost/folder*, where *folder* is the name of a virtual directory. Replace *localhost* with the default web site's domain name if you're testing from a computer other than the one on which the web service resides.

But wait, you can create other sites under Professional...

It is actually possible to create additional sites under Windows 2000 Professional, but not through the IIS console as-is. You can copy the structure of the *iisadmin* folder from a Windows 2000 Server computer to the Pro computer, then browse on the Pro computer to *http://localhost/iisadmin/default.htm*. The administration pages give you the ability to create a new site, among other things. However, Pro only supports one web site running at a time, so you can't start the newly created site until you stop the current site. While this is something of a kludge, you might find it useful if you need to keep several different sites separate on a Pro computer for development purposes.

11.3   Add folders from other computers to your web site

IIS is flexible in the way it enables you to add content to a web site. While each site has a primary home directory, sites can also incorporate other directories as *virtual directories*. This capability enables you to use folders on other local drives or even on other computers across the network within the site structure.

Virtual directories act just like local directories under the home directory, with their *alias* names serving as the logical directory name. You can use them in relative references within your web site page structure (linking to

Web Services and Security

documents in the folders, for example), and users can connect to them by adding the folder to the site's URL.

For example, assume you assign the folder *c:\site\folder* as a virtual directory with the alias *business*. Users could access the virtual folder by the URL *http://YourSite/business*, where *YourSite* is the IP address or name of the web site under which you created the virtual folder.

Create virtual directories for a site

Creating a virtual directory is easy with the help of a wizard in the IIS console:

1. Open the IIS console, right-click the web site under which you want to create the virtual directory, and choose New → Virtual Directory.

2. In the Virtual Directory Creation Wizard, specify the following information:

   Alias
   > This is the name by which remote users will see the folder. It need not have a name relationship to the physical folder name.

   Directory
   > Type or browse to the folder or network share you want to use as the physical folder for the virtual directory.

   Permissions
   > Set access permissions as needed to specify the actions remote users can take within the virtual folder.

3. After the wizard completes creation of the virtual directory, right-click the virtual directory in the IIS console and choose Properties.

4. Configure properties for the virtual directory as needed, such as assigning a default document, assigning directory security, and so on. Assigning a default document through the Documents tab enables users to bring up that default page simply by specifying the URL for the virtual folder, without including any document name in the address.

5. If you need to fine-tune access to the virtual directory, modify the NTFS permissions of the physical folder or its contents (assuming the folder is stored on an NTFS volume).

11.4   Set up SSL for security on a web site

Secure Sockets Layer (SSL) connections provide secured transactions between the client browser and the server. SSL is often used to secure credit card transactions and other e-commerce functions, but SSL can be used to secure the traffic moving between the client and server in any situation in which the traffic must be secure from tampering or interception.

Setting up a web site for SSL isn't exactly intuitive, nor does Windows 2000 automate the process with a wizard. It's mostly a manual process that requires attention to detail to accomplish properly. In addition to obtaining and installing a certificate for the site, you also need to configure various settings in the site to make SSL work.

Obtain and install a certificate

The first step in configuring a web site to support SSL is obtaining and installing a certificate for the site. If your network includes a Certificate Authority (CA) server configured with Certificate Services (either an enterprise or standalone CA), you can obtain the certificate from that server. Otherwise, you'll need to obtain a certificate from an outside CA such as Verisign or Thawte. The following steps assume you're obtaining a new certificate from a local CA and submitting the request through a web browser. Point your web browser to *http://www.verisign.com* or *http://www.thawte.com* if you don't have a local CA.

1. Open the IIS console, right-click the web site, and choose Properties.

2. Click the Directory Security tab, then click Server Certificate to start the Web Server Certificate Wizard. Select the option to create a new certificate.

3. Use the following list as a guide to provide the information requested by the wizard. The result will be a certificate request file:

Prepare the request now, but send it later
Use this option if you have no enterprise CA or need to submit the request to a standalone CA.

Send the request immediately to an online certification authority
Use this option to submit the request immediately to an enterprise CA. This option is dimmed if IIS doesn't detect an available CA.

Name
Specify the friendly name for the certificate.

Bit length
You can use a longer bit length to increase security with a potential minor decrease in performance. The default is 512.

Server Gated Cryptography certificate
Select this option to request an SGC certificate.

Organization
Specify the name of your organization (typically the business name).

Organizational Unit
Specify a department or other OU to further define the certificate.

Common name
Specify the domain name (such as *www.stuffyourhead.com*) for a site hosted on the Internet. You can specify a DNS name or Net-BIOS name for a site hosted on your intranet.

Regional information
Specify country, state, city, or other regional information for your organization.

File name
Specify a filename under which the certificate request will be saved.

4. Point your web browser to *http://ca/certsrv*, where *ca* is the IP address or DNS name of the server providing CA services. In the resulting web page, choose "Request a certificate," then click Next.

5. Select Advanced Request and click Next.

6. Choose the option "Submit a certificate request using a base64 encoded PKCS #10 file," then click Next.

7. Enter the path to the file created in step 3 or click Browse to browse for the file. Select the file and click Read to read the file into the form. If you prefer, you can open the file in Notepad and use the Clipboard to copy and paste it into the form.

8. Select Web Server from the Certificate Template drop-down list, then click Submit.

9. Follow the prompts provided by the CA to complete the request. Depending on how the CA is configured, you'll either be granted the certificate right away or will have to return to the CA's web site to retrieve the certificate after it is issued by the CA's administrator. If you have to retrieve it later, you can download the file in either DER or Base 64 encoded format.

10. Open the IIS console again, open the property sheet for the web site, and open the Directory Security page. Click Server Certificate to run the Web Server Certificate Wizard. The wizard recognizes that a certificate request is pending for the site. Specify the path to the certificate file obtained in step 9. Follow the wizard's prompts to complete the certificate installation.

Configure a web site for SSL

After you install the certificate, you'll probably need to configure a few options to make the site work properly for SSL. You do so through the Directory Security property page, as follows:

1. Click Edit under the Secure Communications group on the Directory Security page to display the Secure Communications dialog box.

2. Use the following list as a guide to configure options:

   Require Secure Channel
   > Select this option to require the client to use SSL to connect to the site. Deselect the option to allow unencrypted access to the site.

   Require 128-bit encryption
   > Select this option to require the client to use 128-bit encryption.

   Client certificates
   > Choose "Ignore client certificates" for a public web site. Select "Accept client certificates" to allow clients to optionally use client-side certificates to authenticate on the site. Select "Require client certificates" to force clients to use a certificate.

   Enable client certificate mapping
   > Select this option to allow clients to use their client-side certificates to authenticate against user accounts on the server, integrating client logon with Windows 2000 user accounts and groups.

   Enable certificate trust list
   > Select this option and use the associated controls to define a list of CAs that are trusted for the site.

3. Test the site to make sure it functions. Point a web browser to *https://site*, where *site* is the IP address or DNS name of the site. Make sure to use *https*, not *http*.

4. If you can't connect to the site, open the Directory Security page again in the site's properties and view the certificate's properties. If Issued To doesn't match the name of the site or the NetBIOS name of the computer (for an intranet site), start over and request a new certificate with the correct name. If the Issued To field shows Administrator or another username, you probably did not select Web Server from the Certificate Template drop-down list when you requested the certificate.

11.5   Manage a web server remotely

If you've done much network administration, you probably know the frustration of having to be in front of a server to make configuration changes. A little experience with remote administration and you'll really come to appreciate the ability to configure a server remotely. Web servers are no exception.

You have a few options for managing a Windows 2000 web server, whether Server or Professional, from a remote location. You can take advantage of the remote administration web site, use the IIS console to connect to other servers on the LAN, or establish a VPN connection and use the IIS console to manage remote servers.

Configure Windows 2000's HTTP-based administration

Under Windows 2000 Server, IIS offers an administration web site you can use to manage many aspects of the web server including adding and modifying sites, stopping and starting sites, and so on. Windows 2000 Professional does not offer the same capability for administration although it does create an *iisadmin* virtual directory just as on Server. The IIS console is more useful for server management, but the advantage offered by *iisadmin* is the ability to manage servers located outside of your network (such as elsewhere on the Internet).

 You can actually connect to two different URLs for the administration site: *http://server/iisadmin* or *http://server:port*, where *server* is the DNS name or address of the server, and *port* is the port assigned to the Administration Web Site.

By default *iisadmin* lets you manage the server locally through *http://localhost/iisadmin*. If you need to manage a server remotely, you must configure that server to allow connections to the *iisadmin* virtual directory from other addresses or subnets. Here's how:

1. Open the IIS console on the Windows 2000 Server computer you want to manage remotely.

2. Right-click the *iisadmin* folder in the Default Web Site or right-click the Administration Web Site and choose Properties. Both point to the same set of folders. The one you choose to modify depends on which method you use to access the administration site. Modify the *iisadmin* folder under the Default Web Site if you connect using *http://server/iisadmin*, or modify the Administration Web Site if you connect using *http://server:adminport* (the recommended method).

3. Open the Directory Security property page and click Edit under the IP address and domain name restrictions group.

4. Verify that Denied Access is selected, click Add, and add the IP address or subnet range for the computer(s) you want to have administrative access to the server.

5. Close all dialog boxes and the IIS console, and then test your ability to connect remotely from the specified computer(s).

Use the IIS console for systems on the LAN

You can manage web servers within your LAN using the IIS console from a Windows 2000 Professional or Server computer, provided you have the necessary permissions on the remote server. Simply open the IIS console on your local computer and choose Action → Connect. Specify the name of the computer you want to manage and click OK. You can perform all of the same administration tasks remotely that you can locally.

Use a VPN and the IIS console for remote systems

The Administration Web Site probably won't fit the bill if you need full administrative control of a server from a remote location, since the admin web site doesn't enable you to control anything other than web sites on the remote server. In these situations, a good alternative to third-party remote control software is a VPN connection and the IIS console. Once you establish a VPN connection to the remote LAN, your computer functions as if it were local to the LAN. This enables you to open the IIS console on your local computer and connect to and manage the remote server.

1. Create a VPN connection to the remote LAN. See Section 10.6, "Create a secure remote connection to your LAN," if you need help setting up the VPN connection.

2. Verify that your current local logon account and password match an account on the remote LAN that has the necessary permissions and rights to manage the remote server. If not, create the account on your local computer, log off, and then log on again using that account.

3. Connect to the remote LAN through the VPN connection.

4. Open the IIS console and choose Action → Connect. Specify the DNS name or IP address of the remote server and click OK.

11.6 A web site you set up returns a 404 or no default page error

The standard 404 error indicates that the page you requested doesn't exist. This can mean that you've either named the default page incorrectly or neglected to configure the default document for the site. In either case it's a quick fix to get the site up and running properly.

Configure default documents

If you receive a 404 error on a site you've recently set up, and the site has never worked properly, the problem is most likely with the name of the home page document or the default document settings. Here's how to rectify the situation:

1. Check the name of the home page document in the site's root folder. If you've named it incorrectly, rename it. Remember that any pages that link directly to the old name must be changed for the links to work correctly.

2. Open the IIS console, right-click the site, and choose Properties.

3. Click the Documents tab and make sure the home page document name is listed (see Figure 11-4). If not, click Add and add the name to the list. Use the arrow buttons to arrange the list so that the added name appears at the top of the list.

4. Close the IIS console and test the site again.

11.7 Create a custom web site error message

IIS provides a set of default error pages it displays when an error occurs. For example, it displays a standard error page when the requested document doesn't exist (the 404 error). While informative, the messages are unimaginative. You might want to add a little sizzle or humor to your site by customizing the error message pages. Or perhaps you want to offer additional help for users who experience specific problems. Whatever the case, it's easy to customize the error messages.

Create custom error pages

The HTML documents that IIS displays for standard errors are stored in *systemroot/Help/iisHelp/common*. You can determine which file is used for a specific error through the IIS console:

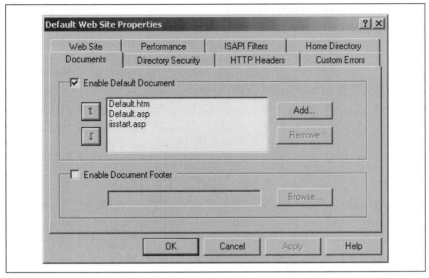

Figure 11-4. You can configure multiple default documents for a site

1. Open the IIS console, right-click the web site, and choose Properties.

2. Click the Custom Errors tab. The list on this page identifies the HTML file associated with each error. Note the name and location of the file you want to modify.

3. Close the property sheet and the IIS console.

4. Open your HTML editor (you can use Notepad, Word, etc. if you don't have a dedicated authoring application) and make the desired changes, then save the file.

11.8   Install and configure FrontPage Server Extensions

Installing FrontPage 2000 Server Extensions on a web site enables you or others to use FrontPage to publish changes to the site. You can enable and disable authoring, set performance options, and configure other settings. The first step is installing the extensions if they are not already installed.

Install the extensions

As with most Windows 2000 components, you install FrontPage Server Extensions through the Add/Remove Programs object in the Control Panel:

1. Open the Control Panel, open Add/Remove Programs, and click Add/Remove Windows Components.

Web Services and Security

2. Double-click Internet Information Services, select FrontPage 2000 Server Extensions, and click OK.

3. Click Next to install the extensions.

Configure a site for server extensions

When you install the server extensions on a Windows 2000 Professional computer, Setup automatically installs the server extensions on the default web site. If you've previously removed the server extensions or you're installing the extensions on a Windows 2000 Server computer, you'll have to add the extensions to each site. You do so through the IIS console:

1. Open the IIS console, right-click the web site, and choose All Tasks → Configure Server Extensions. Click Next when the Server Extensions Configuration Wizard starts.

2. Provide the wizard with the following information:

   Create local machine groups
   Select this option to have Windows 2000 automatically create local Admins, Authors, and Browsers groups for management purposes. Deselect this option if you already have one or more groups created for grouping site managers.

   Begin the group names with this distinguishing label
   You can specify a unique label to begin each group name if you're creating local machine groups. The label is useful when you use different groups to allocate administrative rights in different webs because it helps you differentiate the groups from one another. Omit the label to create the groups without a prefix label.

   Which Windows Group or user account should be the Web Administrator for this web server
   Specify the account that has administrative rights to the web site.

   Who should appear as the author of mail that this web server sends
   Specify the email address to be used when mail is generated by the server.

   If users of this web have problems, who should they contact
   Specify the contact email address displayed to users when they encounter errors in FrontPage when managing or publishing to the Web.

   What SMTP mail server should this web server use to send mail
   Specify the SMTP mail server used to route mail to or from the web server.

After the wizard completes the server extensions configuration, you'll probably want to fine-tune the settings:

1. In the IIS console, right-click the site, choose Properties, and click the Server Extensions page.

2. You can deny authoring access by deselecting the Enable Authoring check box. The other settings under the authoring group should be self explanatory if you're familiar with FrontPage.

3. By default each web site inherits the global security settings of the web server. You can configure security settings individually by selecting the option Don't Inherit Security Settings. The following list summarizes the available options:

Log authoring actions
> Select this option to log all authoring actions to *_vti_log/Author.log*.

Manage permissions manually
> Select this option to prevent the FrontPage Server Administration tools (such as the FrontPage MMC console) from being used to change security settings for the selected web site.

Require SSL for authoring
> Select this option to require the use of Secure Sockets Layer (SSL) connections for authoring. Using SSL adds security to the site and can help prevent hackers from modifying the site.

11.9   Host an FTP site for file transfer

While you can allow others on your LAN access to your local folders and files through the File and Printer Sharing (FPS) service, that method doesn't work for users who are located on the Internet or in a different network segment that isn't supported by FPS. For example, you might be using Net-BEUI for FPS rather than TCP/IP for security reasons, which prevents other users across a router on another network segment from accessing your local resources (because NetBEUI isn't routable). If those users have TCP/IP installed, however, they can access your files if you make them available through File Transfer Protocol, or FTP.

Using FTP has the additional benefit that only those folders and files you place in the FTP folder structure are available to remote users. This helps you protect your other folders and files from unauthorized access, at least through FTP.

Install the FTP service

If your computer doesn't already have the FTP service installed, you need to install it as the first step in setting up an FTP site. As with other Windows 2000 components, you install the FTP service through the Add/Remove Programs object in the Control Panel:

1. Open the Add/Remove Programs object in the Control Panel and click Add/Remove Windows Components.

2. Click Internet Information Services, then click Details.

3. Select File Transfer Protocol (FTP) Server and click OK. If the other required components such as Common Files are not already installed, the Windows Components Wizard will inform you of that and automatically select the additional required components.

4. Click OK, click Next, and follow the prompts to complete the installation.

Set up an FTP site

Setting up an FTP site is relatively easy. Windows 2000 Professional allows you to host only one FTP site, but Windows 2000 Server allows you to host an unlimited number. When you add the FTP service, the setup program automatically creates a default FTP site. The following procedure assumes you're setting up an FTP site on Windows 2000 Server (you don't need to set up a site on Windows 2000 Professional since the default site is created automatically):

1. Open the IIS console, right-click the server where you want to create the FTP site, and choose New → FTP Site.

2. In the resulting FTP Site Creation Wizard, click Next and then provide the following information:

    Description
    This is the description that appears in the IIS console. It is not visible to remote FTP clients.

    IP address
    Specify the IP address on which the FTP site should respond. Use All Unassigned to have the FTP site respond to all IP addresses that are bound to the computer and are not assigned to other sites.

    TCP port
    Specify the port for FTP traffic for the site. The default port is 21.

Path
> Type or browse to the folder to use as the root of the FTP folder structure.

Site access permissions
> Select the type of access (read, write, or both) that remote users should have on a global basis. If the FTP folder is stored on an NTFS volume, you can allow or deny access on a user or group basis and, if desired, apply permissions to folders or individual files.

After the wizard sets up the site you might want to modify a few of its properties. The next section explains how.

Setting FTP site properties and viewing current connections

Whether you've just created a new FTP site on a Windows 2000 Server computer or you need to tweak the settings of the default FTP site on a Windows 2000 Professional computer, the process is the same. Open the IIS console, right-click the FTP site, and choose Properties to display its property sheet. The following lists the properties you'll find on each tab:

FTP Site
> Use this tab to configure the site's IP address, TCP port, maximum number of connections, connection timeout period, and logging options.

Security Accounts
> Use this tab to enable and disable anonymous access to the site, allow only anonymous connections (disable authentication), and grant operator privileges to groups or accounts. Site operators have limited administration abilities for the site.

Messages
> Use this page to define the message that remote FTP users see when they connect to the site, exit the site, or attempt to connect when the maximum number of concurrent connections is reached.

Home Directory
> Specify the location of the site's root folder, its permissions, and the directory listing style (DOS or Unix).

Directory Security
> Use this tab to grant or deny access to remote users based on their individual IP addresses or subnet. This page is disabled in Windows 2000 Professional.

Web Services and Security

In addition to letting you configure the site, the property sheet also lets you view current connections. Just open the FTP Site page and click Current Sessions. You can use the resulting dialog box to disconnect users, if necessary.

11.10 Hide some FTP folders but still have them available

Any folder under the FTP site's root folder is visible to remote users who connect to the site. While you can prevent access to folders or files by applying NTFS object permissions to them, there might be occasions when you want to hide the folders altogether. For example, you might want to ensure privacy for one or more remote users' folders or simply to hide certain content from the general public.

Whatever the reason, it's easy to hide an FTP folder. Just create a virtual directory. The directory functions as a part of the FTP folder structure, behaving like it exists as a child of the root FTP folder. However, the physical directory pointed to by the virtual directory alias can be on a different volume or even on a different computer across the network. Users who know the directory exists can change to that directory using the *cd* command in an FTP console session or include the folder in the URL when connecting via a browser. The virtual directory can still be protected by NTFS permissions for additional security if it resides on an NTFS volume.

Set up a virtual FTP directory

You set up a virtual FTP directory in much the same way as a virtual web directory:

1. Open the IIS console, right-click the FTP site under which you want to create the virtual directory, and choose New → Virtual Directory.

2. In the Virtual Directory Creation Wizard, specify the following information:

   Alias
   > This is the name by which remote users will see the folder. It need not have a name relationship to the physical folder name.

   Directory
   > Type or browse to the folder or network share you want to use as the physical folder for the virtual directory.

   Permissions
   > Set access permissions as needed to determine the actions remote users can take within the virtual folder (read, write, or both).

3. After the wizard creates the virtual directory, right-click the virtual directory in the IIS console and choose Properties.

4. Configure properties for the virtual directory as needed. You can change physical directory location, permissions, and logging of visits to the folder. On a Windows 2000 Server computer, you can also allow or deny access to the folder based on client IP address or subnet (this option is disabled on Windows 2000 Professional).

5. Modify the NTFS permissions of the physical folder or its contents (assuming the folder is stored on an NTFS volume) to fine tune security, if needed.

6. Connect through an FTP console session or browser to test your new virtual directory.

11.11 Place users in specific FTP folders automatically on connection

Directing remote users to their own folders automatically at login serves two purposes: it eliminates the need for relatively inexperienced FTP users to navigate a directory structure, and saves time for advanced users who don't want to have to navigate the directory structure to get to their folders.

Configuring automatic folder direction

Automatic logon in an FTP folder is really a byproduct of the way the FTP server works, not something you need to design into your site. When a user logs in with a given username, the FTP service checks to see if a physical or virtual folder exists by the same name. If so, the service automatically makes that folder the current folder for the user's FTP session. If no matching directory is found, the user is placed in the root FTP folder.

Following are the general steps to make automatic direction to a folder work for FTP clients:

1. Create a physical folder that matches the user's logon name under the root FTP folder, or create it as a virtual directory.

2. Have the client connect to the site. When prompted for a username and password, specify the username that matches the folder name.

11.12 Disconnect users from your FTP site automatically

Windows 2000 Professional is limited to ten concurrent connections. If several users connect to your FTP site but don't disconnect when they finish downloading or uploading, other users could be locked out of the site until a connection times out and becomes available. You can reduce the timeout period so that inactive users are disconnected more quickly. You also can manually disconnect users if needed.

Configure FTP timeout

The default timeout for the FTP site is 900 seconds, or 15 minutes. If this is too long you can decrease the setting so that inactive users are automatically disconnected more quickly. Here's how:

1. Open the IIS console, right-click the FTP site, and choose Properties.

2. On the FTP Site page, enter the desired connection timeout period in the Connection Timeout text box. Click OK.

Disconnect users

In addition to changing the timeout value, you also can disconnect users manually when necessary:

1. Open the IIS console, right-click the FTP site, and choose Properties.

2. On the FTP Site page, click Current Sessions.

3. Select the user you want to disconnect and click Disconnect, or click Disconnect All to disconnect all sessions.

11.13 Allow remote use of your computer

In some situations it's handy to be able to use your computer remotely. For example, you might need to work at home but still have access to your computer as if you were in the office. Or maybe your home computer has a direct Internet connection through DSL or other means and you want to be able to connect to it and use it from the office. Large downloads are another great reason for using Telnet: you can connect to your office computer through your dial-up connection, initiate an FTP session to download files to your office computer, and then copy them to Zip disks or other removable media when you get to the office. Whatever the case, you have a couple of different options for using the computer remotely (or allowing others to do so).

First, you could install a third-party remote control program such as Syman-tec's pcAnywhere on the computer and use it as if you were sitting in front of it. These products are great if you need full access to the system and all the features provided through the Windows interface. In cases where you only need the ability to run a command console, however, Telnet is a no-cost solution.

 There are many good remote control programs now available. Covering their installation and use falls outside the scope of this book.

Set up a Telnet server

The Telnet service enables you to connect to a remote computer and use a command console session on it. You can issue commands as if you were working with the console locally. So anything you can do through a com-mand console locally on the computer you can do remotely through a Tel-net session. Setup installs the Telnet service by default when you install Windows 2000. However, you might need to enable the service if it isn't already running:

1. Right-click My Computer and choose Manage to open the Computer Management console.

2. Open the Services and Applications branch and then open Services.

3. Locate and double-click the Telnet service to open its property sheet.

4. The default startup mode for Telnet is Manual. If you want the service to start automatically at boot, set the startup type to Automatic.

5. Click Start to start the Telnet service.

Configure Telnet authentication

The Telnet service by default uses NTLM authentication, which means the service will automatically attempt to log on the remote user with his current Windows logon account without prompting for an account. If you prefer to have the server prompt for a user account and password, you need to tweak a registry setting on the server. The easiest way to do that is through the TLNTADMN utility, which lets you manage the Telnet service:

1. Open a command console and enter `tlntadmn` to start the Telnet admin-istration console.

2. Press 3 to change registry settings.

3. Press 7 for NTLM.

4. Set NTLM to 0.

5. Exit the TLNTADMN utility.

Windows 2000 sends the username and password in clear text if you disable NTLM authentication for the Telnet service. If this poses a security problem, you should re-enable NTLM authentication.

To prevent specific users or groups from logging in to a computer through Telnet, do not grant those users the right to log on locally to the computer.

Display a message at logon

You can display a message to users when they log on to a computer through the Telnet service. For example, you might want to display a warning message that unauthorized access is prohibited. Or you might just want to use the logon message to offer general information about the server or areas prohibited from remote access.

You configure the logon message by modifying the contents of *%systemroot%\System32\Login.cmd*. Change the existing echo commands or add other echo commands to create the desired logon banner. You can also modify *Login.cmd* to execute commands and perform other tasks automatically at Telnet logon.

 You can configure other Telnet server options through the TLNTADMN command-line utility.

CHAPTER 12

Users, Policies, Certificates, and Security

As privacy concerns grow, security and intrusion protection become increasingly important topics for many people. This chapter provides answers to questions about a broad range of security-related topics.

For example, you'll learn in this chapter how to prevent your email from being forged and assure the recipient of its authenticity. Encryption and digital signatures are also covered in detail, including how to use digital signatures for multiple IDs and ensuring that a digital signature on an incoming message is valid.

Certificates play an important role in Windows 2000 security, and this chapter provides solutions for the more common issues you'll face regarding certificates and Certificate Authorities (CAs). For example, you'll learn how to obtain certificates from a CA and how to move certificates from one computer to another.

Sharing is another topic covered in this chapter. You'll learn how to monitor the users who are accessing your computer across the network as well as the resources they are using. If you're sharing your computer with others, you'll find ways to restrict the tasks a user or group can perform, prevent modification of the registry, and otherwise limit the changes that can be made to your system, whether locally or across the LAN.

The chapter covers additional security topics as well, including how and why to rename the Administrator and Guest accounts, control driver installation, prevent a system shutdown by unauthorized users, and control system behavior when a smart card is removed.

12.1   Protect authenticity of your email

Using a certificate to secure your email prevents someone from impersonating you to send forged email and also assures the recipient that the message is really from you. Whether you are transmitting important documents or simply want to let recipients know your email is authentic, digital signing through a certificate is the way to go.

There are two phases to securing your email. First, you need to obtain the required certificate. Second, you need to configure your email client to use the certificate for digital signing.

Obtain a certificate from a Certificate Authority (CA)

Before you can apply a digital signature to a message, you must first install a certificate that supports that function. You can obtain a certificate from a third-party CA like VeriSign or Thawte (which is now owned by VeriSign). The following explains how:

 Check with your system administrator before obtaining a certificate from a third-party CA. Your network might include an enterprise or standalone CA capable of providing the certificate to you.

1. Connect to the CA's web site, such as *http://www.verisign.com* or *http://www.thawte.com*. You also can connect to *http://www.microsoft.com/windows/oe/certpage.htm* for additional CA choices.

2. Check the site for a link for personal certificates, specifically personal email certificates.

3. Click the link and follow the instructions provided to fill out the required form. Generally you'll need to have a credit card on hand to purchase the certificate.

4. Depending on the CA, you might receive your certificate immediately, or you might have to return to the site after your information is verified. In either case, the site will lead you through the steps to install the certificate through your browser. After the certificate is installed, you can begin using it to send messages.

Send digitally signed messages with Outlook Express

After you obtain the required certificate, it's easy to send digitally signed messages in Outlook Express. It requires only a few extra steps:

1. Compose the message (or reply to an existing message), and in the message window click the Sign button or choose Tools → Digitally Sign.

2. Send the message as you normally would. If the certificate is not installed properly, you'll receive an error message and won't be able to send the email.

Send digitally signed messages with Outlook

Sending a digitally signed message with Outlook is just as easy as with Outlook Express, but the process is slightly different:

1. Compose the new message or reply to or forward an existing message.

2. In the message window click the Options button or choose View → Options.

3. Select the option "Add digital signature to outgoing message," then click Close.

4. Send the message as you normally would.

Reading signed messages

You can read a digitally signed message just like an unsigned message. Just open it as you would an unsigned message. If the sender's digital ID has expired or the message has some other security-related problem, a warning message appears, giving you the option of viewing the message or not.

12.2   Encrypt email so only the recipient can read it

Although adding a digital signature to an email message helps validate the message, it doesn't prevent someone else from potentially viewing the message. You can encrypt messages for further protection, preventing unauthorized recipients from viewing them.

In order to view an encrypted message that you send, the recipient must have a copy of your digital ID with your public key. Similarly, for you to read an encrypted message from someone else, you need his digital ID. There are a couple of ways to obtain it.

Adding IDs of senders to your address book for signed messages

The easiest way to obtain a required digital ID is to exchange digitally signed messages. If someone else will be sending you encrypted messages, have him send you a digitally signed message, which will include his digital ID. If

Security

you'll be the one sending encrypted messages, first send the recipient a digitally signed message so he'll have your digital ID.

In either Outlook or Outlook Express, when you receive a digitally signed message, the digital signature of the sender is automatically added to your address book unless you've turned off that feature. Here's how to re-enable it in Outlook Express:

1. In Outlook Express, choose Tools → Options.

2. Click the Security tab, then click Advanced.

3. Select "Add sender's certificates to my address book," then click OK. Click OK again to close the property sheet.

You can configure the same behavior in Outlook if you're using Outlook in Internet mail mode (but not in corporate workgroup mode). Here's how:

1. In Outlook, choose Tools → Options.

2. Click E-mail Options on the Preferences tab.

3. In the E-mail Options dialog box, select "Automatically put people I reply to in," then click Browse to place the addresses in a folder other than the default Contacts folder.

4. Click OK, then OK again.

If you have a message in Outlook Express whose sender you'd like to manually add to the address book (along with the digital ID), right-click the message and choose Add Sender to Address Book. In Outlook, open the message, right-click the sender's email address, and choose Add to Contacts.

Obtain the public key from a CA

If you can't get a digitally signed message from the sender prior to receiving an encrypted message, you might be able to obtain the public key from the sender's CA. Point your browser to the sender's CA and follow the prompts provided by the CA's web site to obtain the other user's public key.

12.3 Configure digital IDs for one or more email accounts

You can theoretically use the same digital ID for several different email accounts. However, many email clients only recognize the first email address in the certificate, which is a potential problem. Ideally you should obtain a certificate for each account. After the certificates are installed on your computer (through the web browser), you can assign them to individual accounts.

Assign a certificate to an account

You assign a certificate to an email account through the account's properties. Use the following procedure to assign certificates to accounts in Outlook Express:

1. In Outlook Express choose Tools → Accounts.

2. Select an account and click Properties.

3. Click the Security tab.

4. Under Encrypting Preferences, click Select, choose the certificate you want to use with the account, and click OK. Click OK again and then Close to finish.

12.4   Verify that the digital signature attached to an incoming message is valid

The presence of a digital signature in a message doesn't guarantee that the sender's certificate is valid. The certificate could have expired or been revoked. You can configure Outlook Express to use *revocation checking* to automatically check the status of a digital signature. Revocation checking causes Outlook Express to automatically submit a status request to the sender's CA to verify the current status of the certificate. The CA then responds with the certificate's status so you'll know whether the ID is still valid or not. Keep in mind that your computer must be online to perform revocation checking.

Use revocation checking

Follow these steps to configure revocation checking in Outlook Express:

1. In Outlook Express, choose Tools → Options.

2. Click the Security tab and click Advanced.

3. In the Revocation Section, choose "Only when online."

4. Click OK, then OK again.

12.5   Move certificates to another computer

If you use two or more computers, such as a primary computer at the office and one at home or a notebook for travel, you might want to have your

Security

certificates on each one. This simplifies sending and receiving digitally signed or encrypted messages, enabling you to perform those tasks on each machine. You don't need to obtain separate certificates for each computer; you just need to export the certificates to a file.

Export and import certificates

You can export certificates from Internet Explorer, Outlook Express, or the Certificates MMC console. In all cases, Windows 2000 uses the Certificate Export Wizard to accomplish the task. The result is a certificate file that you can copy to and import onto the other computer(s).

Here's how to get your certificates onto a second computer:

1. In Internet Explorer, choose Tools → Internet Options, click the Content tab, and click Certificates.

   In Outlook Express, choose Tools → Options, click the Security tab, and click Digital IDs.

   In the Certificates console, open the branch Certificates\Current User\ Personal\Certificates.

   In IE or OE, select the certificate you want to export and click Export. If you're using the Certificates console, right-click the certificate and choose All Tasks → Export.

2. Click Next after the Certificate Export Wizard starts.

3. Choose Yes, export the private key, and click Next.

4. Accept the default settings for Export File Format and click Next.

5. Specify a password to protect the certificate file and click Next.

6. Specify a filename for the certificate and click Next, then click Finish.

7. On the other computer, follow step 1 to access your certificates. In IE or OE, click Import to start the Certificate Import Wizard. If using the Certificates console, right-click in the right-pane and choose All Tasks → Import to start the wizard.

8. Click Next after the wizard starts. Specify or browse to the path where the certificate is stored, select it, and click Next.

9. Specify the password entered in step 6 and click Next.

10. Click Next when prompted for the location of the certificate (let Windows 2000 place the certificate for you automatically), then click Next again.

11. Click Finish.

12.6 Keep track of who is using your computer's resources across the LAN

Even if you trust the other users who have the ability to access your shared resources, you might still concern yourself with who is using which resources, and when. For example, keeping track of remote connections can alert you to access by unauthorized users.

You can use a couple of different methods to track connections and resource use: actively monitoring connections or using auditing.

View connections dynamically

You can use the Computer Management console to view the current connections and files opened by those connections. While this requires that you take an active role (therefore not the easiest method, particularly if you're busy), you can see the current connections at a glance. Here's how:

1. Right-click My Computer and choose Manage to open the Computer Management console.

2. Open the System Tools\Shared Folders\Sessions branch. Current connections are shown in the right pane (see Figure 12-1).

3. Open the System Tools\Shared Folders\Open Files branch to view open resources by connection.

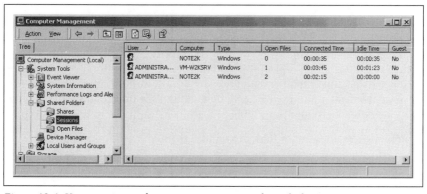

Figure 12-1. You can view and terminate connections through the Computer Management console

Security

Configure auditing

Auditing is a better method than manually monitoring connections because it's always monitoring even when you can't and maintains a record of access. If you have a problem with an unauthorized user accessing your computer, it's imperative that you have a record of the date, time, and other particulars.

When you turn on auditing, you direct Windows 2000 to monitor certain types of events and log those events to the Security event log. But, turning on and configuring auditing is just the first part of the picture. You also need to actively monitor the logs to keep track of events. We'll take a look at that aspect shortly.

In order to monitor resource access, you first need to enable the appropriate audit policy. Here's how:

1. Open the Local Security Policy console from the Administrative Tools folder.

2. Open the Local Policies\Audit Policy branch.

3. Double-click "Audit object access," select both Success and Failure, and click OK.

4. Close the Local Security Policy console.

 You probably realized by looking at the Audit Policy settings that you could audit several other types of events. Some of the other audit policies are discussed elsewhere in this chapter.

Enable auditing for specific objects

In most cases, enabling the audit policy is all you need to do to begin auditing that event type. In the case of folder and file access, however, you must explicitly identify which folders and files to audit. So it's a two-phase process: enable folder and file auditing by enabling the object access policy, and then specify which folders and files you want to audit.

You configure auditing of folders and files through the Explorer interface:

1. Open My Computer (or Windows Explorer) and locate the folder or file you want to audit.

2. Right-click the folder or file and choose Properties.

3. Click the Security tab, click Advanced, and click the Auditing tab.

4. Click Add, select the user or group you want to monitor, and click OK.

5. In the Auditing Entry dialog box (see Figure 12-2), select the specific events you want to audit, then click OK.

6. Add any other users or groups as desired, then close the Access Control Settings dialog box.

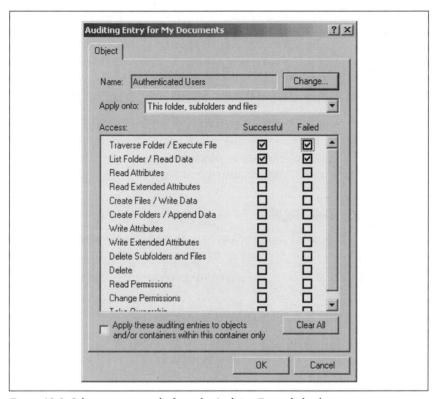

Figure 12-2. Select events to audit from the Auditing Entry dialog box

Configure and monitor the Security log

After you enable and configure auditing, you need to begin monitoring the Security event log. You can use the Event Viewer console, located in the Administrative Tools folder, to view all of the system's logs. Monitoring the log is simply a matter of reviewing it periodically to scan the events stored in the log.

As audit events begin to pile up in your Security log, however, you might need to tweak the configuration of the Security log to enable it to hold more events, clear events automatically, and so on.

Security

Follow these steps to configure the Security event log:

1. Open the Event Viewer console from the Administrative Tools folder.

2. Right-click Security Log and choose Properties.

3. Configure the log settings, including the maximum log size and what action Windows 2000 takes when the log reaches its maximum size. These options are generally self-explanatory.

12.7   Keep track of who uses your shared computer locally, and when

If you share a computer with other users and you're the primary user, you might want to keep track of who else is using your computer and when. You do so by auditing logon and logoff, which logs these events to the Security log. You can then monitor the Security event log.

Audit logon and logoff

Unlike with object access, all you need to do to make Windows 2000 start auditing logon and logoff events is to enable the appropriate audit policy:

1. Open the Local Security Policy console from the Administrative Tools folder.

2. Open the Local Policies\Audit Policy branch.

3. Double-click Audit account logon events, select Success and Failure, and click OK.

4. Close the Security Policy Console.

 The audit policy Logon Events tracks non-local authentication such as network use of a resource or a remote service logging on using the System account. You might want to enable this audit policy as well to track remote access to your computer.

12.8   Prevent someone from modifying your registry

It's possible for remote users to connect to your computer's registry from across the network and make changes to your computer's configuration. In some cases, this is a good thing—administrators can make needed changes or repairs to your system remotely. The ability for remote users to access and modify your registry remotely can, however, be a security risk, particularly if your local administrator account is compromised.

If you share a computer with other users, you might also be concerned that they could make unwanted changes to the registry. So protecting the registry locally is also a consideration. Auditing is a third line of defense that enables you to keep track of registry changes.

 Be careful when modifying the registry. An incorrect change can render your system unusable. You should make a backup of the registry through the Backup accessory before making any changes.

Disable remote registry access and modification

When someone tries to connect to the registry remotely, Windows 2000 checks the permissions of the following registry key:

HKEY_LOCAL_MACHINE\System\CurrentControlSet\Control\
SecurePipeServers\winreg

If this key doesn't exist, all users can access the registry remotely, subject to the permissions assigned to individual registry keys. Those permissions then determine what actions the remote user can take within the key (adding values, deleting values, deleting the key, and so on). If the key does exist, the permissions assigned to that key determine whether the remote user can gain access to the registry at all.

 You should allow at least the local Administrator account the ability to connect to the registry remotely in case your system needs remote administration to fix a problem that can't be fixed locally (such as the inability to log on locally with the Administrator account).

You can prevent remote access to your registry by setting the permissions on the winreg key so that only the required local accounts have permission to modify the registry. Or you can restrict remote access by setting permissions to grant only those authorized remote users access to the registry. Here's how to set permissions on the winreg key:

1. Click Start → Run, and enter **regedt32** in the dialog box.

2. Locate and select the following key:

   HKEY_LOCAL_MACHINE\System\CurrentControlSet\Control\
   SecurePipeServers\winreg

3. Choose Security → Permissions.

Security

4. Use the Permissions dialog box to set permissions as needed on the registry key, granting access only to those users you want to authorize for remote registry access.

5. Click OK and then close the Registry Editor.

Apply permissions to registry keys

In addition to restricting remote access, you might want to configure permissions on various registry keys to restrict who can modify the keys locally. Here's how:

1. Click Start → Run, and enter **regedt32** in the dialog box.

2. Locate and select the registry key you want to protect, then choose Security → Permissions.

3. Use the Permissions dialog box to assign permissions to the key as desired (see Figure 12-3).

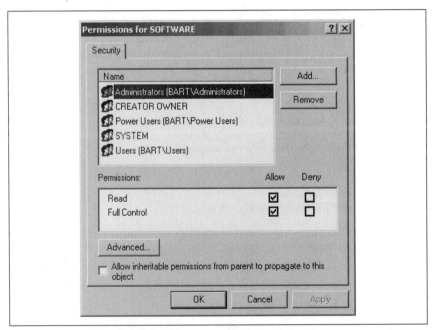

Figure 12-3. You can configure permissions on individual registry keys with Regedt32.

Audit registry changes

If you allow remote editing of the registry or simply want to keep track of who is making registry changes and when, you should enable registry auditing. As with object access, you enable auditing of registry changes by enabling the appropriate audit policy.

1. Open the Local Security Policy console from the Administrative Tools folder.

2. Open the Local Policies\Audit Policy branch.

3. Double-click Audit object access, select Success and Failure, and click OK.

4. Close the Local Security Policy console.

5. Click Start → Run, and enter `regedt32` in the dialog box to start the Registry Editor.

6. Select the key you want to audit and then select Security → Permissions.

7. Click Advanced and click the Auditing tab.

8. Click Add and add the users and groups whose access to the registry you want to audit. Add the Everyone group to audit all registry access.

9. Close the Access Control Settings dialog box and close the Permissions dialog box.

10. Repeat steps 6 through 9 to configure auditing for other keys and then close the Registry Editor.

12.9   Restrict what can be done on your computer

If you share your computer with others and you are the primary user, you might want to exercise some control over the tasks other users can perform when logged onto the computer. In a home office where the kids also use the computer, you're sure to want to apply some restrictions to the actions the kids can take.

Restrictions are easy to achieve in a domain environment because you can apply them on a group or user basis through group policies applied at the domain or organizational unit (OU) level. It isn't quite as easy without a domain, but it can be done. On a standalone computer in a workgroup, you can ensure different levels of restriction and protection through a handful of different methods, starting with user accounts and groups.

Configure user accounts and groups

First and foremost, you need to make sure the other users are not using your account. It's important that each user has a unique account to enable you to apply rights and permissions differently for them. Using unique accounts is also important if you want to audit logon, logoff, resource access, and so on. You use groups to further segregate permissions and rights if you have many users who work on the same computer. Or create a shared account with the necessary permissions and rights for those users who require the same settings and restrictions.

You create user accounts and groups through the Users and Passwords object in the Control Panel. This object also gives you access to the Local Users and Groups console, which offers additional options for creating and configuring user accounts and groups.

Protect the filesystem by using NTFS

The next step you should take in protecting your system from unauthorized or unintentional access or changes by other local users is to apply appropriate restrictive permissions to your folders and files. Review the permissions of all folders to make sure other users have at most read permission in any folder where they should not be able to make changes, removing write, change, or delete permissions as necessary. Also, consider removing read permission (denying access) to any folders and files the other users should have no need to see or modify.

In order to configure local restrictions on folders or files, you must be using NTFS on the affected volumes rather than FAT. If your volumes are currently formatted as FAT, use the *convert* utility to convert them to NTFS. See Chapter 1, *Installing and Booting Windows 2000*, to learn how to convert a FAT volume to NTFS. Although a backup is always a good idea before any major filesystem change, the conversion process is safe and you should have no problems converting.

Apply restrictions through policies and rights

Perhaps the most useful means of restricting what other users can do on your computer is group policy. In a domain, group policies can be applied at several levels: domain, site, OU, and locally. At the domain, site, and OU levels, you have the ability to apply policy settings on a user- or group-basis. However, the local group policy is intended to apply to all users, but there's a little trick you can use to apply local group policy to selected local users. For example, you might give your account full access but considerably restrict what all other users can do.

You can use the local group policy to apply a number of different restrictions. The following list summarizes just a handful:

Hide drives in My Computer
> Prevent users from accessing certain drives (or any drive) through My Computer. Doesn't affect the ability to access the drives through other means, such as a command console.

Hide My Network Places
> Help keep other users from browsing the network.

Hide the Internet Explorer icon
> Help keep other users off the Internet. You could also apply permissions to the Internet Explorer executable to prevent other users from running it.

Disable Add/Remove Programs
> Prevent other users from adding or removing currently installed programs.

Disable changes to the taskbar
> Prevent intended or accidental modification or deletion of toolbars on the taskbar.

Remove Run from the Start menu
> Prevent users from bypassing restrictions you've placed on access to applications by starting programs through the Start menu.

Disable and remove the Shutdown command from the Start menu
> Prevent other users from shutting down or restarting your computer, disrupting needed services such as Fax.

The additional restrictions you can apply are too numerous to detail here. Spend some time reviewing all the settings in the local group policy to decide which ones you want to apply.

You configure the group policy through the Group Policy console. As you work through the following steps, keep in mind that the changes you make will initially affect the Administrator account as well. Make sure you don't make any changes that will prevent you from logging back on as Administrator, opening the Group Policy console, and removing the restrictions for the Administrator account.

1. Log on as Administrator.

2. Click Start → Run, and enter `gpedit.msc` in the dialog box to start the Group Policy console.

3. Open the User Configuration\Administrative Templates branch and change restriction settings as needed. The settings for each restriction vary from one to another.

4. Close the Group Policy console and log off, then log back on again as Administrator to apply the change.

Security

5. Log off and log on as another user to verify that the restrictions are applied. Log off and then log on as each of the other users to whom you want to apply the restrictions.

6. Log on as Administrator and copy the file *systemroot\System32\GroupPolicy\User\registry.pol* to a backup location and name it *userreg.pol*. Copy the file *systemroot\System32\GroupPolicy\Machine\registry.pol* to the same backup location and name it *machinereg.pol*.

7. Open the Group Policy console and remove the restrictions applied in step 3. In some cases, you might need to use the opposite setting from the one applied in step 3. For example, if you selected Enable to apply a given restriction, choose Disable to remove the restriction rather than Not Configured, which applies no change to the registry.

8. Close the Group Policy console and then copy the backup *userreg.pol* file created in step 6 back to *systemroot\System32\GroupPolicy\User\registry.pol*, making sure to rename the file *registry.pol*. Copy the backup *MachineReg.pol* created in step 6 back to *systemroot\System32\GroupPolicy\Machine\registry.pol*, making sure to rename the file *registry.pol*.

9. Log off as Administrator and log on as one of the restricted users to verify that the restrictions are in place. Log off and then back on as Administrator to verify that the restrictions are not applied to the Administrator account.

As long as you didn't use your own non-Administrator account to log on in step 5, that account will not have the restrictions applied.

12.10 Prevent changes to your system

If other users share your computer, you might be concerned that they are able to make changes to it. In most cases, simply preventing the other users from logging on as Administrator will prevent them from making most changes. However, some changes are still possible depending on how you've configured permissions of folders and files, whether the Control Panel objects are accessible, and so on. You can use a combination of permissions and local security policy to prevent unwanted changes to your system's configuration.

Prevent changes to your system

The procedures for accomplishing the lockdown of your computer have been covered either in this chapter or in earlier chapters. The following list summarizes the tasks you can perform to lock down your computer and where to go in Windows 2000 to accomplish those tasks:

Use NTFS and apply permissions to folders and files to prevent access or changes

Use the *convert* utility to convert your FAT volumes to NTFS (see Chapter 1). Then apply permissions as needed to prevent other users from reading or changing folders or files that should be off limits to them.

Prevent other users from logging on as a member of the Administrator or Power Users group

Use the Local Users and Groups console (right-click My Computer and choose Manage) to change group membership so that other users belong only to the Users group.

Disable the Control Panel

Use the domain or local group policy to disable the Control Panel for all accounts other than your own and the administrator's. See the earlier section, "Apply restrictions through policies and rights," to learn how to apply local policies selectively.

Hide pertinent desktop icons

Use the domain or local group policy to hide any desktop icons to which other users should not have access.

Hide drives in My Computer

Use the domain or local group policy to hide the icons for any drives that other users should not have access to.

Restrict access to run command and command console

Use the domain or local group policy to remove the *run* command from the Start menu. Apply permissions to *cmd.exe* in the *systemroot\System32* folder to prevent execution by any account other than your own and the administrator's.

Apply other restrictions through the group policy

Review all the settings in the Group Policy console to determine which additional restrictions you need to set to prevent changes to your system. See the earlier section, "Apply restrictions through policies and rights," to learn how to apply local policies selectively.

12.11 Can't eject a removable NTFS media unless you're logged in as Administrator

By default, Windows 2000 allows removable NTFS volumes to be ejected only by members of the Administrators group. This helps ensure that casual or unauthorized users don't inadvertently eject an important media from a

Security

system. If you need to give other users the ability to eject NTFS media, you can do so through a simple security policy change.

Configure the security policy

You can select which types of groups have the ability to eject NTFS media by modifying the local security policy. If the domain policy is defined, it takes precedence over the local policy.

1. Open the Local Security Policy console from the Administrative Tools folder.

2. Open the branch Security Settings\Local Policies\Security Options.

3. Double-click the policy "Allowed to eject removable NTFS media."

4. Select the desired groups from the Local policy setting drop-down list. You can choose Administrators, Administrators and Power Users, or Administrators and Interactive Users.

5. Click OK and close the console.

12.12 Specify when you'll be prompted to change password prior to its expiration

By default, Windows 2000 prompts you for a new password 14 days prior to password expiration. However, you might want to change that period, particularly if you've changed the password age limit. For example, if you've decreased the maximum password age from its default of 42 days, you'll probably want to decrease the notification period as well. Or perhaps you don't want to be prompted until just a few days before expiration. In any case, it's a relatively simple change.

Change security policy

The security policy defines how soon Windows 2000 prompts you to change your password before expiration. If domain policies are set, they override the local setting.

1. Open the Local Security Policy console from the Administrative Tools folder.

2. Open the branch Local Policies\Security Options.

3. Double-click the policy Prompt user to change password before expiration.

4. Set the number of days prior to expiration that you want to be notified then click OK.

5. Close the console.

12.13 How (and why) to rename the Administrator account

Any hacker or intruder knows that on Windows 2000 systems the Administrator account gives him full access to the system if he can just guess, hack, or steal the password. Knowing the account name is a big step to breaking in, so changing the name of the Administrator account—particularly to something relatively cryptic—can go a long way toward keeping unwanted "visitors" out of your system.

Changing the Administrator account name is relatively easy. However, you should change it to something that you can remember, since you will have no other way to determine a forgotten account name unless you have another account on the system that is a member of the Administrator's group.

Change the Administrator account name

You change the Administrator account name through the Local Security Policy console. As a reminder, make sure you can easily remember the new Administrator account name, or make another account a member of the Administrator's group prior to changing the Administrator account name. This will enable you to log on with that account and view or change the Administrator account later if needed.

1. Open the Local Security Policy console from the Administrative Tools folder.

2. Open the branch Local Policies\Security Options.

3. Double-click the policy Rename administrator account.

4. Type the new Administrator account name and click OK.

5. Close the console.

12.14 How to rename or disable the Guest account

Windows 2000 creates a Guest account automatically when the operating system is installed. Although the Guest account is disabled by default (unless you upgraded from a Windows NT installation that had the account

Security

enabled) and has limited rights and permissions, the account can still pose a security risk. If the account is configured incorrectly, it can serve as a "back door" to enable unauthorized access to your system.

You can take two steps to lock down the Guest account: rename, disable it, or both. Rename the account if you still want authorized users to be able to connect or log on using the Guest account. Disable the account if you don't need it.

Rename the Guest account

As with most security options, you rename the Guest account through the Local Security Policy console. Here's how to make that change:

1. Open the Local Security Policy console from the Administrative Tools folder.

2. Open the branch Local Policies\Security Options.

3. Double-click the policy Rename guest account.

4. Type the new Guest account name and click OK.

5. Close the console.

Disable the Guest account

If you don't need the Guest account, it's a good idea to disable it. This prevents other users from logging on locally with the account or using it to connect remotely. You disable the Guest account through the Local Users and Groups console.

1. Right-click My Computer and choose Manage, then open the Local Users and Groups branch.

2. Double-click the Users folder to open it, then double-click the Guest account.

3. Select the option Account is disabled and click OK.

4. Close the Computer Management console.

12.15 Control what happens when your smart card is removed

If you use a smart card to log on to your computer, you should concern yourself with the implications of removing the smart card. For example, you should keep your smart card with you at all times for security reasons. This means that if you leave your computer, you should remove your smart card and take it with you.

By default, Windows 2000 takes no action when you remove the smart card. However, since you're probably leaving your workstation unattended, you should have Windows 2000 either lock the workstation or force a logoff.

Configure smart card removal behavior

You use the Local Security Policy console to specify the action Windows 2000 takes when you remove your smart card. If a domain policy is configured for this option, it overrides the local policy setting.

1. Open the Local Security Policy console from the Administrative Tools folder.

2. Open the branch Local Policies\Security Options.

3. Double-click "Smart card removal behavior."

4. From the Local policy setting drop-down list, select No Action, Lock Workstation, or Force Logoff, as desired.

5. Click OK and close the console.

12.16 Prevent unsigned drivers or services from being installed

If other users have administrative access to your computer they can install applications and device drivers. In most cases that isn't bad per se, but someone installing a noncompatible or buggy driver could wreak havoc with your system.

Microsoft has implemented a new feature in Windows 2000 called *driver signing* that enables a driver developer to certify that its driver has been tested and certified by Microsoft. This helps protect against incompatible and buggy drivers and services by ensuring that the driver has been through a testing and certification process. When you install a driver, Windows 2000 checks the driver to determine if it has been signed. If not, Windows displays a warning message and gives you the option of installing the driver anyway. You can change this behavior to prevent unsigned drivers from being installed. You can also configure how Windows 2000 handles other non-driver installation (such as services).

Prevent unsigned driver and service installation

You can configure two policies to define how Windows 2000 handles installation of drivers and non-driver applications such as services. As with most policies, if a domain policy is configured, it takes precedence over the local

Security

security policy. You use the Local Security Policy console to change the settings:

1. Open the Local Security Policy console and open the Local Policies\ Security Options branch.

2. Double-click "Unsigned driver installation behavior."

3. Select "Do not allow installation," then click OK.

4. Double-click "Unsigned non-driver installation behavior."

5. Select "Do not allow installation," then click OK.

6. Close the console.

12.17 Keep another user from shutting down your system

If you share a system with other users, and if your system provides local or network services that need to be up all the time, you might need to prevent other users from shutting down the system. For example, if you use the Fax service to accept incoming faxes, shutting down the system means you'll miss faxes sent to you while the system is down. Or perhaps you share folders that need to be available all the time to other users on the network. Shutting down makes those folders unavailable. Preventing other users from shutting down the computer means they can log off, but they can't shut down the computer.

Prevent system shutdown

The ability to shut down the computer is one of the many rights that can be assigned to a group or user. By default, on a Windows 2000 workstation, members of the Users, Power Users, Administrators, and Backup Operators groups can shut down the computer. The most straightforward way to prevent others from shutting down the system is to limit the groups that have that right. For example, you could remove the right from the Users group, or even remove it from all but the Administrators group, depending on which users still need the ability to shut down the computer.

You configure rights through the Local Security Policy console. As with other security settings, rights can be inherited from the domain security policy; if one exists, it overrides locally defined rights. Here's how to reassign the right to shut down the computer:

1. Open the Local Security Policy console and open the Local Policies\User Rights Assignment branch.

2. Double-click "Shut down the system," then use the resulting dialog box to select which groups have the right to shut down the system. Deselect those groups (such as Users) that you do not want to be able to shut down the computer.

3. Click OK, then close the console.

Security

CHAPTER 13

Backup, Recovery, and Repair

Backup and recovery are two hand-in-glove topics that most users never think about. Unfortunately, they are two of the most important topics for ensuring your data and system are safe from a catastrophic failure or gross user error.

This chapter offers tips on several data security issues including how to perform backups in Windows 2000 and what to back up, how to schedule backups to occur automatically, and how to back up to devices other than a tape drive.

You'll find several tips for recovering the system in the event of a problem. These options include recovering from a backup set, restoring the registry both through the GUI utility and the Recovery Console, and using the Emergency Repair Disk (ERD).

Troubleshooting is another topic covered in this chapter, and you'll find helpful solutions to address issues such as the inability to boot Windows 2000, how to create a boot disk, how to install and use the Recovery Console, and how to repair a corrupted registry.

13.1   Protect your system against catastrophic failure

Although it isn't common, a complete, catastrophic failure of your system is certainly possible through hardware failure, virus or worm, or even user error. Even a minor malfunction or mistake can take a big bite out of your day or even your week. So backing up your system and planning for catastrophe, even if it doesn't occur, is important.

Back up critical data

First and foremost, you need to back up your critical data. This means backing up any documents or applications that can't be restored or at least restored easily. You can use the Backup utility included with Windows 2000 to back up your critical data and applications to a file on a local or network hard disk, diskette, or tape. You'll find Backup under Start → Programs → Accessories → System Tools → Backup.

Back up the registry

The registry serves as the database for your computer's hardware and software configuration. If the registry becomes corrupted or damaged you could have a hard time booting the system. So it's important to make regular backups of the registry. You can restore from the backup with the Recovery Console if the registry becomes corrupted or damaged or if you simply want to restore the system to a known good state. You can also use the repair data in conjunction with the Setup program to repair your Windows 2000 installation. Just run Setup from the CD and choose the Repair option.

You have two methods for backing up the registry. The first makes a backup copy of the registry in the *\%systemroot%\repair* folder. You can boot the system using the Recovery Console, copy the registry files from the *repair* folder back to the *\%systemroot%\System32\config* folder to restore them, and reboot to recover the system.

Here's how to update the registry files in the *\%systemroot%\repair* folder without creating or modifying the Emergency Repair Disk (ERD):

1. Open the Backup utility and make sure there is no disk in the floppy drive.

2. On the Welcome page click Emergency Repair Disk.

3. Select the option "Also back up the registry to the repair directory" and click OK.

4. Click OK when informed by Backup that the ERD disk is not ready.

 Unlike Windows NT, the Windows 2000 ERD doesn't include a copy of the registry. Use this method when you want to back up the registry without also modifying the ERD. See the upcoming section, "Create an emergency repair disk," to learn more about the ERD.

Back up system state data

The *system state data* comprises the registry, COM+ class registration database, the system boot files, and protected files in the *dllcache* folder. These critical files essentially define Windows 2000, and any disaster recovery plan should include regular backups of the system state data.

The system state data can include 200MB or more of data, so you'll have to back it up either to a file on a local or network drive or to tape. Here's how:

1. Open the Backup utility, click the Backup tab, then select System State in the left pane.

2. Select any other files you want to back up, then start the backup.

You can back up the system state data separately from your other data or include the system state data in your regular backups. In either case, you can recover the system state data either along with or separately from your other data in the backup set. Just run Backup, click Restore, locate the appropriate system state data, and restore it.

Create an emergency repair disk

The Emergency Repair Disk, or ERD, contains a copy of your system's *autoexec.nt*, *config.nt*, and *setup.log* files. You can use the ERD in conjunction with the Windows 2000 Setup program from the Windows 2000 CD to repair your system should the need arise. You should also have a good copy of the registry in the \\%*systemroot*%*repair* folder to use along with the ERD.

Follow these steps to create or update the ERD for your system:

1. Insert a blank, formatted disk in the floppy drive.

2. Open the Backup utility, click the Welcome tab, then click Emergency Repair Disk.

3. It's a good idea to back up the registry too, so select the option "Also backup the registry to the repair directory," then click OK to create the ERD.

If you later need to use the ERD to repair the system, run the Setup program from the Windows 2000 CD and select the Repair option.

13.2 Perform backups automatically

The Backup utility includes the ability to schedule unattended backups, enabling you to back up your system automatically at regular intervals. This is particularly useful for backing up the system in the evenings or on weekends when you're not using the system.

Schedule automatic backups

The Backup utility provides a wizard to automate the process of defining a backup job and scheduling it for execution. Follow these steps to define and schedule a backup:

1. Open the Backup utility.

2. Click the Schedule Jobs tab.

3. Click Add Job.

4. Click Next to start the wizard.

5. Use the wizard to define what to back up, the backup type and location, and other general backup options.

6. The wizard displays a When to Back Up dialog box enabling you to run the backup job now or schedule it for later execution. Select Later, type a name for the job in the Job Name text box, and click Set Schedule.

7. Use the resulting Schedule Job property sheet to specify how often to run the backup job, at what time to start it, the first execution date, and various options that determine how Backup runs the automated job. The options are generally self-explanatory.

8. When you're satisfied with the schedule click OK. Click Next and then Finish to schedule the job.

Deleting a scheduled job

You might change your mind about when you want a backup job to execute or need to redefine it. You can delete the backup job and create a new one with the desired properties. Here's how to delete an existing job:

1. Open the Backup utility and click the Schedule Jobs tab.

2. Locate the scheduled job in the calendar and click the job's icon.

3. Click Delete then click Yes.

Then follow the steps in the previous section to create a new backup job with the desired properties.

13.3   You can only back up when logged on as Administrator

Backing up the system requires access to files that are normally restricted from normal users. In order to successfully back up anything other than your own files, your account or group must be assigned the "Back Up Files And Directories" right.

Configure backup rights

You can assign the Back Up Files and Directories right to an individual user (such as your own regular user account) or to a group. But Windows 2000 already has a predefined group called Backup Operators that has the necessary rights to back up the system, and you can simply make yourself (or the required account) a member of that group. Here's how to add an account to the Backup Operators group:

1. Log on as administrator, right-click My Computer, and choose Manage to open the Computer Management console.

2. Open the Local Users and Groups\Groups branch.

3. Double-click Backup Operators.

4. Click Add and add the user account(s) that you want to have backup rights on the computer.

5. Close the console when finished.

13.4 Back up to writable or rewritable CD (CD-R/RW)

Although Backup doesn't directly support backup to writable or rewritable CD media, you might still be able to use those media types for your backups. Determine if your CD-R or CD-RW hardware supports the ability to act like a standard writable drive, enabling you to write directly to it through the standard Windows interface. For example, many drives support Adaptec's DirectCD software that enables them to act just like any other drive. You can drag files to the drive, copy them from a console prompt, and so on.

Set up the device

Check the drive's software to make sure it is compatible with Windows 2000. If you're running DirectCD, you need version 3.01c or higher, which you can obtain from your drive's manufacturer or directly from Adaptec. Install the updated software and verify that you can copy files to the drive outside of the CD creation software. For example, try dragging files to the drive in My Computer to verify that the drive works like a standard hard drive.

Back up to a file

When you can successfully copy files to the CD using the Windows interface, you can use the drive in the Backup utility as the backup destination media:

1. Open the Backup utility and select the files you want to back up.

2. In the Backup Destination drop-down list select File.

3. Click Browse and browse to the CD-R/RW drive.

4. Click Start Backup and complete the backup as you would when backing up to a local or network disk.

13.5 Back up critical Windows 2000 data without using the Backup utility

While the Backup utility does a good job of backing up your system's configuration, you might prefer to use a different method in cases where the Backup utility might not be available to restore the system. For example, if you can't boot the system you won't be able to use Backup to recover your registry or other configuration data.

Manual backup of the system state data requires that you manually copy the registry files, boot files, and files in the *\%systemroot%\System32\dllcache* folder. You can use a couple of different methods to back up those files outside of the Backup utility.

Recovery Console method

The *copy* command in the Recovery Console doesn't support wildcards, so you have to copy files one at a time or use a batch file. The *\%systemroot%\ System32\dllcache* folder can contain well over 1000 files, so the batch file method is the only practical method.

1. Open a console prompt and type the following commands:

```
cd \%systemroot%\system32\dllcache
dir /a /b > sysbackup.bat
```

This creates a file containing a list of all the files in the *dllcache* folder.

2. Edit *sysbackup.bat* to add the appropriate *copy* command information to each line. (Add the *copy* command in front of the filename and the proper backup destination after the filename.)

3. Add additional commands in *sysbackup.bat* to copy the following boot files from the root folder of the boot volume to the backup destination:

ntdetect.com
ntldr
boot.ini
ntbootdd.sys (if present)

4. Add additional *copy* commands to *sysbackup.bat* to copy the files in the \%*systemroot*%*System32\Config* folder to the backup destination.

5. Boot the Recovery Console and run *sysbackup.bat* to test it for problems.

Boot to another OS (FAT/FAT32 volumes only)

If you don't have the Recovery Console installed on your system, you can still use the *sysbackup.bat* file described in the previous section to back up your system's configuration files, provided the following are all true:

- The files to be backed up are stored on a FAT/FAT32 volume.

- The backup destination is not NTFS.

- You can boot the system using a DOS diskette or dual-boot to Windows 9x.

Here's how to back up your system's configuration in this situation:

1. Create the *sysbackup.bat* file as described in the previous section.

2. Boot the system using a bootable DOS diskette or dual-boot installation of Windows 9x.

3. Run the *sysbackup.bat* file to back up the system's configuration.

13.6   Another user's system won't boot normally so I need to repair its registry

The registry comprises multiple *hives*, stored in files in the \%*systemroot*%\ *System32\config* folder. It's possible to repair a system's registry by editing the system's registry files on a different computer. To do so, however, you must be able to copy the affected registry hive file from and to the problem computer. This means you must be able to at least boot the system with a diskette or dual-boot OS (Windows 9x), gain access to the problem file, and be able to copy it to a removable media with sufficient space to accommodate the file (or copy it across the network). The third restriction is that you can only modify the HKEY_LOCAL_MACHINE and HKEY_USERS hives.

Editing a single hive

You can use one of the two Windows 2000 Registry Editor programs to modify an external registry hive file. Use the following steps to move the hive file from a problem computer, modify it, and restore it:

1. Boot the problem computer with a boot diskette or dual-boot OS, then copy the problem hive file to a removable media. (If using a dual-boot configuration with network capability, copy the file directly across the network to the system on which you'll repair the file.) See Table 13-1 for a list of hive files.

2. On the working system, boot Windows 2000, log in as administrator, and run *regedt32.exe*.

3. In the Registry Editor, select either the HKEY_LOCAL_MACHINE or HKEY_USERS window and choose Registry → Load Hive.

4. Locate the file you copied in step 1, select the file, and click Open. This loads the hive into the local registry as a subkey of the selected key.

5. Make the necessary changes to the damaged hive and choose Registry → Unload Hive.

6. Copy the hive file back to its original location on the problem computer and restart to test the system.

Table 13-1. Registry hive files

Hive	Files
HKEY_LOCAL_MACHINE\SAM	*sam* and *sam.log*
HKEY_LOCAL_MACHINE\SECURITY	*security* and *security.log*
HKEY_LOCAL_MACHINE\SOFTWARE	*software* and *software.log*
HKEY_LOCAL_MACHINE\SYSTEM	*system* and *system.alt*
HKEY_CURRENT_CONFIG	*system* and *system.log*
HKEY_CURRENT_USER	*ntuser.dat* and *ntuser.dat.log*
HKEY_USERS\DEFAULT	*default* and *default.log*

13.7   Restore settings after a problem occurs

The unthinkable has happened: your system is hosed and you can't boot it. Or perhaps it boots but the system is hopelessly messed up and you can't get it to work properly.

You have a handful of things you can do, assuming you've backed up your registry, backed up the system state data, and/or made a full backup of the system. The following sections offer steps you can try, in order of least aggressive to most aggressive, to fix the problem.

Use the last known good configuration

You have two options for booting Windows 2000: use the default registry configuration or use the *last known good configuration* (LKGC). Both configurations are stored as control sets in HKEY_LOCAL_MACHINE\SYSTEM. The last known good configuration is the system configuration from the previous boot, prior to any changes made in the last session. Here are a few examples of when the last known good configuration can save the day:

- You install an application, device driver, or service, and the system stops responding. The last known good configuration was created at boot, prior to installing the new software, so it isn't affected. Booting with the LKGC lets you restore the system to the way it was before the problem.

- You install a new display driver but can't see the display after boot because the new settings are incompatible with the display adapter. Rather than log on, which would cause the current settings to replace the LKGC, shut off and restart the computer, then boot with the LKGC to recover the system.

- You or an application has disabled a critical device driver and the system won't boot normally. In this case, Windows 2000 automatically reverts to the LKGC.

When it becomes necessary, you can boot with the LKGC through the Windows 2000 startup menu:

1. Restart the system and press F8 as soon as the BIOS message disappears (you might need to press F8 a few times for it to be recognized on some systems).

2. Windows 2000 should display a boot menu (called the Advanced Options menu) in which one option is Last Known Good Configuration. Select that option and press Enter to boot the system with the LKGC.

Restore the registry from the Repair folder

If booting from the LKGC isn't an option or doesn't properly restore the system, you can restore the registry from a backup to recover the system. How you restore the registry depends on how you saved it. If you have the Recovery Console installed and have a recent registry backup in the Repair folder, one of the quickest ways to restore the registry is simply to copy the files into place:

1. Restart the system and boot the Recovery Console. Log on as Administrator to the appropriate Windows 2000 installation on the computer (if there are multiple installations).

2. Navigate to the *\%systemroot%\repair* folder.

3. Use the *copy* command to copy all the files in the folder to the \
%systemroot%\System32\config folder.

4. Restart the system and boot normally.

Restore system state data

If you don't have the Recovery Console installed but can boot the system and log on as Administrator, and you also have a recent copy of the system state data backed up, you can restore the system state data to restore the registry. Here's how:

1. Start the system and log on as Administrator.

2. Open the Backup utility and click the Restore tab.

3. Locate the backup set containing the system state data you want to restore. Select the data you want to restore. At a minimum, select the system state data.

4. Click Start Restore.

Use the ERD

If all of the previous options fail to get your system back to normal, you can attempt to restore the system using the Emergency Recovery Disk (ERD). You'll need the Windows 2000 CD to proceed as follows:

1. Insert the Windows 2000 CD and restart the system, booting either from the Windows 2000 Setup disk or the CD.

2. Run Setup again, and when prompted to select the type of installation, choose Repair.

3. Follow the prompts provided by Setup to run the Repair procedure.

13.8   Create a bootable Windows 2000 disk

In some situations you might not be able to boot the system from the hard disk. For example, the Master Boot Record or Partition Boot Sector might be corrupted. Or a hardware problem is preventing the system from starting from the hard disk. Whatever the case, having a bootable system disk will help you begin to troubleshoot and recover the system.

Whether your system uses FAT/FAT32 or NTFS, you can create a diskette to boot the system in the event you can't boot from the hard disk. The process for creating the disk varies, however, depending on the filesystem(s) in use.

Create a bootable disk for FAT/FAT32

Because FAT and FAT32 are supported by DOS and Windows 9x, you can use a bootable system diskette created with either of those operating systems to boot and begin troubleshooting and recovering your Windows 2000 system. Open a command prompt on a working DOS or Windows 9x system with a diskette in the drive and type the following command to create a bootable system disk:

```
format a: /s
```

where a: is the drive letter for your floppy drive.

Create a bootable disk for NTFS

If your system uses NTFS volumes or if you don't have access to a DOS or Windows 9x system to create a bootable disk for FAT/FAT32 volumes, you can create the boot disk on a Windows 2000 system. The process is a little more involved and requires that you format the diskette, then manually copy files from your system to the floppy.

Follow these steps to create a bootable disk from Windows 2000 to support NTFS volumes:

1. Open My Computer or a console prompt and format a disk in the floppy drive.

2. Configure folder options to show all files including hidden and protected system files.

3. Copy the following files from the root folder of the boot volume to the diskette:

    ntldr
    > This is the Windows 2000 boot loader.

    boot.ini
    > This file defines the location of the boot partitions.

    ntdetect.com
    > This file performs hardware detection during the boot process.

    bootsect.dos
    > This file enables dual boot of another operating system when using the boot diskette.

4. If your system uses the scsi( ) syntax in *boot.ini* rather than the multi( ) syntax, you'll also need to copy *ntbootdd.sys* to the disk. This is a renamed copy of the driver for your system's SCSI adapter. For example, if your system uses an Adaptec 1542 host adapter, copy the file *aha154x.sys* to the diskette and rename it *ntbootdd.sys*. Use either of the following methods to determine which file to copy:

— Check the value in the registry key HKEY_LOCAL_MACHINE\
  HARDWARE\DeviceMap\SCSI.

— Right-click My Computer and choose Manage, then open the Device Manager branch. Open the SCSI and RAID Controllers branch, double-click the boot SCSI adapter, and click the Driver tab. Click Driver Details to view the driver name and path.

13.9   Your only volume is NTFS and Windows 2000 won't boot

When your system uses FAT or FAT32 volumes you have some additional options for booting the system. You can use a bootable DOS or Windows 9x diskette to boot the system and potentially fix whatever is preventing the system from booting normally. When your only volume is NTFS, however, you need to use other methods to boot and troubleshoot the system.

Boot from a diskette

If your system isn't booting because of a problem with the boot sector, or if the system disk is on a different volume from the boot volume and the boot volume has failed, you need to use a Windows 2000 boot diskette to start the system. Just insert the diskette in the system and restart.

If you don't have a bootable Windows 2000 diskette, you'll need to create one. See the previous section, "Create a bootable disk for NTFS," to learn how. Since you can't boot your own system, you'll have to create the diskette using another system. If your system uses the scsi( ) syntax in *boot.ini*, make sure to copy the correct SCSI driver to the diskette.

Use the Recovery Console

If your system won't boot because of a hard disk corruption or failure, you probably won't be able to boot using the Recovery Console even if it is installed. If it is installed and the system does at least attempt to start, you can press F8 after the initial BIOS message disappears to display the boot menu and select the Recovery Console. Once the Recovery Console is loaded you can begin troubleshooting and repairing the system.

If a hard disk problem prevents the system from booting with the Recovery Console, or if the Recovery Console isn't installed, you can run the Recovery Console from the Windows 2000 Setup disks:

1. Insert the Windows 2000 Setup boot disk in the floppy drive and restart the system.

2. Provide the other Setup disks when prompted by Setup.

3. When prompted to install or repair Windows 2000, select the repair option.

4. Windows 2000 Setup gives you two repair options: use the Recovery Console or use emergency repair process. Press C to use the Recovery Console.

Use the Windows 2000 Setup disk and ERD

If neither of the previous options works to get your system booted and repaired, you can try repairing the system with the ERD. See the section "Use the ERD," earlier in this chapter, for specific steps for starting and repairing the system with the ERD.

Install another copy of Windows 2000

If you have a relatively current backup that you want to restore to recover the system, another potential solution is to install another, minimal copy of Windows 2000 and use it to restore your system from the backup:

1. Run Setup again by booting from the Windows 2000 CD or the Windows 2000 Setup disks.

2. Follow the installation procedure and install another copy of Windows 2000 in a new folder. Do not choose the same folder as your existing installation.

3. After installation, restart the system and boot the newly installed copy of Windows 2000.

4. Run the Backup utility and restore the files and system state data from the backup to their original locations.

5. Edit the *boot.ini* file in the root folder of the boot drive to help you easily identify the old and new installations of Windows 2000.

6. Restart the system and choose the appropriate option from the boot menu to boot the original copy of Windows 2000.

Index

A

absolute path, 31
Accessibility Wizard, 70
Accessories, 70
Active Directory (AD), 82
active partition, changes in, 32
ActiveX controls, 71
AD (Active Directory), 82
adapters, multiple, 3
Add/Remove Programs object, 12, 48
address lease, 170
address reservation, 174
administrative shares, 157
Administrator account, renaming, 255
Administrator password, 24, 67
Administrators group, 121
Advanced Multiple Website
    Configuration dialog box, 217
Advanced TCP/IP Settings property
    sheet, 178
AGP adapters, 84
aha154x.sys, 271
alias names, virtual directories and, 219
allusersprofile variable, 88
Always on Top option, 90
anonymous access, 110, 214, 231
Anonymous Access and Authentication
    Control group, 113
APIPA (Automatic Private IP
    Addressing), 145, 171
applications
    avoiding reinstallation for dual-boot
        systems, 16
    document association, 102

non-driver, 257
run automatically at logon,
    disabling, 85
third party, 63
attrib command, 21
auditing, 244–247
    registry, 248
authentication
    certificate-based, 189
    encrypted, 187
    smart cards, 190
author mode, consoles, 73
Author.log, 229
autoexec macros, 106
autoexec.bat, 13
autoexec.nt, 47, 262
autohide, 90
automatic backups, 262
automatic caching, 80
automatic logon account, 147
Automatic Private IP Addressing (see
    APIPA)
Automatic startup, 65
automatic startup type (services), 65
automatic synchronization, 81
autorun, 54
    preventing, 15
    setting, 125

B

background color, 131
backups
    automatic, scheduling, 262
    Backup utility, 35, 45, 262, 265

E

EAP (Extensible Authentication
    Protocol), 189
Effects page, Display properties, 95
EFS (Encrypting File System), 37
email
    encryption, 239
    forgery, preventing, 238
    notification, 70
Emergency Repair Disk (see ERD)
enabling/disabling
    applications at startup, 85
    context menus on taskbars, 76
    incoming connections, 205
    NetBEUI, 146
    network interfaces, 138
    print sharing, 118
    protocols, 141, 163
    registry, remote access to, 247
    services, 63
    visibility, 100
encrypted messages, reading, 239
Encrypting File System (EFS), 37
encryption, 35, 187, 202
    128-bit encryption, 223
ERD Commander Professional, 26, 27
ERD (Emergency Repair Disk), 15, 261
    recovery, 269
    registry backups, 47
    updating, 262
error messages
    404 error, 226
    customizing, 226
Everyone group, 121
.exe file extension, 104
expand command, 31
expanding menu items, 94
Extensible Authentication Protocol, 189

F

FAT (File Allocation Table) file
    system, 34, 48
FAT32 file system, 34
Favorites
    expanding, 95
    Start menu, 93
Fax service, 64, 70
faxsetup.inf, 72

fdisk.exe, 6, 33
File Allocation Table (see entries at FAT)
File and Printer Sharing service, 229
    disabling for dial-up
        connections, 191
    unbinding from TCP/IP, 192
file name completion, 133
File Transfer Protocol (see FTP)
files
    archiving, 48
    auditing, 244
    cleaning out, 48
    color-coding compressed, 102
    disabling sharing, 164
    hidden, 100
    in use, 156
    offline, synchronizing, 80
    ownership, 51
filters, IP, 143
firewalls, 142, 180, 192
fixboot command, 24
folders
    access restrictions, 159
    appearance, customizing, 101
    auditing, 244
    background, customizing, 100
    color-coding compressed, 102
    comments, adding, 101
    hiding shared, 156
    options, 13
    shared, 80
    Sharing property page, 154
foreground color, 131
Format dialog, 35
Forward Lookup Zones, DNS, 76
FQDN (Fully Qualified Domain
    Name), 181
FrontPage 2000 Server Extensions, 212,
    227
FTP (File Transfer Protocol), 64, 212,
    229
    automatic folder direction, 233
    folders, hiding, 232
    service, 230
    site, 230
    timeout, 234
    users, disconnecting, 234
    virtual directory, 232
FTP Site Creation Wizard, 230

W

WAN (wide area network), 66
Web servers, remote management
      of, 224
web sites
    default, 214
    hosting, 212
wide area network (WAN), 66
wildcards, 16, 55, 161
win command, 14
Win2k folder, 12
Win9x folder, 12
Win9xBootfiles, 13
Win9xipp.cli, 109
WinBootDir, 13
WinDir, 13
window position, 128
window size, 128
Windows 2000
    installing, 1–37
Windows 2000 boot diskette, 271
Windows 2000 components, removing
      unnecessary, 49
Windows 2000 GUI, 22
Windows 2000 Professional, 12, 211

Windows 2000 Resource Kit, 129
Windows 2000 Server, 12
Windows 3.x, 11
Windows Components Wizard, 70
Windows folder, 12
Windows ME, 11
Windows NT Challenge/Response, 215
Windows NT, dual-boot systems, 10
Winnt folder, 12
winnt32.exe, 4, 5
winnt.exe, 4, 5
WinntSystem32config folder, 16
Winternals, 26, 36
Word, 102
workgroups
    changing, 139, 161
    creating, 139
World Wide Web Server, 111

X

xcopy command, 54, 123, 132
xcopy32 command, 13

Z

Zip disks, 46, 234

About the Author

Jim Boyce is a former contributing editor and monthly columnist for *Windows* magazine. Jim has authored and co-authored over 40 books about computer software and hardware. He has been involved with computers since the late seventies as a programmer and systems manager in a variety of capacities. He has a wide range of experience in the DOS, Windows, Windows NT, Windows 2000, and Unix environments. In addition to his full-time writing career, Jim is a founding partner and vice president of Minnesota Webworks (*http://www.mnww.com*), a Midwest-based web development firm.

Colophon

Our look is the result of reader comments, our own experimentation, and feedback from distribution channels. Distinctive covers complement our distinctive approach to technical topics, breathing personality and life into potentially dry subjects.

Leanne Soylemez was the production editor and copyeditor for *Windows 2000 Quick Fixes*. Jane Ellin, Clairemarie Fisher O'Leary, and Catherine Morris provided quality control. Pamela Murray wrote and Brenda Miller edited the index.

Hanna Dyer designed the cover of this book. The cover image, a stopwatch, is from the Stock Options Sports CD and is used with permission. Michael Snow used Adobe Photoshop to tweak the image for the cover. Emma Colby produced the cover layout with QuarkXPress 4.1 using Adobe's ITC Garamond font.

David Futato designed the interior layout. Mike Sierra and David Futato implemented the design in FrameMaker 5.5.6. The text font is Birka, and Franklin Gothic Condensed is used for headings; the code font is TheSans Mono Condensed. The illustrations that appear in the book were produced by Robert Romano using Macromedia FreeHand 8 and Adobe Photoshop 5.

Whenever possible, our books use a durable and flexible lay-flat binding. If the page count exceeds this binding's limit, perfect binding is used.

Nineteenth century wood engraving
of a bear from the O'Reilly &
Associates Nutshell Handbook®
Using & Managing UUCP.

BUSINESS REPLY MAIL

FIRST CLASS MAIL   PERMIT NO. 80   SEBASTOPOL, CA

Postage will be paid by addressee

O'Reilly & Associates, Inc.
101 Morris Street
Sebastopol, CA 95472-9902